CALIFORNIA DESERT RESORT CITIES
Reflections & Visions

PUBLISHER AND EDITORIAL DIRECTOR

Victoria J. Bailey

DESERT SPRINGS PUBLISHING

AND

HUNT WEBER CLARK ASSOCIATES, INC.

2003

*"Once you've experienced a deep purple sunset

and a clear desert night with a gentle warm breeze,

you'll have 'sand in your shoes.' Wherever you go

a little piece of this desert paradise will stay with you."*

DESERT SPRINGS PUBLISHING
Victoria J. Bailey, Publisher and Editorial Director
Michael G. Morein, Associate Publisher
Joyce Sunila, Managing Editor
Marc L. Thompson, Consultant

CONTRIBUTING HISTORICAL WRITERS
Pamela Bieri, Gayl Biondi, Valerie Bizier,
James W. Cornett, Chris Manes, Evan Trubee

CONTRIBUTING PROFILE WRITERS
Suzanna L. Braum, Jennifer C. Leibrum,
Carol Lyn Moloshco, Rommi O'Brien,
Karen Oppenheim

CONTRIBUTING PHOTOGRAPHERS
Paul Ames, Tom Brewster, James W. Cornett, Ned Redway

CONTRIBUTING PHOTOGRAPHS
Coachella Valley Historical Society and Cultural Museum,
Coachella Valley Water District, Palm Springs Historical Society

ART DIRECTION, DESIGN AND PRODUCTION
Hunt Weber Clark Associates, Inc.
Nancy Hunt-Weber, Jim Deeken, Laura Pellegrini, Yan Wu

Desert Springs Publishing
78365 Highway 111, #340
La Quinta, CA 92253
760-219-7008
Email: victoria@desertspringspublishing.com
www.desertspringspublishing.com
www.californiadesertresortcities.com

Hunt Weber Clark Associates, Inc.
2410 Alhambra Drive
Palm Springs, CA 92264
760-318-6548
415-546-2091
www.hwcinc.com

Cover Photo: Tom Brewster Photographer
Mesquite Golf & Country Club, Palm Springs, CA
www.tombrewsterphotographer.com

ISBN 0-9727572-0-1 First Edition
Library of Congress Control Number 2003091238

Copyright © 2003 by Desert Springs Publishing

All rights reserved. No part of this book may be reproduced in any form or by any means, electronic or mechanical, including photocopying, without permission in writing from the publisher. All inquires should be addressed to Desert Springs Publishing, 78365 Highway 111, #340, La Quinta, CA 92253

Published 2003
Toppan Printing Company of (HK) Ltd.
Printed in China

Table of Contents

The Canvas
A DESERT'S NATURAL HISTORY
BY JAMES W. CORNETT

Page 7

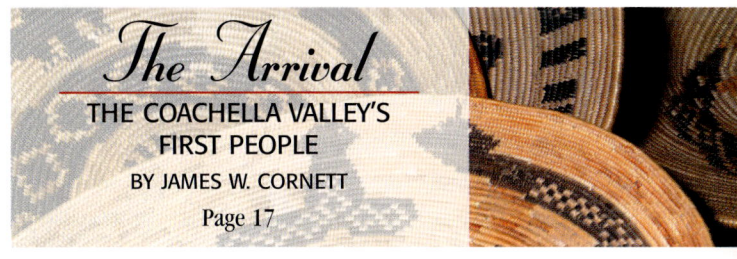

The Arrival
THE COACHELLA VALLEY'S FIRST PEOPLE
BY JAMES W. CORNETT

Page 17

Agriculture
THE GREEN END MEETS THE GOLF COURSE FROM HEAVEN
BY CHRIS MANES

Page 27

Visitors
THE MAGIC AND THE WAY OF LIFE
BY EVAN TRUBEE

Page 41

Celebrities
TO SEE AND BE SEEN
BY VALERIE BIZIER

Page 53

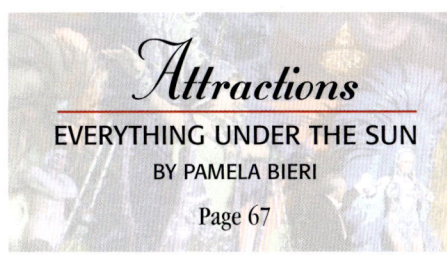 

Attractions
EVERYTHING UNDER THE SUN
BY PAMELA BIERI

Page 67

Valley Cities
A FAMILY ALBUM
BY GAYL BIONDI

Page 81

Commerce
IN PARADISE
BY GAYL BIONDI

Page 93

Profiles
OF EXCELLENCE
Page 103

INDEX OF PROFILES
Page 182

It is with heartfelt gratitude that I celebrate my many new friends who gave so generously of their time to make this book a reality.

This truly was a leap of faith and I thank you all for your warm encouragement throughout the journey.

Victoria J. Bailey

The Canvas

A DESERT'S NATURAL HISTORY

BY JAMES W. CORNETT

Photographer James W. Cornett

San Andreas Fault in Painted Canyon.

The San Andreas Fault forms the eastern boundary of the great Pacific Plate and the western boundary of the North American Plate.

The earth is made up of a series of "plates" that float atop the hot molten magma which forms the core of the earth.

Photographer Paul Ames

San Jacinto Mountains.

BEFORE IT BECAME A DESERT

The natural history of this region begins approximately 20 million years ago, with the formation of the San Andreas Fault. Forces deep within the earth created a fissure in the planet's crust that slowly tore away the western edge of our continent and began sliding it northward. The friction along either side of the San Andreas Fault occasionally buckled the land into lofty mountains that today line the Coachella Valley on the north, south and west.

That this has been a geologically recent event is clear from the precipitous drop along the north face of the San Jacinto Mountains, which nearly touch downtown Palm Springs. The north face rises 10,000 feet in just seven horizontal miles, making it the steepest escarpment anywhere in North America — steeper even than California's Mount Whitney or Sierra Nevada, Wyoming's Grand Tetons, or even Alaska's Denali Peak, the highest point on the continent. What's more, the entire range continues to rise today, though at a rate imperceptible in a human lifetime.

San Jacinto Peak, the highest point in the range, towers 10,831 feet above sea level. This is not, however, the highest peak bordering the Valley. That designation goes to San Gorgonio Peak in the San Bernardino Mountains. At 11,502 feet, it is the highest point in Southern California.

Over the past five million years these two peaks and their respective ranges have risen so high that they now form a barrier to eastward-traveling storms coming in off the Pacific Ocean. In fact, few storms are massive enough to successfully pass over the San Jacinto and San Bernardino mountains. Most are forced to drop their load of moisture before they reach the Coachella Valley.

As westerly winds force storms upward and over the peaks, the air cools, moisture condenses, and most of the water load falls as rain and snow on the western or

Desert Sunflower.

Calico Cactus.

Sand Verbena.

windward side of the mountains. By the time the air mass finally succeeds in surmounting the ranges, there is little moisture left in the storm. Thus, a vast desert extends east of the mountains. Climatologists call this a rain shadow desert. Biologists call it the Sonoran or Colorado Desert.

The San Jacinto and San Bernardino mountains that form the Coachella Valley's western barrier have been high enough to create a rain shadow desert for at least the last two million years. The Coachella Valley, however, has only continuously received less than 10 inches of annual precipitation (the criterion for desert designation) for the last 10,000 years. Why?

Scientists have determined that during the last Ice Age, which ended 10,000 years ago, large storms were more frequent than they are today. Many penetrated into interior California, bringing twice as much rain to the Coachella Valley as it sees now. These more frequent storms, as well as colder ocean water off the coast, combined to ameliorate high summer temperatures, reduce evaporation and make the increased rainfall even more accessible to plant life. The result was a savannah-like environment with tall grass, scattered oak trees, and a year-round river through the center of the Valley. At this same time, elephant-like mammoths, sabre-toothed cats and giant ground sloths traversed the Coachella Valley.

Researchers have not yet unraveled the mystery of why the storm path moved to the north or what caused the disappearance of the giant ice-age animals. Suffice it to say that by 10,000 years ago the savannah was gone, replaced by a region of meager rainfall, hot summers, and a multitude of cacti and dwarf shrubs.

HOW HOT – HOW DRY

Today each city in the Coachella Valley experiences true desert conditions: average annual precipitation of only four to five inches, and summer temperatures routinely exceeding 105 degrees. Most of the rain falls in the winter months, although there are occasional summer thundershowers.

In some years, winter precipitation exceeds four or five inches and the bounty of colorful springtime wildflowers that results brings tourists not just from southern California, but as far away as Europe. So dense are the displays of sand verbena that the Coachella Valley takes on a pink hue when recorded by satellite photography.

WHEN THE DESERT IS IN COLOR

The pink-flowered sand verbena is the Valley's most notable wildflower, although over 300 species of flowering annuals have been recorded from the region. Other beautiful species not to miss include the yellow desert sunflower, the red indian paintbrush, the purple canterbury bells, the white dune primrose, and the orange mariposa lily.

In the minds of most visitors deserts are synonymous with cacti, and the Coachella Valley boasts a variety of sizes, shapes and floral color of these succulent, spine-covered plants. Largest of the local cacti are the barrels. Some barrel cacti stand six feet tall with a diameter of nearly two feet. Barrel cactus flowering commences in late March, with each cactus displaying a perfect circle of brilliant yellow flowers at the top of each stem.

Barrel Cactus.

Although the other Coachella Valley cacti are smaller, their flowers are no less beautiful. The several-stemmed calico cactus produces brilliant magenta flowers that contrast dramatically with the pale green flowers of the teddy-bear cholla. The beaver-tail is the most common and widespread cactus, but its flowers are not nearly so red as are the flowers of the Mojave mound cactus. In all, there are more than 20 species of cacti in the region.

The Colorado Desert, of which the Coachella Valley is part, is often referred to as the "tree desert" because of the several species of woody plants that can be found abundantly in the dry washes or arroyos. Best known is the green-trunked palo verde that turns bright yellow in late spring with the appearance of thousands of blossoms. In May the ironwood tree, named for its incredibly hard wood, breaks out in multitudes of pink blossoms, followed in June by the blossoming of the desert willow, with its pinkish-lavender flowers. Most impressive is the gray-foliaged smoke tree that turns deep blue when it is reproductively ready to be visited by pollinating insects.

All images Photographer James W. Cornett

THE PALMS OF PALM SPRINGS

No discussion of Coachella Valley plant life would be complete without mention of the tallest plant native to the deserts of California. With some individuals reaching 90 feet in height, the desert fan palm towers above all other plant species. Known to botanists as Washingtonia filifera, these desert fan palms occur only where natural springs bring water to the desert's surface.

Many such springs exist along the San Andreas Fault in the Valley center and in drainages of the Santa Rosa Mountains behind Palm Desert, but most occur in canyons near the base of the San Jacinto Mountains bordering Palm Springs. In fact, the largest natural desert fan palm oasis in the world lies just a few miles south of that city, in Palm Canyon, a part of the Indian Canyons Tribal Park.

It requires many superlatives to adequately describe this remarkable tree. Not only is it the tallest plant anywhere in the California deserts, it is also the only species of palm in the world that has its trunk completely obscured by dead, hanging fronds throughout its life. These fronds form a kind of interlocking skirt that rests firmly on the ground and is quite unfettered even by powerful desert winds. Only fire can destroy the skirt.

Desert fan palm oases.

In prehistoric times, lightning was the most frequent cause of palm oasis fires. Later, after the arrival of Native Americans, humans most often ignited the oasis vegetation. Indians started oasis fires to increase palm fruit production. Today, thoughtless vandals occasionally set palms on fire. Fortunately, the palms survive a fire and are, in fact, the only oasis plant species that is still standing after an oasis conflagration.

The palms survive because of the tremendous amount of moisture in the trunks. After flames consume the dry leaf skirts, and the thin outer "bark"

Indian Canyons Tribal Park contains three of the ten largest Desert Fan Palm Oasis in existence.

The Western Yellow Bat only roosts in the dry leaf skirts of the Desert Fan Palm. It is found nowhere else in the world.

Western Yellow Bat.
Photographer James W. Cornett

is burned away and the flames encounter the moist tissues just beneath the trunk surface. The heat of the fire causes the water to evaporate, moistening the flames which soon flicker out. It's like a built-in fire extinguisher.

Although most first-time visitors to the desert are surprised to discover such a green, water-loving plant growing in the middle of such a hot, arid environment, many visitors already know Washingtonia filifera. In fact, they may have one planted in their yard.

So taken with this tree were 19th and 20th century horticulturists that they collected seeds and distributed them worldwide. The result was that the desert fan palm became one of the world's most widely planted tree species. Today, they line not only Palm Canyon Drive in downtown Palm Springs but the avenues of Sydney, Australia, Rome, Italy, Nairobi, Kenya, and Barcelona, Spain, to name only a few locations.

The bird most closely associated with desert fan palm oases is the beautifully black, white, and orange hooded oriole. Pairs of these create a basketlike nest beneath a green palm frond. Other birds often found in palm oases include the western bluebird, cedar waxwing, house finch, ladderback woodpecker, and great horned owl.

For those who associate life with moisture, the diversity of plant forms and species in the Coachella Valley must be surprising. But what our desert lacks in water it more than compensates for in diversity of landscapes.

The mountain ranges that nearly encircle the Valley are just one aspect of Coachella Valley geography. Sandwiched among these ranges are a variety of topographical features including deep canyons, alluvial fans, dry wash beds, stony flats, plant-held hummocks, and sand dunes. These varied features support a diversity of not only plant but animal life as well.

We have over 20 kinds of snakes in the Coachella Valley, but the chances of seeing one on a hike or nature excursion are very small (less than 5 percent).

This is true even in spring when they are most active. Part of the reason for this is that most species are nocturnal.

Photographer Tom Brewster

Desert Kangaroo Rat.
Photographer James W. Cornett

Many animal species are closely associated with particular kinds of habitats — unique assemblages of surface features and their associated plants. Only by visiting a palm oasis, for example, is one likely to encounter the beautiful orange and black hooded oriole during the day, and the rare western yellow bat at night. Only in a rocky canyon with permanent or near-permanent water can one find the California tree frog and the southern alligator lizard. The desert kangaroo rat and the officially threatened Coachella Valley fringe-toed lizard are confined to the dunes and sand hummocks of the Valley floor.

THE FRINGE-TOED LIZARD AND HABITAT PRESERVATION

Fringe-toed Lizard.

The Coachella Valley Fringe-toed Lizard is king of the dunes. It shows myriad adaptations for life on a soft, ever-moving substrate — and adaptations are important to a reptile that spends its life not only running lickety-split over the dunes but diving under it when danger approaches. The fringed scales on its toes have not only given the lizard its name, but also increase the surface area of each foot, thereby increasing traction when running across the soft sand. The scales serve the same function as the wide tires of a dune buggy.

The lizard also has overlapping eyelids that make a double seal guaranteed to keep sand grains off the eyes. A check of the ears reveals that they, too, are protected — in this case with finger-like scales that collapse over the ear opening when the lizard dives into the sand. Particles are kept out of the nose by valves, and should any sand make it past these valves there is a kind of sink trap that prevents grains from proceeding further down the breathing passages. A healthy nasal exhale when the lizard pops out of the sand ejects the sand grains in the nasal trap.

The final adaptation to life on the dunes involves the jaws. The lower jaw doesn't just meet the upper jaw but actually fits up into it. So adapted to a sandy environment is the fringe-toed lizard that individuals of this species are almost never found anywhere else.

The hummocks and dunes that were once the dominant features of the Valley floor are now mostly gone — a result of resort and residential development. Unfortunately for the lizard, it lives only in the Coachella Valley and only on the sandy desert floor.

What man has taken away, however, man can preserve. In 1986, government wildlife biologists, local naturalists, politicians and the Nature Conservancy joined together to do something to protect the unusual reptile, as well as the many other plants and animals that live in the same habitat. They created the Coachella Valley Preserve, 19 square miles of relatively undisturbed desert landscape in the center of the Valley. The preserve encompasses not only the last remaining sand dunes but also portions of the fault-torn Indio Hills, several palm oases, canyons, alluvial fans, bajadas (two or more alluvial fans joined together), dry washes, and mesquite hummocks as well. It's a magnificent assemblage of desert habitats that is to be preserved for all time.

Held within its boundaries are numerous rare plants and animals, several of which were already officially threatened or endangered when the preserve was created. Perhaps best known is the Desert Tortoise, an affable, plant-eating creature that is the state's largest reptile. Less

---

The Coachella Valley Preserve provides 19,000 acres of habitat for the Coachella Valley's fringe-toad lizard.

The Bureau of Land Management California is part of a public and private cooperative effort to protect the unique sand dune habitat of the fringe-toad lizard.

Desert Tortoise.

Coachella Valley Ground Squirrel.

Honey Mesquite Flowers.

All images Photographer James W. Cornett

familiar is a plant known as the Coachella Valley Milk Vetch. This is an endangered species found nowhere else in the world. Although the tortoise occurs on the rocky, compacted soils of the northern part of the preserve, the milk vetch shares with the fringe-toed lizard the sandy habitat in the southern portion of the preserve.

Additions to the preserve are continually being made, and several satellite preserves have been created in recent years. Today, the goal of professional naturalists is to establish a preserve network that ensures the survival of not just the lizard, tortoise and milk vetch, but an additional 24 rare plants and animals as well – such creatures as the Flat-tailed Horned Lizard, LeConte's Thrasher and the Coachella Valley Ground Squirrel.

The plan is called the Multiple Species Habitat Conservation Plan, and it is an ambitious attempt to protect these rare organisms, link already established preserve lands together and preserve large tracts of natural open space for future generations. Animals would theoretically be able to move between the Santa Rosa – San Jacinto Mountains National Monument along the southern boundary of the Coachella Valley to Joshua Tree National Park along the Valley's northern boundary. Additionally, the connecting of the existing preserves and parks with undisturbed corridors would provide dissemination avenues for not just animals but plants and their seeds as well.

In the final analysis, the MSHCP would allow for genetic exchange between all the areas, a necessity to prevent inbreeding and insure the long-term vigor of all plant and animal populations. Only time will tell if this ambitious plan will succeed.

BIGHORN SHEEP

The magnificent, statuesque bighorn sheep have roamed the lower slopes of the Coachella Valley mountains for centuries. They thrive only on the open, sparsely vegetated foothills. They eat just about any desert plant, including barrel cacti.

A large bighorn ram with massive curled horns can approach 200 pounds, making it the largest animal found in our desert region. Female bighorn sheep have horns, though much smaller than the male's.

Every year it seems another new development is proposed in or adjacent to the mountainside habitat of the bighorn sheep, and every year more hikers, horseback riders, and mountain bikers innocently enter the sheep's domain. Not surprisingly, sheep numbers are decreasing rapidly.

The bighorn sheep population in the San Jacinto Mountains has decreased by 90 percent since 1975, and in the Santa Rosa Mountains by an even higher percentage. The magnificent, hardy animals could probably handle the intrusion of the hikers on trails, but they have not been able to handle the diseases introduced by domestic livestock, which have been grazed in bighorn habitat. Over the last four decades, these have been the leading contributors to death among the bighorn. So serious is the situation for sheep on the south side of the Valley that the state government has listed these populations as threatened and the federal government listed them as endangered in 1997.

However, there is hope for the sheep. Bighorn sheep living in the mountains of Joshua Tree National Park on the north side of the Valley are thriving. With the passage of the Desert Protection Act in 1993 and the creation of a new national monument in the San Jacinto and Santa Rosa mountains in 1999, their future seems secure. The two acts have cordoned off large parcels of the bighorn sheep's favorite habitat – lower mountains slopes and alluvial fans – as protected land.

Run by the federal government's Bureau of Land Management, the new national monument includes plans to provide better protection for sheep. Today biologists count 19 sheep in the San Jacinto Mountains and 48 sheep in the Santa Rosa Mountains. Although sheep are not tagged, more than a dozen have radio collars and their whereabouts are tracked in order to learn more about their needs. Lambing sites (a mature female sheep can give birth to one lamb per year) and critical waterholes are already being identified and made accessible only to sheep. In addition, the private, nonprofit Bighorn Institute in Palm Desert is now breeding sheep in captivity and releasing healthy animals into the Santa Rosa and San Jacinto mountain ranges to replenish those lost through disease and other causes.

Bighorn Ewe (Female).

THE SALTON SEA AND LAKE CAHUILLA

Lake Cahuilla reservoir.

Photographer Paul Ames

Imperial Dam near Yuma.

Congresswoman Mary Bono speaking about the Salton Sea.

Courtesy of Coachella Valley Water District

In 1998 the Salton Sea was approximately 227 feet below sea level and salinity: 44,000 to 45,000 parts per million (ppm).

Salinity of seawater is about 35,000 parts per million (ppm).

Oddly, faults are responsible for both lifting rock high into the air – as with the San Jacinto Mountains – as well as dropping land below the level of the oceans. In the Coachella Valley, the San Andreas Fault has had it both ways.

In the Western Hemisphere, the most remarkable example of land dropping as a result of movements along faults is the Salton Trough, home to the Salton Sea. In all, more than 2,000 square miles of Sonoran Desert terrain, including the Salton Sea itself, lie below the level of the Pacific Ocean. The lowest point in the trough is at the bottom of the Salton Sea at 273 feet below sea level. (Although Badwater in Death Valley is somewhat lower – minus 282 feet – the number of square miles of land below sea level is far less in Death Valley.)

Careful examination of topographic maps, complete with contours and elevations, reveals that the Salton Trough and Coachella Valley are really extensions of the Gulf of California, part of the Pacific Ocean. Were it not for sediments deposited at the mouth of the Colorado River, together with some slight uplifting along the San Andreas near the head of the gulf, the Pacific Ocean could easily push northward all the way to Palm Desert.

In fact, in past geological times that was exactly the case. Two million years ago the gulf extended into the Coachella Valley. If that seems difficult to believe, just drive to Garnet Hill immediately south and east of the intersection of Interstate 10 and Indian Avenue north of Palm Springs. Walk into any ravine that cuts into the hill, and brush away the sand until you reach the harder material beneath. You'll find numerous fossils of clams, sea urchins and perhaps even a shark tooth or two. These fossils are actually less than two million years old, and clearly indicate that ocean-going creatures occupied the Coachella Valley in prehistoric times.

Ancient shoreline of Lake Cahuilla.

Coachella Valley Water District

Photographer Darrel Bennett

Salton Sea.

Why did the ocean retreat? As mentioned earlier, the sediment-laden waters of the Colorado River deposited their load at the northernmost point of the Gulf of California. The simple piling up of these sediments could have cut off the gulf from the Coachella Valley. But accumulating sediments were assisted by some minor uplift along the San Andreas Fault as well. Together, these forces eventually cut off the Coachella Valley from the gulf. All this had happened by at least half a million years ago, perhaps earlier. With no source of water, the northward finger of the gulf evaporated away.

The story of the Salton Trough might have ended at that point, too, had it not been for the persistence of the Colorado River and its load of sediments — sediments that originated primarily from the carving of the Grand Canyon. The accumulation of sand, silt and clay continued after the retreat of the gulf waters, and from time to time built up so high that it was easier for river water to flow into the below-sea-level Salton Trough than it was to empty into the Gulf of California. For hundreds of years at a stretch, river water would flow into the Coachella and Imperial valleys, forming an enormous inland lake more than ten times the size of today's Salton Sea.

Geologists call this extinct body of water Lake Cahuilla, after the indigenous people of the area. There were, in fact, several Lake Cahuillas, since the same sediments that blocked the flow or river water into the gulf would just as often block the flow of water into the trough. Without river water, each lake eventually evaporated away under the hot desert sun. Evidence for the last Lake Cahuilla can be seen along the hillsides behind the cities of Coachella and La Quinta. As you drive or walk along these hillsides you can see the ancient shoreline — a light/dark interface that runs along the mountain base 40 feet above sea level. The shoreline level indicates that at one time Lake Cahuilla was more than 300 feet deep!

About 400 years ago natural processes changed the course of the Colorado River for the last time. Sediments had accumulated near the present day Mexican city of Mexicali, and river waters flowed back into the Gulf of California. Left without a permanent source of water, Lake Cahuilla slowly evaporated away, leaving an enormous saltpan in its place.

The story of the Salton Trough might have ended here, yet again, had it not been for the arrival of settlers of European ancestry at the end of the 19th century. Realizing that the mild winter temperatures of the Imperial and Coachella valleys allowed for the growth of agricultural crops year-round, they foresaw a fortune in crop yields if a reliable source of irrigation water could be secured. These early investors and farmers turned to the nearby Colorado River that separated Arizona from California. The idea was to create diversion structures and canals that would siphon off a portion of the river's flow. Since the Salton Trough was lower than the level of the river, gravity alone would bring fresh water to the two valleys.

The engineers had a new channel cut into the side of the riverbank. But heavy winter snows and a rapid spring thaw in 1905 resulted in floodwaters reaching the channel and overwhelming it. Much of the river's flow rushed into the Imperial Valley, flooding farmland and making a beeline for the low-lying Salton Basin.

Try as they might, hundreds of laborers were not able to stem the flow of water. For two years, Colorado River waters flowed unchecked into the basin, forming what would become the Salton Sea. Eventually, in 1907, work crews patched the breach using trainloads of enormous boulders. The river was sent back into its proper channel.

Today, the Colorado River flows into the Coachella and Imperial Valleys but is kept in check by concrete-lined canals. Along with the water delivered by the canals, the dream of a vast agricultural cornucopia has come to fruition. So successful has this been that today most of America's fresh winter vegetables come from the Imperial and Coachella Valleys.

A byproduct of agricultural development and the need for irrigation has been the Salton Sea, the largest body of water contained within the boundaries of California. By all rights, the sea should have evaporated away after the closure of the breach in 1907. But unused irrigation water and wastewater from flooded fields is allowed to run into the basin. Inflow and evaporation have kept the sea's level more or less in balance ever since.

From the outset, the lake formed inside the Salton Basin was fairly salty. With thousands of years of salty ocean water overlying the basin sediments, then with continual deposition of mineral-laden Colorado River waters and the repeated evaporation of the ancient Lake Cahuillas, a vast saltpan had developed by 1905. When river water once again flowed onto the basin, the salts quickly dissolved in the fresh water. Additional salt was added by the flow of irrigation waters flushed from surrounding farmland, as well the salts carried by the river itself. By 1980, the sea was saltier than the ocean.

Many Coachella Valley civic leaders hoped to prevent the sea from dying, but even with federal monies it's a nearly impossible battle, uphill and expensive all the way. There is no way to rid desert lakes of salt. Eventually they become too salty to support most kinds of life. Such is the case with California's Mono Lake and Great Salt lakes in the Great Basin Desert of the western U.S., as well as the Dead Sea separating Israel and Jordan in the Mideast.

WATER SUPPLY

Throughout the late Pleistocene and early Recent times, the Colorado River has changed its course quite often, and whenever it has flooded into the Coachella Valley the floodwaters could reach as far as present-day La Quinta. This water seeped into the ground, creating an aquifer. More than 90 percent of the domestic water supply used in the Coachella Valley comes from this aquifer.

Hydrological researchers believe the most recent inundation of this type occurred less than 1,000 years ago.

Ever since 1918, when human consumption began lowering aquifer levels, the Coachella Valley Water District has made efforts to replenish the aquifer. The first major replenishment effort began when water flowed through the Coachella branch of the All-American Canal in 1949. In response to this new supply, groundwater levels rose in the southeastern part of the Valley. In the more heavily populated western part of the Valley, water replenishment programs have been in place for over 30 years.

Northern part of Whitewater River being released from the Colorado River Aqueducts flowing to recharge ponds.

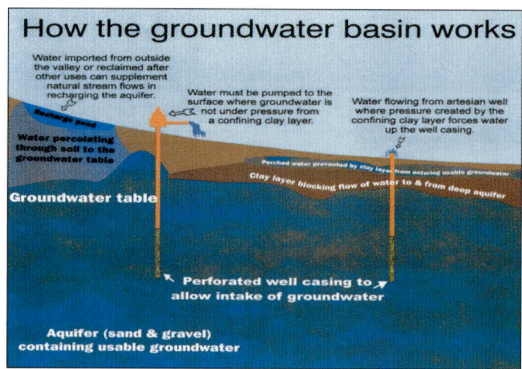

How the groundwater basin works.

In the 1960s, with increasing urbanization and new agricultural irrigation techniques, groundwater levels began declining again in the southeastern Valley. The Valley's two largest water agencies have pooled their entitlements to state Water Project water, and have used that water to replenish the aquifer from Palm Springs to Indian Wells. In all, more than two million acre-feet have been percolated into the ground so far, and other replenishment programs are in the planning stages. The Water District recently released a water management plan for the entire Coachella Valley for the next 30 years.

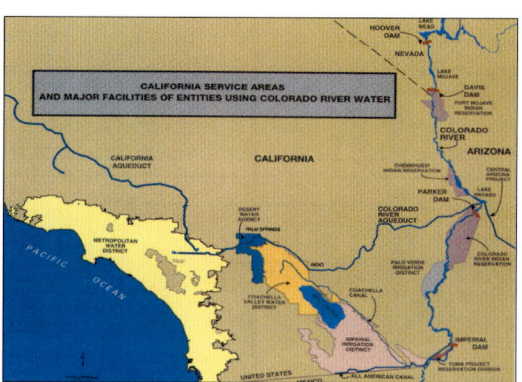

California service areas and major facilities of entities using Colorado River water.

Although there is abundant water in the aquifer (there are 39 million acre-feet in the first 1,000 feet below ground level alone), the Coachella Valley Water District believes that conservation is important. They have published a guide to gardening with low-water-use plants called "Lush and Efficient Gardening." The guide offers a landscaping model that's less taxing on water supplies than the traditional one.

With adequate monitoring and sensible planning, the aquifer will continue to serve the needs of the Valley's growing population for many years to come.

Images courtesy of Coachella Valley Water District

The Arrival

THE COACHELLA VALLEY'S FIRST PEOPLE

BY JAMES W. CORNETT

THE ARRIVAL

Archaeologists debate about the exact timing of human arrival in the Coachella Valley, but there is general consensus that by 1,000 B.C. the first Americans had reached the deserts of southeastern California. Here they hunted game, gathered a remarkable array of wild plant foods, and lived in permanent villages at several desert localities. They lived around a lake that no longer exists – Lake Cahuilla, which was located about where the Salton Sea is today. These people would become known as the Cahuilla (pronounced Ka-wee-ya) Indians.

THE CAHUILLA

The Cahuilla language is linguistically related to the languages of several well-known tribes in the Southwestern United States and Mexico. Their language shares many features with the Aztecan family of Mexico, the Comanche, the Hopi and Pima of Arizona, the Ute of Colorado and Utah, and the Paiute and Shoshone of Nevada. Approximately 35 members of the Cahuilla tribe speak their native tongue today. With linguists' help, both the written and spoken Cahuilla language is being documented and preserved for posterity.

At the time of the arrival of the first European explorers in 1774, about 7,500 Cahuilla-speaking people lived in the desert lands now known as the Coachella Valley. These people are often referred to as the Desert Cahuilla and Pass Cahuilla (Agua Caliente), to distinguish them from Cahuilla living in the San Jacinto and Santa Rosa mountains, the San Gorgonio Pass near Banning and on the plains near what are today the cities of Riverside and San Bernardino.

Fig Tree John wearing his dress uniform, with his grandchildren and his wife, circa 1927.

Photos Courtesy of Coachella Valley Historical Museum

While Alluvial Fans do form in other regions, they are especially noticeable in flat-bottomed desert valleys.

Fig Tree John and his wife, circa 1906.

THE ARRIVAL OF STRANGERS

In 1774, the Spanish explorer Juan Batista de Anza made contact with the Cahuilla in what is today the town of Borrego Springs just south of Palm Springs. De Anza came in search of an overland route from Mexico to California to supply the Catholic missions that had been established in both Baja and Alta California. Prior to de Anza's expedition, the only way to travel from Mexico to California was by ship — a long, expensive, and sometimes hazardous journey. A safe land route would allow more people and livestock to live near these missions.

Although de Anza was eventually successful in finding a reasonably safe route, his arrival in Cahuilla territory would change the lives of the Cahuilla people and culture forever. With their horses, steel swords, and firearms, de Anza's men were imposing intruders. They viewed the Cahuilla as godless inferiors who needed to be shown the correct way to live — through force and enslavement if necessary.

Significant change for the Cahuilla was not immediate, however. Most of the Spanish, and later Euro American, activity remained along the coast, where the missions and ranches were built. Compared to natives inhabiting the coastal regions, the Cahuilla were able to maintain their culture and traditions relatively intact. To be sure, they had occasional contact with the Spanish and other persons of European ancestry, and were aware of Christianity and the new religious traditions. Many Cahuilla also began using some of the new technology, including guns and steel blades. By in large, however, the Cahuilla continued to embrace their own religious traditions, still relied upon the natural environment for food, and continued to make pottery and baskets using the old techniques.

Courtesy of Coachella Valley Historical Society

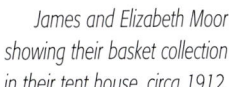

James and Elizabeth Moor showing their basket collection in their tent house, circa 1912.

Dolores Patencio, circa 1920.

Large grain baskets were used for storing dried plant food and were made by men using willow twigs. The baskets were placed on platforms to protect the contents from rodents and other animals.

Courtesy of Palm Springs Historical Society

Ceremonies were held for important foods, such as the first acorn, agave, mesquite and piñon crops.

MESQUITE

Mesquite is the most common shrub / small tree of the Desert Southwest. There are three species of mesquite: Honey Mesquite, Screwbean Mesquite and Velvet Mesquite. All three are deciduous and have long been used by humans, wildlife and livestock as a food source. Native Americans relied on the mesquite pod as a dietary staple from which they made tea, syrup and a ground meal called pionle. They also used the bark for basketry, fabrics and medicine. This giant shrub or small tree was scattered throughout the Coachella Valley and was one of the most reliable sources used for food even in years of severe drought.

This is because mesquite plants have extraordinarily long roots, sometimes reaching downward over 200 feet to the underground aquifer. With its roots in water, the mesquite produces fruit pods even in years of little or no rainfall.

When no other desert plant was producing fruits and seeds, and when game populations were severely depressed, the mesquite would provide food in the form of long pods filled with protein-rich seeds. These "beans" as they are often called, could be pulled off the branches and eaten green or, more frequently and more importantly, dried and stored for later use. Pods to be stored would not be picked until they had dried and turned brown, indicating they were ripe.

After they were plucked from the branches, the pods would be stored in huge baskets, called granaries. The granaries were made from the branches of the desert willow or true willow and were spectacular in size, with diameters of up to 6 feet and depths of nearly 4 feet. Once filled, the baskets were set out in the open on wooden stands to keep the pods off the ground. This allowed them to quickly dry if it rained, and made it more difficult for rodents and rabbits to make off with the food.

Often the dried mesquite pods were processed immediately. Entire pods and enclosed seeds were ground into flour with a cylindrical stone – a pestle – that was pounded in a mortar.

The mesquite flour was mixed with water and the resulting paste molded into cakes. The cakes were then placed on a sunlit rock surface until they had become dry and brittle. Like whole pods, mesquite cakes could be stored for later use. The dried cakes were a particularly useful food for men embarking on lengthy trading or hunting trips. The cakes were nutritious, light in weight and would not spoil.

Today Cahuilla use mesquite flour in baking.

The Smoke Tree is often found along sandy or gravelly flats and derives its name from its plume-like growth and golden color, which give the tree the appearance of smoke.

LIFE IN THE DESERT

The Cahuilla lived in scattered villages, usually consisting of several families numbering less than 60 individuals. Village locations were dictated by the availability of permanent sources of water and proximity to the Cahuillas' most important food plant, the mesquite.

No permanent settlement was ever far from a reliable source of water. Most often the water source was associated with a spring or a small stream emanating from one of the canyons of the San Jacinto and Santa Rosa mountains. Typical of this type of settlement was the village, consisting of several dozen people, that sprang up at the mouth of Andreas Canyon just four miles south of today's downtown Palm Springs. Here a year-round stream provided all the water needed for the inhabitants, even in the driest of years.

Other village sites took root in Tahquitz, Palm, Chino and Snow Creek canyons. Palm Canyon is three miles south of downtown Palm Springs, and separates the Santa Rosa from the San Jacinto Mountains. Chino Canyon is one mile northwest of downtown Palm Springs, and is the canyon that harbors the Palm Springs Aerial Tramway. Snow Creek Canyon is five miles northwest of downtown Palm Springs, at the northern face of the San Jacinto Mountains.

Cahuilla living in the area known today as Indian Wells didn't depend on streams because they were aware of the underground aquifer, which is unusually close to the surface in Indian Wells. With shovels made from palm fronds they were able to dig wells, complete with staircases, that allowed them to walk to a depth of 20 feet, where water would percolate upward to form small ponds. Then they descended into a well with a large earthen pot or water jug, an olla, (pronounced oi'ya) and scooped up the water. The small mouth of an olla helped to prevent evaporation, and the narrow neck was easy to hold for carrying and pouring. Ollas were smoothed and shaped by hand. Baking or firing hardened the clay and made them watertight. In about 1918 a prehistoric olla was found in a cave in San Andreas Canyon, measuring 13 3/4" high by 12 1/2" in diameter.

As far as is known, the Cahuilla are the only American natives who constructed wells to tap subsurface supplies of water. Indian Wells is indeed an appropriate name for the city.

More than anything else, what characterized Cahuilla territory was diversity of landscape and climate. The region was, and is today, topographically and environmentally varied with low, hot and barren desert in the Coachella Valley; pine-covered slopes and valleys in the San Jacinto Mountains, and grasslands to the west of the mountains. Indeed, no other cultural group in North America occupied such a diverse environment. All of these were available to the Cahuilla because of the steepness of the terrain. Rapid changes in elevation meant rapid changes in environments, and these habitats were in close proximity to the net. In a single day, a Cahuilla could walk from the sandy desert floor to a lush pine forest. Hikers still do it today.

The Cahuilla living in the desert organized their year to utilize the seasonal plant foods at different elevations. On the Valley floor in winter the fruits of the bladder-pod bush could be picked, nectar of the Chuparosa could be collected, and stems of the joint-fir could be gathered, placed in water and heated to make tea. In spring, the Cahuilla moved upward to the alluvial fans at the base of the mountains to gather fruits from succulents such as the beavertail cactus, barrel cactus, and calico cactus. At the base of the mountains they could also gather the fruits and flowers of several species of yucca including the Mojave yucca and Whipple yucca.

In summer the occupants of many villages traveled into the high country of the Santa Rosa and San Jacinto mountains to collect the fruits of the desert apricot, or into palm oases to gather the berries of the thornbush. Fall was a bountiful time to travel once again into the mountains to harvest the savory nut of the pinyon pine and acorns from oak trees. The number of plant species utilized by the Cahuilla was truly astounding, numbering in the hundreds.

Pedro Chino stands in the doorway of his home, his wife Marie by a large basket, circa 1898.

Courtesy of Palm Springs Historical Society

"Shatta" was a Cahuilla basket weaver and she was Ruby Modesto's grandmother. Ruby Modesto (1913-1980)

Courtesy of Palm Springs Historical Society

The art of basketry was considered a gift to the Cahuilla from Menily the moon maiden.

The Cahuilla ancient tradition of oral history continues today through the singing of songs and is known in English as "bird songs."

CAHUILLA BASKETS

Among museum-goers, the Cahuilla are best known for their beautiful and functional baskets. Every respectable collection of North American Indian baskets contains at least one Cahuilla basket. A permanent display of Cahuilla basketry is found at the Palm Springs Desert Museum and the Agua Caliente Museum in downtown Palm Springs.

Dolores Patencio is one of the many remarkable artisans known for her intricate and colorful basket designs. One of her baskets, usually on public view, at the Desert Museum is a giant Cahuilla bowl basket over three feet high. During her life, which ended in the early 20th century, Dolores was responsible for making hundreds of baskets.

Cahuilla baskets are known for their fine and tight weaves, intricate designs, and subtle but beautiful colors. Designs woven into the basket were of animals and plants representing the environment. Animal motifs included such designs as rattlesnakes, eagles, scorpions and lizards.

The foundation for a coiled basket was usually a bundle of deer grass, or sumac. Plant material of different colors were used or dyed naturally for colors. An example: for black they would use sulphur or an iron-rich mud. These fine-coiled baskets were used for cooking, storing and serving food, gifts and ceremonies. Many were custom made for tourists in the early 20th century.

Indian baskets today often sell for thousands of dollars each.

Kermit Maxwell, son of the Indian agent, in front of a ceremonial round house.

Courtesy of Palm Springs Historical Society

THE HUNT FOR FOOD

The Cahuilla ate the meat of animals, birds and insects, in addition to a diet of many plant foods. Many animals could be hunted throughout the year by journeying into different elevations and habitats. All manner of creatures were consumed, from the bountiful larvae of sphinx moths in years of abundant winter rain, to the majestic mountain sheep (bighorn). (Contrary to popular belief, meat from hunting was not an important source of protein. Plants harvested by Cahuilla women accounted for over 90 percent of the nutritional requirements of village members.) Hunters often hunted small rodents such as woodrats and ground squirrel. These rodents were an important source of animal protein. The hunters would often build small fires near rodent burrows and blow the smoke into the hole to drive out the small mammals. Sometimes they would use sticks to dig the rodents out. The rodents were turned over to the women who would skin them and then throw them, whole, into clay cooking pots. The pots contained boiling water and various plant parts to add flavor to the rodent stew.

Jackrabbits and cottontails were the most frequent animals to be taken – not just for their meat but for the pelts as well. Cahuilla rabbit-skin blankets were legendary for their warmth, and often consisted of over 100 individual pelts. Rabbit-skin blankets were a popular trade item between the Cahuilla and their neighbors, the Serrano to the north and Kumeyaay and Luiseno to the south.

The three large game animals hunted were mule deer, mountain sheep (bighorn) and antelope (pronghorn deer). Large animals were elusive and difficult to bring down. Hunting big animals required endurance and skill, which was the domain of mature Cahuilla men. A hunter armed with a bow and arrow would hide behind a boulder near a known waterhole. When a mountain sheep (bighorn) or deer came to drink, an arrow was launched. (The knowledge of how an arrow was used was considered a gift to the Cahuilla.) The hunter knew that a strike would probably not kill the animal but rather wound it. The prey would flee, and the hunter would follow it until it could run no further.

Cahuilla storytellers often described chases that might last up to three days. To minimize the pursuit, arrows were usually dipped in some kind of poison. The mashed bodies of black widows were a commonly used poison. This slowed the victim and hastened its demise. It did not contaminate the meat, since the venom breaks down into harmless components in the human digestive tract. When a hunter finally caught up to the deer or mountain sheep (bighorn), a blow to the head often killed the animal. Long chases were particularly fatiguing because the hunter still had to carry the animal all the way back to the village. If the animal was particularly large, the hunter might use a smoke signal to ask for help carrying the animal.

Game hunting was so demanding that a successful hunt was a usually a cause for much excitement.

THE DESERT FISHERMAN

Perhaps the most surprising Cahuilla food was fish. A desert people eating fish might seem illogical, but in fact for many centuries there was a freshwater lake in the middle of the Colorado Desert called Lake Cahuilla. This lake was 10 times the size of today's Salton Sea, had a depth of over 300 feet, and was chock full of fish. However, Lake Cahuilla dried up some 400 years ago. Prior to that time, however, the Cahuilla Indians lived around the lake, where fish could be captured at any time of year by spear, net or fish trap. The Cahuillas' fish trap, referred to as a weir, was a structure made of rocks piled into a U-shape and open at one end.

The weir formed a mini-cove of calm, warm water accessible to the fish via the opening. Many of the fish traps still exist today. (However, exactly how the fish trap functioned is still unknown.)

Stagecoach road through the desert.

THE NEW CENTURY

History records events that changed California in the late 19th century. In 1848 the Mexican-American War ends. Then in 1849 the California Gold Rush began on a global scale and the world rushed in.

In 1850, California becomes a state. Many Americans passed through the area in increasing numbers on their way to find gold and make a new life for their family. Despite the existence of effective vaccines, smallpox epidemics often wrecked havoc, particularly among Mexicans and Native Americans. An outbreak in 1862 killed hundreds in Southern California. Among the Cahuilla population, the death toll was as high as 6,000 to 10,000 people before the epidemic ended. The remaining Cahuilla numbered approximately 2,500.

The administration of President Ulysses S. Grant established the first Cahuilla Indian Reservation from 1875 to 1877, including Cahuilla, Cabazon, Morongo, and Torres-Martinez tribes. These new reservations were managed by the Bureau of Indian Affairs to supervise U.S. government programs. The person appointed to supervise was called an Indian agent.

It was not until the early 1880 that the U.S. Congress pressured the Indian Advocacy Groups and formed the Mission Indian Commission.

Finally, in 1891, Congress passed the Act for the Relief of Mission Indians giving further authorization for allotments or at least definitive Indian reservations were formed in Southern California. It was at this time that the boundaries for nearly all of the Coachella Valley reservations were established, including those for the Morongo, Torrez-Martinez, Cabazon, and Agua Caliente tribes. These boundaries have survived to the present time.

An assistant to the net who helped conduct ceremonies, solve disputes, organize hunting parties, and fulfill other duties was called a paxaa.

Frontier Photographer Edward S. Curtis
Courtesy of Palm Springs Historical Society

Marcos Belardoa, a Cahuilla Indian, was the "paxaa" at the Agua Caliente Reservation, circa 1924.

Chief Cabazon was a 19th century Cahuilla leader.

Agua Caliente Band of Cahuilla Indians, Kermit Maxwell on the bike, Adrian his father (the agent), Alice his mother, and Ellen his older sister. Photo taken next to the bathhouse, circa 1912.

THE RESERVATION

Unlike most Indian reservations in the United States, several of the reservations in the Coachella Valley region – particularly those of the Agua Caliente Band of Cahuilla tribe – were not comprised of a single, large block of land. Rather, the reservation consisted of a checkerboard pattern of land with only every other section of land being designated as part of the reservation.

This strange arrangement was the result of a prior agreement the federal government had made with the Southern Pacific Railroad Company. In 1860 an exchange for building railroad lines out West, the company was awarded huge quantities of land, usually alternating, 640-acre sections of land over vast areas of many western states. This encouraged railroad development, but kept the company from completely dominating the economy of any particular region.

This had been done in the Palm Springs region, so when the federal government decided to create a reservation for Indians living in Palm Springs, all it had left to give in 1876-77 were alternating sections of land. In the decades that followed, and even up to the present time, this was to cause many problems in the planning and development of Palm Springs and the reservation.

CABAZON BAND OF MISSION INDIANS

The Cabazons and their Cahuilla relatives have a rich history. The Cabazon Band is a politically independent unit of the Cahuilla cultural group. Tribal members of the Cabazon Band of Mission Indians are direct descendants of Chief Cabazon, the leader of the Desert Cahuilla Indians from the 1830s until the 1870s. Chief Cabazon was also a traditional leader and performed the ceremonial duties of the net in several villages. Cabazon Band descendents lived in and controlled an area that stretches from east of the Salton Sea to west of Indio toward the San Gorgonion Pass.

There were 600 tribal members when the Cabazon Reservation was defined as three parcels of raw desert totaling 2,400 acres. The Southern Pacific Railroad later claimed 700 acres to create a railroad and interstate highway.

Today, there are fewer than 50 members of the Cabazon tribe, but owing to perseverance and a diversified economic base, their future is bright. Their business enterprises includes Fantasy Springs Casino, Fantasy Lanes Bowling Center, and Cabazon Resource Recovery Park which includes the tribe's First Nation Recovery Inc., (which is a tire recycling operation). For more information contact the Cabazon Culture Museum in Indio.

Courtesy of Palm Springs Historical Society

Courtesy of Palm Springs Historical Society

Palm Canyon, circa 1900s.

Cahuilla were able to make money by charging for their labor as well as the use of springs on their land, and by selling food to visitors.

Mount San Jacinto, Indio, the sunset route reached by Southern Pacific Railroad.

SOVEREIGN STATES

All Indian reservations are like states within a state. Reservations are, in general, only subject to federal law, and are exempt from state, county and city laws, regulations and taxes. The Indian reservation sovereignty was established by Congress, and the Supreme Court allowing the present rights of tribes to govern their members and their territories with the same rights of sovereignty that was established in place before European arrival. This sovereignty has been limited over the years, but never taken away, by the fact that the tribes' territory was included within the territorial boundaries of the United States. Consequently, tribal sovereignty means that Indian tribes have the right to govern their internal affairs; the state cannot interfere with the tribes' self-government; but that Congress can limit tribal sovereignty. The government has established a policy of tribal self-determination, which has created opportunities for tribes to remain independent and overcome many of the limits imposed either arbitrarily or improperly over the years. Indian tribes understand this inter-governmental attitude and realize that it will always be present and that their sovereignty may always be in jeopardy from various factions.

GAMBLING ON INDIAN LAND

Native American Indians contend that building gambling casinos is their right, since federal law does not specifically prohibit gambling on Indian land. State governments, on the other hand, have always been reluctant to support most kinds of gambling, whether on Indian land or not. In some cases, states have attempted to prohibit some or all types of gambling on Indian land. The situation has been exacerbated by Interior Department rulings that have generally required tribal and state governments to work out compromises. In California, a compromise has been reached that allows each reservation to build two casinos.

The types of games played at casinos are dictated by agreements between tribes and their state government. For example, you can play craps at Arizona casinos but not in California. From time to time agreements change. The trend today is towards more and more Las Vegas-style gaming.

Needless to say, gambling casinos have been a boon to tribal governments, bringing in huge sums of money and providing many Indians as well as non-Indians with jobs. In some places they are the largest industry in their communities.

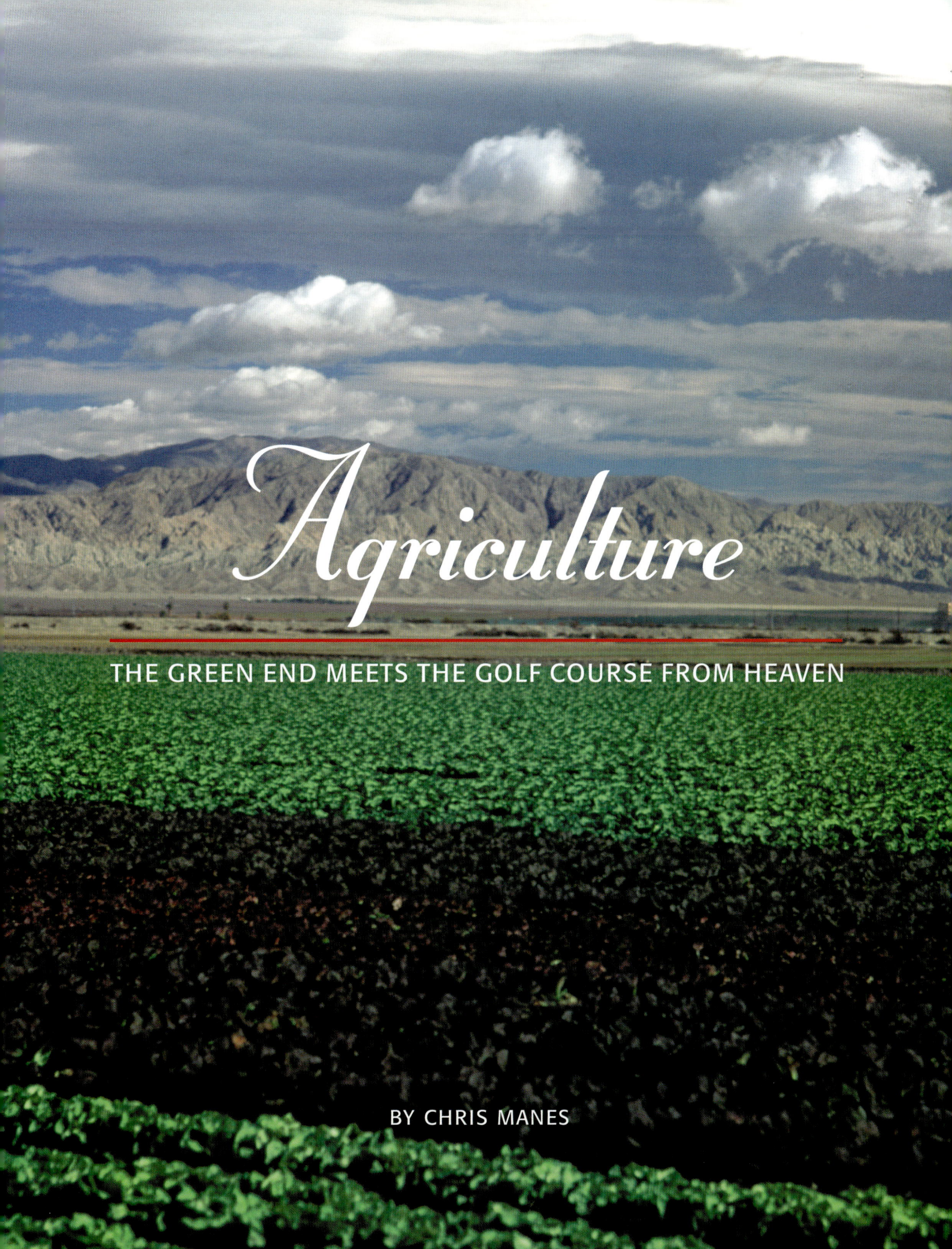

Agriculture

THE GREEN END MEETS THE GOLF COURSE FROM HEAVEN

BY CHRIS MANES

THE GREEN END

Satellite photos show the lower Coachella Valley, from Indio to Thermal, as a lush green swathe surrounded by a garden wall of bare brown rocky hills. These images of what local farmer and real estate developer, Paul Ames has termed "The Green End of the Valley" suggest the prominent role agriculture has played in shaping the area's history, as acre after acre of desert gave way to an empire of grapes, citrus, melons, dates and broccoli, the envy of agribusinesses around the country. "You can grow almost anything here," says Ames, a lifelong Valley resident who began his farming career as a sharecropper more than half a century ago.

"Almost anything" includes a long list of more than 50 varieties of fruits, vegetables, and flowers. Credit fortunate geography, a few visionaries (often derided as crackpots or worse), and water from the Colorado River.

The Cahuilla Indians who preceded the white man cultivated California fan palms in the Palm Canyon area for centuries, harvesting the abundant small sticky black dates. The fan palm — Washingtonia filifera — is California's only indigenous palm and is not to be confused with the date palm — Phoenix dactylifera — which was imported from Northern Africa early this century. The fruit was crushed on mortar stones, seeds and all, to form a syrupy-flavored paste. Various lineage groups within the tribe demarcated and laid claim to individual palm groves, which were managed by controlled burning (a technique that increases the date yield) and other methods. This is one of the few known instances of private property rights arising among Native Americans before Columbus.

But even after the Valley passed successively into the hands of Spain, Mexico, and the United States, large-scale farming was unknown here until the beginning of the 20th century. Like most of early California, the Valley was dominated by cattlemen, who bought up the limited riparian water rights, which basically meant the Whitewater River, the only significant source of flowing water in the area. And just as important, the Valley was truly the middle of nowhere at the time: while cattle could come and go on their own four legs, crops needed to be transported. Homesteaders trickled into the desert early on, lured by its beauty and government sales of land at $1.25 an acre, no money down. But to make a go of anything beyond a vegetable patch and a few fruit trees, farmers needed a railroad and a reliable supply of water. They got both in that order.

The Fan Palms.

Satellite photo of the Salton Sea and the Coachella Valley.

Since the Salton Sea was re-formed in 1905, the sea's existence has been maintained primarily by agricultural flows from the Imperial, Coachella and Mexicali Valleys.

Lake Cahuilla reservoir was the largest soil-cement lined reservoir in the world when constructed in 1969.

THE VALLEY GETS WHEELS

Because the Coachella Valley is a natural corridor between neighboring Arizona and the Los Angeles Basin, it wasn't long after California entered the Union that stage coaches began making regular runs through the Valley, with depots at either end at Indio and Snow Creek. In 1853 Congress authorized a series of surveys for determining the best southern (snow-free) route for building a railroad to the Pacific Coast. In that same year, William R. Blake, a survey geologist who would also play a central role in bringing irrigation to the Coachella Valley, explored the barren Salton Basin (there was no Salton Sea there at the time) for the most likely passage for a line.

By 1876, the Southern Pacific Railroad was in place, and Indio was on the verge of becoming a major rail center. A two-story depot, both a freight station and a hotel for passengers, was built in 1887, surviving until it was destroyed by fire in 1966. When the trains started rumbling past Palm Springs, railway rates were at an all-time low: you could travel from the Missouri River to the beaches of Southern California for all of $1.

Suddenly, the Valley was connected with the rest of the country by cheap, dependable transportation. One could, theoretically, pull up stakes and make oneself a home here – although people mostly just passed through, no doubt deploring the heat as they fanned themselves furiously. For most, all they saw outside their coach window was a desiccated inferno.

But in fact, more water than they could imagine lay right beneath their feet.

William P. Blair, an early settler in the Indian Wells area, circa 1909.

Southern Pacific Steam Engine in the early 1900s.

HIDDEN BLUE

Steam engines (like farmers) crave water, and after the line through the Coachella Valley was built, the Southern Pacific began looking for it desperately. In 1894, the company struck aquatic gold when a drill rig in Mecca hit a gusher of pure water. Government scientists later confirmed that the water was of remarkable purity, not the alkaline brew often dredged up in other Southwest deserts. The railroad was the first to tap into a gigantic aquifer underlying the Coachella Valley.

The desert was literally floating on a giant subterranean lake nourished by the Whitewater River draining the snow-capped San Bernadino, San Joaquin and the Santa Rosa mountain ranges.

The Coachella Valley is part of a geologic depression with a bottom some 265 feet below sea level. Periodically, the Colorado River in flood stage (before dams were built) would flow into this depression filling the Valley as far as Indio and La Quinta, depositing its load of clay and silt. This is where a lot of the Grand Canyon ended up.

As the Colorado River then shifted back to its normal course flowing straight into the Gulf of California, ancient Lake Cahuilla would vanish into the desert as a mirage, only to reappear like a Phoenix when the river reached another flood stage years later and forced its way back into the basin. This repeated filling and draining deposited salt along hundreds of feet of clay and silt, overlaying the aquifers below and trapping water under artesian pressure. The railroad and early pioneers learned that by drilling wells a couple of hundred feet deep, they could tap this artesian pressure and have unlimited quantities of beautiful sparkling water for free. This was the impetus for harnessing the agricultural proclivities of this remarkable desert valley.

Built in 1887 the Southern Pacific Depot Clubhouse and Restaurant in Indio.

Well drilled by Martin & Sandford in 1910 on Thayer Brothers Ranch at Avenue 61 and Pierce.

Cahuilla oral history memorialized the great lake, whose last incarnation may have been as recent as the 1500s. Indeed, Cahuilla legend refers to a vessel carrying strange men into the Valley, possibly a reference to a wayward expedition led by Spanish explorer Hernando de Alarcon around 1540. This expedition scoured the Gulf of Mexico for pearls and may have been driven by a storm up into the waters of Lake Cahuilla. It is a remarkable image for the mind's eye: a Spanish galleon laden with pearls slowly drifting up the Coachella Valley on the endless blue inland sea, its sails blindingly white in the desert sun, its confused crew peering at the 11,000-foot peak of San Jacinto up ahead, wondering if they would ever see home again. Legend has it that the ship eventually ran aground near the mouth of the Colorado, where it is now buried in the sands, pearls and all.

Shortly after water was discovered in Mecca, the first date and citrus groves were planted, and the Valley was on its way to being transformed from pristine desert to agricultural powerhouse. As might be expected, the well-drilling business also boomed.

But farming from wells had its limitations. Wells were expensive to drill and unpredictable, often running dry as the local water table dropped. The underground lake gave agriculture a foothold in the Valley, but it could not sustain it.

This is where William Blake, the railroad surveyor, comes back into the picture. Blake, a trained geologist, observed that the Cahuilla Indians raised a variety of crops from corn to barley, using ditch irrigation to bring water from local springs. Obviously there was nutrient-rich soil here, despite the outward appearance of a sandy no-man's land. Blake was first to theorize that an extinct lake had left arable sedimentary soil under the surface layer of sand (he in fact gave Lake Cahuilla its name). This "Death Valley," as he called it in his survey report, might possibly be made to bloom by building irrigation canals from the Colorado River.

He wrote prophetically, "With water, it is probable that the greater part of the desert could be made to yield crops of almost any kind."

Some early intrepid farmers tried to build their own irrigation projects. Most notably, "Judge" John Guthrie McCallum, a San Francisco attorney and one of Palm Springs founding settlers, built a 19-mile flume from the Whitewater River to his land in the late 1800s, as part of a real estate venture that resulted in some orchards being planted. This was the first concerted effort to promote agriculture in the Valley through irrigation. But it was short-lived, as floods destroyed the flume and drought destroyed the settlers' will to continue.

But Blake's ambitious vision of a blossoming desert went forward nonetheless, though it would take decades before it came to fruition. Setting the stage for successful irrigation of the Coachella Valley was another visionary with a passion for water and farming.

A 28-year-old schoolteacher named Charles Wright went to the state legislature with a mission to free up water rights owned by land and cattle barons. He authored a statute, the Wright Act of 1887, which for the first time allowed farmers and other local citizens to establish municipal irrigation districts, essentially taking local control of water supplies by funding and building dams, canals, and reservoirs through a tax on land values. The Wright Act was intended to aid small farmers, and in fact it broke the stranglehold the cattle ranchers and land speculators had on the state's water resources. With the Wright Act in their pockets, the Coachella Valley settlers could begin making water policy on their own. Indeed, the Coachella Valley Water District came into existence when the local citizens

An artesian well in the Coachella Valley at Cawthon Ranch.

Pre-cast pipe sections used to bring water to the Imperial Valley.

Mules take a drink from an irrigation ditch at E.N.T. Burnett's farm, 1915s.

learned of a developer's scheme to pipe water from the Whitewater River to Imperial Valley, which might have doomed the area to become another Owens Valley.

Washington and Sacramento entertained various proposals in response to Blake's water epiphany, with a combination of enthusiasm and skepticism. One of them was the brainchild of Dr. Oliver M. Wozencraft, a prominent San Francisco physician, who felt so strongly about the agricultural possibilities of the desert that he proposed to build a canal from the Colorado River with his own money, but only if the government agreed to grant him six million acres of land to build it on. This transfer would have included virtually the entire Salton Basin and would have made him the largest individual landowner in the nation.

The California legislature agreed to the so-called Wozencraft Plan without blinking an eye, but Congress had some lingering doubts and got sidetracked by the Civil War before it could act. After the War the federal government seemed poised to adopt the Wozencraft Plan,

Early photos of the Coachella Valley Canal.

Photographer Paul Ames

but the good doctor suddenly died, ending his dream. It is sobering to think that if Congress had proceeded, Palm Springs today might be called Wozencraft City.

Eventually, Washington settled on a project to build an aqueduct, following the path originally proposed by Blake's engineer, Ebenezer Hadley (no relation to Paul and Peggy Hadley, who founded the famous Hadley Fruit Orchards in 1931, selling fruits and dates made possible by the very canal their namesake suggested). The result was the All-American Canal, completed in 1940, which brought Colorado River water to the Imperial Valley. The Coachella Canal, completed a few years later, extended the water's reach into the lower Valley through Mecca, terminating at Lake Cahuilla (not the great fugitive prehistoric lake, but a small man-made reservoir in La Quinta, near PGA West, which is about 12 feet deep and hardly deserving of the name).

The whole project is 159 miles long and has the capacity to deliver almost one million acre-feet of water a year (an acre-foot equals 325,851 gallons). It takes an entire day for the water to move from its source at the Imperial Dam to its endpoint in the Coachella Valley. To prevent aquatic weeds from clogging the system, the canals were eventually stocked with sterile grass carp, giant plant-eating fish that can reach 100 pounds.

When water officials first opened the spigot, the green revolution envisioned by Blake exploded.

A DATE WITH DESTINY

"It's impossible to overestimate the effect the bringing of Colorado River water had on the Valley," says Paul Ames, who at 79 and still in the industry is the *eminence gris* of the old generation of farmers. Ames began his farming career in 1949, the year the All-American Canal water started to flow (and was recognized in 1958 as one of the four "Outstanding Young Farmers of the USA," an award he certainly lived up to). "It meant the difference between life and death for farming here," he adds. Ames also played a significant role in the Valley's water history. Once the farmers got access to water, they needed to store it, which is quite a trick in the desert's sandy soil. Ames invented a system for lining reservoirs and ponds to prevent the water from percolating away.

One of the first crops to benefit from the waves of water flowing into the Valley was dates. Today, dates are the third most valuable farm product in the Valley, grossing almost $63 million in revenues in 2001, a figure bested only by bell peppers and table grapes. The

Early 1900s Bernard G. Johnson planted an offshoot of dates. He was called the "Father of California's Date Business."

Date trees are among the oldest cultivated trees and are believed to have grown in North Africa for at least 8,000 years.

There are 60 references to date palms in the Old Testament.

Dates were found buried with King Tutankhamen.

stately palms are also the most water intensive, using 9.5 acre-feet per acre annually (two or three times the amount of most vegetables and fruits). Eighty to 90 percent of America's date crop is grown here, earning the Coachella Valley the title of undisputed Date Capital of the World, though some Middle Eastern countries might take issue.

But, at the turn of the 20th century, there wasn't a single commercial date grove in the Coachella Valley, or anywhere else in North America for that matter. While the Franciscan and Jesuit missionaries had nostalgically planted date palms at their Spanish missions around the Southwest, none were commercially viable, since the trees required just the right combination of ferocious heat, abundant water, extreme sunshine and skilled labor. Date palms like their "heads in the fire and feet in the water," as an old Arab saying goes. At that time, this magic combination was found only in Middle Eastern countries and Northern Africa.

In the early 1900s, Bernard G. Johnson, inevitably called the father of California's date business, set about to change things by bringing commercial date production from the lands of Araby to the American Southwest. At the time, this was no mean feat. It meant traveling to distant oases in French-governed Algeria and Tunisia, whose people were restive over colonial misrule, hardly inclined to part with the cultivation secrets of the quasi-sacred palm for the benefit of foreign competitors. Since agricultural enthusiasts like Johnson acted under license from the French colonial government, they were sometimes viewed with suspicion. On one occasion, the sale of palm saplings for date production in the Valley generated a minor uprising by tribesmen, who felt their way of life was being betrayed by local officials. It was, in short, more like Lawrence of Arabia than agronomy.

From desert wastelands to date gardens.

Others before Johnson had tried to bring date production to the desert, but with little success. They brought back inferior stock from their travels (apparently duped by the indigenous growers with their superior

Grading and sorting table, California Date Growers Association Packing Plant, Indio circa 1948.

A palmero is collecting pollen to pollinate the tree.

Valerie Jean Date Shop at the Riverside County Fair circa 1950s.

knowledge of palms) and lacked the expertise to raise dates. One of the earliest date palm ventures failed to properly take into account that date palms are "dioecious" – like people, having male and female gender. Only the female trees, which must be hand pollinated, produce fruit, and optimally a grove will, harem-like, have one male palm for every 40 or 50 females. Some of the early settlers who bought the saplings found out after a few years that their groves consisted almost entirely of useless males.

"Date production isn't for amateurs," notes Dick Wilson, owner and operator of Shields Date Gardens on Highway 111. Shields has been a landmark in the Valley for decades, most notably for its suggestive sign tempting visitors to enjoy a video called "The Romance and Sex Life of the Date" created by Floyd Shields, the original owner of the company, and business partner with Wilson's father, Frank.

Besides requiring botanical knowledge, raising dates is plain hard work. The unsung heroes of the date industry are the palmeros, skilled workers who climb the trees on 50- or 60-foot ladders or ropes, often in 110 degree or more temperatures, to collect pollen, pollinate the female trees, prune fronds, wrap the ripening fruit bunches in paper to protect them from rain and pests, and finally to harvest the crop.

So it's easy to see what Wilson means. And Bernard Johnson was no dilettante when it came to dates. A robust, red-bearded man, he traveled through the rugged back country of French Algeria in 1903 and several years thereafter, to make his dream of dates groves in America a reality. In 1904, the Department of Agriculture established an experimental date station near Mecca under Johnson's leadership, to study the feasibility of commercial date growing in the area. A few years later the experimental station was moved to Indio – out of fear that the rising waters of the newly created Salton Sea, the result of a dike breach that diverted a flood-swollen Colorado River – would overtake the station.

The efforts of Johnson inspired a "date boom" of sorts. Soon a number of adventurer-agronomists were donning pith helmets and making pilgrimages to Arab lands in search of superior date stock and the secrets of the trade. Paul and Wilson Popenoe, Henry Simon, and others began importing palm offshoots by the tens of thousands. The local Indio newspaper, The Date Palm, covered the arrival of each new shipment as front-page news.

As has often happened in the history of California agriculture, real estate promoters got into the action. To lure would-be settlers to buy parcels of its land, Southern Pacific issued a pamphlet in 1912 bruiting the Coachella Valley as the "Best Date Lands in the World." "Someone is going to make a lot of money during the next few years out of dates," the pamphlet inveigled. "Why not secure your share?"

Riverside County Fair, National Date Festival circa 1950s.

Very few farmers got rich on dates in those early years, but those who stuck it out created a leading industry in the Valley. By 1913, eight growers – the founding date fathers, so to speak – formed the Coachella Valley Date Growers Association. In the 1920s, packing houses were springing up in Mecca and environs. The early farmers relied on wells; but with the completion of the Coachella Canal and the flow of cheap and abundant water, production increased phenomenally. Forty-one million pounds were produced in 1966, as compared to one million pounds in 1926. In 2001 it was 56 million pounds.

There are now about a quarter of a million bearing trees in California and Arizona, where there used to be none. Every February since 1947 the National Date Festival in Indio has celebrated the harvest, often drawing as many as 250,000 visitors. And in 2002, in what might be called poetic justice, Sun World International, a large Coachella-based producer of dates, merged with an Egyptian company controlled by a Saudi Arabian prince, Alwaleed Bin Talal Bin AbdulAziz Alsaud.

Johnson's vision of bringing Araby to the Valley has come true in ways he could never have imagined.

Pre-World War II Kitagawa family and their date farm.

The Coachella Valley produced over 20,000 tons of potatoes and 2,000 tons of okra in 2001.

In 1905 the Salton Sea was created when the Alamo Canal, a private canal, was built to supply water to the Imperial Valley. The Canal silted up, then flooding the Colorado River, which flowed into the Salton Basin.

Trini Alvarez looking over the oranges just picked on a Valenica Orange Ranch near Mecca.

EVERYTHING GROWS HERE

In the wake of the success of date production, farming in the Valley flourished. Almost all the early farms were family businesses, with a surprising mix of Anglos, Latinos, Filipinos, Japanese, Chinese, and others from around the world involved in the industry. And there was a surprising degree of solidarity, as borne out by the oral histories collected by Cecelia Foulks in her book, "A History of Mecca" (and by the generally low murder rate for a frontier town in the West!).

When World War II struck and Roosevelt signed the notorious Executive Order 9066 authorizing the internment of Americans of Japanese descent, there was very little pandering to racial stereotypes in the Valley. People knew better. The desert had a significant community of gifted Japanese farmers, founded by Joe and (his mother) Kiyoko Kitagawa, who bought their first farm in the Valley in 1919. By the beginning of the war, the number of Japanese growers had increased to the point that there was a Japanese Christian Church in Coachella. In the wake of Pearl Harbor, the Kitagawas, along with the other Japanese-American farmers, were detained by the government and interred for the duration of the war. But afterward the Kitagawas, and many other Japanese farmers, returned to the Valley to find their property intact (something not always true for internees elsewhere). Title to their land had been preserved by the Coachella Bank, now Valley Independent Bank, and neighbors had looked after their belongings.

The Valley's crops were as diverse as its people. Oranges came to Riverside County in the 1870s, under the auspices of Eliza Tibbets, who obtained from the Department of Agriculture stock of what was then a curiosity: a seedless Brazilian citrus, which would become known as a navel orange. The trees prospered under desert conditions, and news of its superior qualities spread, bringing would-be citrus ranch barons flocking to California. The orange boom found satiric expression in the 1934 W.C. Fields film, "It's a Gift," where the henpecked Fields buys a California orange grove, which after much browbeating from his wife, he's able to sell at a huge profit and retire to the good life of squeezing fresh orange juice as a gentleman farmer. This orange bonanza has been called California's second gold rush.

Today oranges, tangerines, grapefruit, lemons and limes, are the Valley's fourth most important product.

Valley growers also raise specialty products, such as sweet corn (considered to be some of the highest quality in the nation) and turf.

All of this is in flux. Turf, once a minor product, now is nipping at the heels of staple crops. "Turf is

West Coast Turf was founded in 1990 and offers more than 20 varieties of top-quality sod.

Early crate labels.

really beginning to take off big time," says Jose L. Aguilar, a farm advisor for the Riverside County office of the University of California Cooperative Extension. West Coast Turf, the largest Coachella Valley grass grower, is world famous among those in the know about sod, providing turf for innumerable professional and college baseball and football teams (Angels, Padres, USC), Disneyland, some of the world's most beautiful golf courses, not to mention its crowning glory – laying down the gridiron for NFL Superbowls XXVII, XXIX, XXV, and XXXII. As Danielle Marman, West Coast marketing coordinator, puts it, "We take sod seriously. If the NBA played on grass, we'd supply it."

But if the Valley has a signature crop, it would be table grapes. About 14 percent of all California table grapes are grown here. In 2001 grapes were the second most valuable crop in the Valley. And in particular the Valley is known for its seedless varieties, especially the Red Flame and Thompson, which found a home in the hot sands of the desert.

Seedless grapes – once known as Sultanas – like almost everything in the Valley are immigrants brought here by the immigrants. They originated in Western Asia, some say in Asia Minor or Afghanistan, and were favored by Armenian émigrés. But originally Sultanas were used mostly for making raisins, since they were bland and small. William Thompson, who farmed near Yuba City, brought a superior strain to California in 1878, giving rise to the Thompson grape. But it was still too small for table use. Growers discovered a way to increase the size by girdling – cutting off a narrow ring of bark around the trunks of the vines increased the berry's size. And then in 1957 researchers increased the size further by spraying vines with gibberellic acid, a naturally occurring plant growth hormone (grape growers now call the treatment "gibbing").

Red Flames were introduced in 1973, the culmination of crossbreeding research by the legendary professor of viticulture, Harold Olmo of the University of California at Davis. Today more than 90 percent of the grapes consumed in California are seedless.

If the Valley had champions of the seedless revolution, they would be Howard Marguleas and Lionel Steinberg.

Marguleas formed Sun World International. As its C.E.O., he introduced the Flame Seedless to the Coachella Valley and became one of its primary pioneer promoters. Marguleas also introduced seedless watermelons, which have become increasingly popular with consumers and are a major part of today's mix of Coachella fruits and vegetables. Lionel Steinberg was equally successful at one time commanding 10 percent of the Coachella Valley's table grape acreage.

As cropping and market conditions changed, some commodities disappeared and new products took their places. Some crops like carrots, corn and tomatoes are permanently ensconced as staples year after year, but we find that asparagus is no longer a commercial crop of the Coachella Valley and there are no more dairies. On the other hand, along with the seedless grapes and seedless watermelons, we find that beautiful new varieties of yellow and red peppers along with strawberries and artichokes have been recently added.

More and more we see acre after acre of greenhouses growing off-season crops and various flowers. There are new varieties of grapefruit and tangerines along with a significant acreage of especially fine lemons and Valencia oranges.

All in all, Coachella Valley agriculture is a fascinating and evolutionary industry dominated by innovative and hard working, progressive agribusiness men and women.

Field workers picking green beans.

FIELD WORK

The unsung hero, the missing man and woman, in most depictions of the Valley's agriculture is the farm worker. The fact is, the availability of large numbers of low-paid workers, knowledgeable in farming techniques, was just as important to the blossoming of the Valley's agriculture as water and the coming of the railroad. Fieldwork is often denigrated as "unskilled labor," but in fact it often requires significant training and experience.

Because of their hard-earned knowledge of date production, palmeros – the date tree workers – sometimes become growers themselves. CalSunGold, the largest independent producer of dates in the Coachella Valley, which produces six million pounds of dates annually, was founded by the Castro family, who immigrated from Mexico to the desert in the 1950s to work as palmeros.

Palmeros are not the only skilled farm workers. Many farm crops such as artichokes, citrus and tomatoes require a sensitive eye or touch at harvest time to determine that the individual fruits are at their peak readiness for consumer satisfaction. Other products require a very deft and expert hand to efficiently and economically pack the produce at a price the consumer can afford. Many crops like carrots and corn have been fully mechanized while other crops such as broccoli and onions only lend themselves partially to mechanization.

In the early 60s Caesar Chavez, a graduate of the infamous Saul Alynski School of Revolutionary

Farmland in the Coachella Valley covers almost 60,000 acres.

One male date palm tree produces enough pollen to pollinate one acre or 48 female date palm trees.

The rich soil of the Imperial and lower Coachella Valley was built from river slit deposited on the floor of ancient Lake Cahuilla.

Pollen from a date palm tree, which has been hung, to dry. Photographer Paul Ames

Science formed the United Farm Workers and started agitating to unionize farm workers. Despite burned packing houses and chopped down vineyards, he failed to elicit a significant number of workers to his cause. It was then that Chavez instituted a national boycott against California grapes.

This unfair boycott lasted five years and affected the whole nation devastating California's table grape growers who found it more and more difficult to market their product. Most of the grape growers fought the UFW tooth and nail, and on more than one occasion violence erupted in the fields. Lionel Steinberg, one of the fathers of the Flame Seedless grape, but a liberal thorn among mostly conservative roses in the farming community, and is well remembered for his role in one of the most dramatic episodes in the Valley's agricultural history as one of the first growers to sign a contract with the UFW. Other growers in the Valley and throughout the state were forced to follow and the UFW did prevail for a time. When it became apparent that Chavez did not have a good hold on his members, the Teamsters Union mounted a campaign to take the farm workers away from the UFW. In the final analysis, both unions failed to lure a permanent membership and today the agricultural worker scene is quite stable with only scattered union representation. Growers point out "Chavez had his chance and he blew it".

But adversity has its uses, and one of the side effects of the grape boycott was to gather together and unify the first organized group of women in the agriculture business, California Women for Agriculture. "At first we called ourselves CROP," recalls Beth Sfingi, a founding member of the group. "It stood for the Committee to Relieve Organized Pressure." The acronym reflects Sfingi's view that there was nothing grassroots about the grape boycott at all. In her view it was pressure from union organizers that stood behind the boycott — pressure that was often applied with violence. "We talked to the farm workers every day and they would tell us about threats being made against them by the union organizers, about the tires of their cars being slashed and so forth. They felt they were being forced to join the UFW. You'd see Cesar Chavez on TV preaching nonviolence, but we were seeing something very different out in the fields.

National Grape Boycott circa 1970s.

"We got this idea that if the media wouldn't listen to the farmers, maybe they'd listen to their wives." The women tried a variety of approaches for getting their message out through the media, but few reporters were willing to paint the UFW in a negative light. At one point the women called a press conference, inviting the television networks to come to the east Valley to listen to women grape pickers, whose view of the boycott differed substantially from what most people were reading in the papers and hearing about on TV. The TV crews came out, "but they wouldn't listen to the women," says Sfingi. "They got diverted by an argument over an ad that had appeared in the Riverside Press Enterprise." The women left, deflated.

"We weren't successful in stopping the boycott," concludes Sfingi, "but we found something valuable in working together and sharing our views. California Women for Agriculture is still going strong. Today women come from all over the country when we have our conferences. And it all started with trying to get the media to see another side of the grape boycott."

National Grape Boycott, United Farm workers, Riverside County Sheriff and Teamsters.

Photographer Paul Ames

The growing of artichokes is relatively new to the Coachella Valley. In 2000, 800 acres produced more than 7,000 tons of artichokes and contributed $4.5 million to the Valley's economy.

GOLF COURSES FROM HEAVEN

As agriculture has morphed from remote, rural date oases in turn-of-the-century Mecca to modern corporate businesses trading in world markets, the challenges it faces have become more and more complex. The list is fearsome: a receding water table, competition from foreign producers, pests introduced from overseas, loss of family farms to consolidation, and the spectre of rampant development.

Table grape growers, who used to count on getting their sun blessed grapes to market before northern growers, now find their harvest lagging behind imports from even earlier-ripening grapes from Mexico and Chile. The glassy-winged sharpshooter has appeared in the Valley, an insect that carries a wilt disease fatal to grapes.

Patricia "Corky" Lason, Executive Director of the Coachella Valley Association of Governments.

"Yes, it can look a little scary out there for growers," says Patricia "Corky" Larson, the executive director of the Coachella Valley Association of Governments. Partly for that reason, she and five other Valley women founded the California Women for Agriculture. Its purpose is to promote an understanding of farming among consumers and elected officials, with a particular emphasis on women's role in the industry. The group has expanded nationwide, and now gives scholarships and provides teaching materials to schools concerning agriculture. "But like farmers everywhere," she concludes, "the growers of Coachella Valley know how to take care of their own in the face of adversity."

Perhaps, however, the biggest challenge for the Valley's farmers is not adversity, but rather their own good fortune. The lower Valley, where almost all the area's crops are raised, lies cradled between the picturesque Santa Rosa Mountains on the one side, and the Mecca Hills on the other, opening out to the mirage-like Salton Sea. Ironically, this very natural beauty may do farming in. As country clubs and housing subdivisions march inexorably down-Valley and bang at their doors, it is hard for farmers to say no to the huge buyout offers. And many, if not most, want positively to say yes.

They have a phrase for it: "The golf course from heaven." Rather than passing on the family business to their children, many of the current generation of growers hope to sell their highly appreciated farmland to developers (which often means country club developers), fetching prices that will allow them to retire as millionaires, or at least be well off.

Ted Nishikawa, a third-generation Japanese grower, explains, "Most third generation farmers want to move to the big city and become professionals, not farmers." Nishikawa has stuck it out, but even he and his father decided to sell the family acreage to a corporate grower, for whom he now works.

But there are diehards who will never forsake the farming life. Paul Ames insists that the "golf course from heaven" view represents a skewed vision of the future. According to him, "the land that's been turned into country clubs so far has been sand dunes or otherwise non-farm land. Look at PGA West, for instance. It's built on land that had been abandoned for farming because of its marginal productivity and vulnerability to winter frost.

But the land on the slopes of the southern end of the East Valley is where the best crops are grown. There, where the danger of winter frost is minimized, is where most of the 500 million dollars per year of new money is generated to benefit the economy of the Coachella Valley. The land remains in the hands of the farmers, and agriculture will be a significant part of the Coachella Valley's economy for a long time to come."

Mark Nickerson, managing partner of Prime Time in Coachella, sees a future of vast potential and constant change. "This is a resilient place that has always adapted to change quickly," he says. "Whether the change has been stimulated by technology, by changing markets or whatever, we have always been able to adapt and remain competitive. The uniqueness of this place lies in its sunshine, its water availability and its temperature, which aren't duplicated anywhere else. It allows for a wide range of products being grown. That range is one of the reasons we are able to change and adapt so nimbly to outside conditions."

In addition, he points out, agricultural production per acre in the Coachella Valley has doubled in the last 20 years. "And I see it continuing to multiply, as we

Paul Ames The Ames Group
Photographer Allison Mc Bee

Table Grapes produced more than 93,870 tons and contributed nearly $100 million to the Valley's economy in 2000.

take advantage of new technologies like mesh houses and greenhouses."

Nickerson doesn't deny that agricultural land will be bought up by developers, and he regrets the loss of open land for purely aesthetic reasons. "But that won't spell the end for farmers. There are still many acres that aren't being utilized. Farmers will just move on to the new acreage and continue to increase their productivity."

"This is like a great laboratory for agricultural experimentation. We've developed varieties in the Coachella Valley that couldn't have been developed anywhere else, we're using insect and weed control that's more environmentally safe than in the past, and we are getting more out of every acre of land all the time. It's great industry all around. It's got no place to go but up."

Crates of Red Flames

Photographer Paul Ames

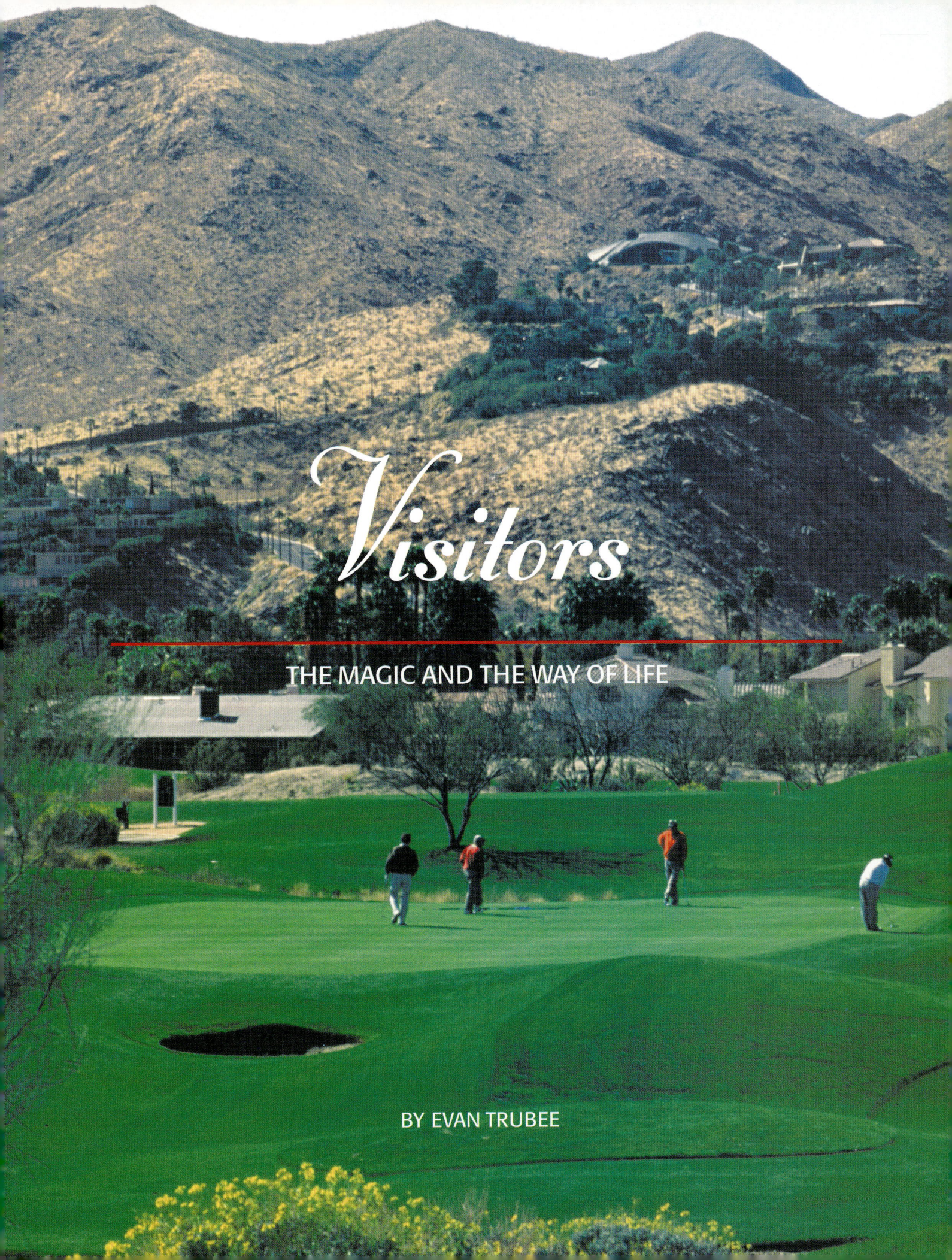

Visitors

THE MAGIC AND THE WAY OF LIFE

BY EVAN TRUBEE

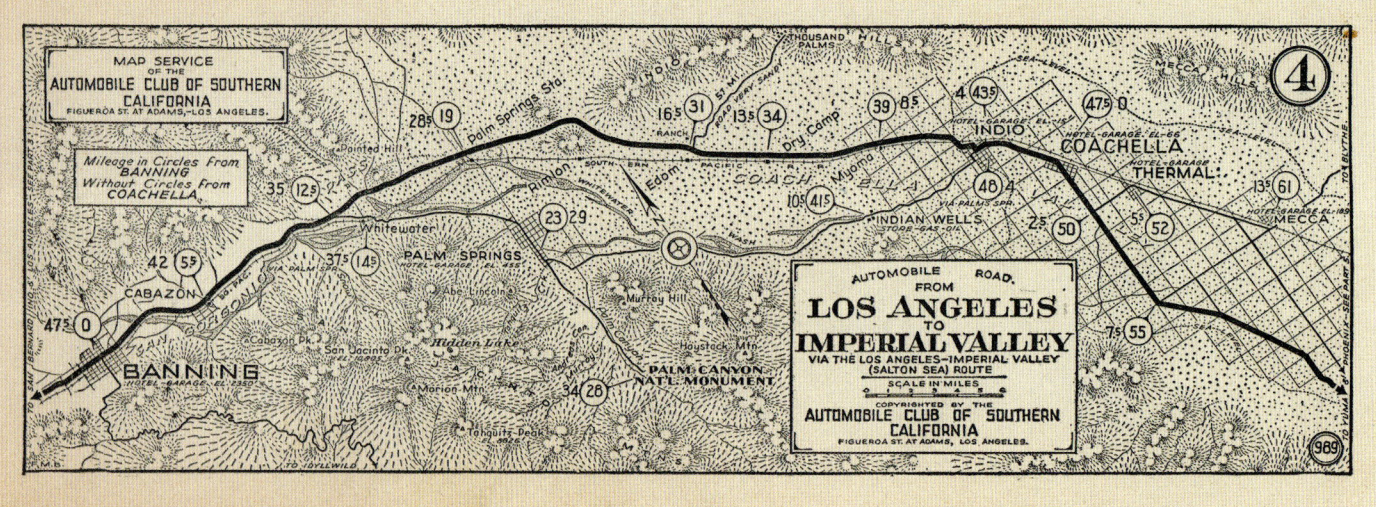

An early map from the Automobile Club of Southern California for members. The official hotel was the Desert Inn and the official garage was Bunker's Garage in Palm Springs.

Irving Berlin is said to have written "White Christmas" while staying at the La Quinta Hotel.

Frank Capra, a regular visitor to the La Quinta Hotel, considered it his good luck charm and wrote several screenplays while staying there, including "It Happened One Night" and "Lost Horizon."

THE MAGIC AND THE WAY OF LIFE

The Coachella Valley's first visitors came not for its glamour, nightlife, tennis or golf. They came for relief.

They arrived in the late 19th century when tuberculosis was a common affliction for which there was no known cure. The only deliverance tuberculosis sufferers could hope for was warm, dry air. Doctors also recommended soaking the body in hot mineral springs.

The desert had both in abundance.

Palm Springs first hotel wasn't so much a hotel as a sanatorium. Built in 1887 by Dr. Welwood Murray, it attracted visitors from the world over. Their deepest desire was to breathe in the desert's crystalline air, to bask in its constant sunshine and to "take the waters." For diversion, these early visitors might take a buckboard ride into the mountains and enjoy a picnic in the spectacular Indian Canyons.

The desert's weather was so helpful that more sanatoriums soon sprang up. Lavinia Crocker opened a convalescent home in 1898 which Nellie and Harry Coffman bought in 1909, renaming it The Desert Inn and Sanitorium. There were also the La Palma Hotel, the Tauchers' Wintergarden, the Goff family's hotel, and the Monte Vista apartments. All advertised themselves as havens for those with tuberculosis, asthma, arthritis and other ailments. The Desert Inn's advertisements claimed it was "...first class in every respect, rooms with private baths and all of the conveniences of the City without the City's Nervous Tension."

Many came from the cold, moist cities around San Francisco. Round trip train fare from San Francisco to Palm Springs in those days cost $25. Round trip from Los Angeles cost $3.50.

The Desert Inn, Palm Springs circa 1920.

ARTISTS SPREAD THE WORD

During this early, quiet period, noted artists, photographers and naturalists began visiting the desert, creating works that piqued the curiosity and wonder of people across the nation. The beauty and sensuality of the Palm Springs Valley, its spectacular mountains and unusual scenery were remarked upon, sketched and photographed.

Early Palm Springs circa 1940s.

The great naturalist John Muir himself visited The Desert Inn in 1905 for the benefit of his sick daughter, Helen. Carl Eytel, a Los Angeles Times artist, fell in love with the desert and ultimately became better known as a desert landscape artist than a newspaper artist, traveling the country to sing the desert's praises. He contributed over 300 sketches of the Valley to a 1906 book by George Wharton James called "Wonders of the Colorado Desert." A prominent newspaper cartoonist, Jimmy Swinnerton, came to Palm Springs in 1907 to recover from tuberculosis, and spread the news of the desert's wonders to the entire nation through the Hearst newspapers.

With ambassadors like Swinnerton, Wharton and Eytel, the desert's charms did not remain secret for long.

Soon the convalescent population was outnumbered by ordinary travelers wanting to see the storied wonders of the desert for themselves. The awe-inspiring Indian Canyons were the great jewel that drew them. By the 1920s, the Indian Canyons were a major tourist attraction, particularly for day-trippers from Los Angeles. Frank Bogert recalls how every Sunday night "the little towns of Banning and Beaumont were filled with bumper to bumper traffic, with tourists heading back to Los Angeles after a Sunday hike in the Indian Canyons." In the winter of 1924, over 35,000 people visited the startlingly beautiful oasis.

Diving exhibition at the El Mirador Hotel, now Desert Regional Medical Center circa 1940s.

THE FIRST HOTELS AND LEGENDARY RESORTS

As the Modern era dawned, the desert's image began to change. The first hotel to attract a new type of visitor appeared in La Quinta, not Palm Springs. Harry Morgan, the son of a wealthy San Francisco businessman, settled in an area 30 miles east of Palm Springs known as Marshall Cove, building a secluded retreat in the rustic Mission style in the north end of "The Cove."

His La Quinta Hotel opened in 1927 with 20 casitas and a golf course. Prized for its seclusion and quiet (it was literally out in the middle of nowhere, with only a dirt road connecting it to the city of Palm Springs) it was nonetheless much more than a simple retreat. It was the first desert hotel to gain a reputation as a place where movie stars and the rich and famous came to relax and recreate. Today the La Quinta Resort and Club has grown to 640 casitas and is known as one of the Valley's premier resorts.

A year after the La Quinta Hotel was built the elegantly Moorish El Mirador Hotel opened up in Palm Springs. By the mid-1930s this hotel was making history as the winter playground of wealthy industrialists, high-living politicians and the Hollywood elite. Avidly promoted by its owner and master publicist Walter Pinney, the El Mirador helped to establish the desert's early reputation as an enchanting, exclusive paradise.

Mecca, circa 1915, Hotel which served breakfast of ham and eggs for 45 cents and a regular dinner for 50 cents.

Frank Bogert, who served as the El Mirador's public relations agent from 1934 to 1936, recalls how he used the media to broadcast the high-living image of El Mirador. "Every time a guest checked in to the hotel, I would look them up in Poore's 'Directory of Directors' to see if they were someone notable," he recalls. "One time, Dan Bull came in from Minneapolis in the middle of winter. He was one of the big shots from the Cream of Wheat company and one of the few people who came from Minneapolis that year. Well, I took a picture of him sunning by the pool and sent it to the papers back in Minnesota. The next year we had 30 guests from Minneapolis."

RUSTIC PLEASURES

Hotel Indio a modern inn located in the heart of California's winter playground circa 1947.

El Mirador Hotel in Palm Springs circa 1940s.

La Quinta Resort and Club built in 1926 has a history as the deserts hideaway for celebrities and visitors.

Despite Palm Springs growing reputation as a cosmopolitan playground, the Coachella Valley remained a mostly rural place. Sally McManus, Director of the Palm Springs Historical Society whose family moved here in the 1940s, recalls those early days: "Most people even in the '40s got around on horseback. There was no TV and only one radio station (its call letters were KCMJ and it was a CBS affiliate), so there was no way to follow the trends of the day. It was all so free. We could spend all day running around in our bare feet."

This pastoral quality, and the townspeople's disinterest in big city goings-on, in a sense made the desert's Hollywood high life reputation possible. Says McManus, "We respected the privacy of the celebrities, which made them like it here."

Another tourist industry began to thrive 11 miles east of Palm Springs in an area known as Rancho Mirage. There, dude ranches and rustic hotels began to spring up, drawing in the kind of visitors who wanted nothing more than to ride horseback and take in the desert's natural beauty.

Rancho Mirage had begun as an agricultural town, with the DaVall family establishing the Wonder Palms Date Ranch in the area below Magnesia Falls Canyon. But the rugged pastoral beauty of the place inspired hotel developers. William Everett was the first to buy hundreds of acres and build a dude ranch, which he named the Eleven Mile Ranch. He had ambitious plans to create a kind of Nile Valley in Rancho Mirage, but those plans crashed along with the stock market in 1929.

However, that didn't stop Rancho Mirage from eventually becoming a popular retreat for the horsey set. After World War II The Desert Air Hotel made its debut. A totally unique hostelry, it included a private plane airport, hotel, and polo field. The Desert Air Hotel became legendary among a certain type of rarefied traveler, who could fly in, walk from their plane to the registration desk and check in for a few days of polo and relaxation in the sun. Today the Marriott Rancho Las Palmas Hotel, off Highway 111 on Bob Hope Drive, occupies the land formerly owned by the Desert Air Hotel.

Eventually the White Sun Guest Ranch was built where the Eleven Mile Ranch had been, and it, too, became a legendary spot for desert idylls. As Rancho Mirage grew, dude ranches and rural hotels were eventually replaced by golf courses and homes, and guests were replaced by well-heeled residents (both the late Walter Annenberg and former President Gerald Ford have made homes in Rancho Mirage).

One very special type of guest tended to frequent Rancho Mirage, burnishing its reputation as a playground for the elite: the city has hosted every single president since Harry Truman.

With radio, movies, newspapers and magazines spreading images of sunny high jinks and poolside pleasures across the land, Palm Springs gradually entered the forefront of the nation's consciousness as "America's Foremost Desert Resort City."

General Patton and General McNair photographed at the Desert Training Camp, established in late March 1942. Patton made Camp Young his headquarters. Preserving the past for the future, visit the Patton Army Air Field and the General George Patton Memorial Museum.

Courtesy of Palm Springs Historical Society.

THE POSTWAR BOOM

Andy Rolan known as "Andy the Donkey Man" who was a prospector in the area and would come into town and offer children rides on his donkey for 50 cents. Andy was struck and killed by an automobile on New Years Day, 1974. circa 1950s.

A few years after World War II ended, in a community 20 miles east of Palm Springs known as Palm Village, a man by the name of Cliff Henderson had a vision for a new kind of resort development. He teamed up with Hollywood entertainer Edgar Bergen (without his famous dummy, Charlie McCarthy) and in 1948 they opened the Shadow Mountain Resort in what today is Palm Desert.

His plan didn't follow the traditional resort plan, with a hotel, tennis courts and golf course. It was a resort consisting of cottages, a figure-eight swimming pool and a dining room. It was called the Shadow Mountain Resort.

Current Shadow Mountain Resort & Club, General Manager, Stephen Frisbee describes Henderson's plan this way: "Everything bought and built here was a cottage to be used between December and March. The Los Angeles market was the source of all the early business, and it was originally just a social club with a pool and communal dining where people could buy lots." After building cottages on their lots, people could come back year after year to see the same friends, enjoy the desert weather and play in the Club's figure-eight-shaped pool.

A hotel was built on the property in the 1950s, and Henderson began staging diving exhibitions and water ballets in the pool. These were performed by world-class athletes, whose feats were captured on film. The film was sold to newsreel companies that soon broadcast the Shadow Mountain lifestyle to audiences across the country.

Courtesy of Andy Hollinger

By now Palm Springs had lost some of its original hotels, the El Mirador was turned into a hospital during World War II while The Desert Inn was torn down in the 1950s. With the advent of the Shadow Mountain Resort, development shifted to the central Coachella Valley. Palm Desert's Shadow Mountain Resort was soon followed by the Eldorado Country Club in Indian Wells and the Indian Wells Country Club. The Eldorado was and still is home to some of the nation's most prominent citizens. President Eisenhower is said to have written his memoirs at Eldorado. The two clubs established Indian Wells as a prestigious community where the wealthy came to enjoy the desert's wintertime climate.

El Mirador Hotel was turned into a hospital during World War II, circa 1942.

Boat Races on the Salton Sea circa 1940s.
Courtesy of The Coachella Valley Historical Society

Twenty-One world records were set at the Salton Sea Regatta in 1951.

New world records for airplanes were also set over the Salton Sea. An F-100 Super Sabre hit 767 miles per hour on one pass and averaged 754.98 over a 15 kilometer course.

Date Palm Beach on the Salton Sea.

A BOATER'S PARADISE

In 1926 a pair of San Francisco developers named Eilers and Goldthwait set about to develop the north shore of the Salton Sea, encouraging boaters to begin racing on the waters. Other developments sprang up – Salton City, Desert Beach – and the town of North Shore emerged. Elaborate yacht clubs were built, including the two million dollar North Shore Yacht club, boasting one of the largest marinas in Southern California.

By the 1940s, the Salton Sea was enjoying a heyday as a boater's paradise.

Stars like Jerry Lewis, the Beach Boys, and the Marx Brothers came to visit the club or kept boats at the marina. A championship golf course was built in Salton City. The Salton Sea was proclaimed the "fastest body of water in the world" by National Motorist magazine. Because of the lake's high salinity and the desert's low barometric pressure, racers were able to set dozens of world records speeding along its surface. Soon speedboaters from around the country were coming to Southern California to race on the Salton Sea. At one point, a local newspaper took the State Park to task for allowing too many boats on the lake – the boats were endangering swimmers trying to enjoy the beach.

Anglers and hunters also discovered the Salton Sea's bounty. Headlines of the day raved about the Coachella Valley as a "True Sports Wonderland" and a "Fisherman's Paradise."

But the Sea's salinity would eventually spell its doom. Headlines from the 1960s and '70s tell the story: "Salt Mars Salton Sea Sports," said one, and "Salton Sea Brine Threatens Fish Life." The Salton Sea was labeled as polluted and dirty, its luxurious resorts were abandoned, and boaters headed over to Lake Havasu and the Colorado River.

Today the Salton Sea State Park still attracts several hundred thousand visitors every year, and there are local residents who swear the area is a diamond in the rough. Norm Niver, a 30-year resident of West Shores, still takes a daily swim in the Sea and says, "It is an absolutely beautiful place to live."

TENNIS ANYONE

During the 1970s, tennis surged in popularity across the United States and nearly equaled golf in popularity. One local observes that, "When tennis was on the rise in the United States, every hotel, country club, condominium and many private homes built courts. The Davis Cup Tournament was played at the Racquet Club; other tournaments were staged at courts all over the city. For a while, tennis almost equaled golf in popularity."

Besides the Davis Cup, other major tournaments that came to the desert included the 1981 Grand Marnier ATP and the Congoleum Classic in 1982-84, renamed the Pilot Penn in 1985 and '86.

Pilot Penn was sponsor when Charlie Pasarell announced plans to build a 10,000-seat stadium across from the old Erawan Garden Hotel (now the Miramonte Hotel). The world's two best players, Boris Becker and Stefen Edberg, competed in the 1987 finals at the Hyatt Grand Champions Hotel stadium court. Pasarell increased the size of the stadium to 11,500, but that still wasn't big enough.

In the year 2000 Pasarell and partner Raymond Moore achieved an even higher benchmark for tennis, when they built the $70 million dollar, 16,000-seat Indian Wells Tennis Garden. The stadium's inauguration coincided with the 2000 Newsweek Tennis Masters Series. The tournament gained a new sponsor in 2001, becoming the Pacific Life Open, presented by the City of Indian Wells.

Bob Hope and Charlie Farrell at the Racquet Club in Palm Springs.

First ever held Easter Bowl Doubles Title Tennis Tournament was held at the Palm Springs Riviera Resort & Racquet Club in 1996. Andy Roddick of Wesley Chapel Florida (far right) and partner Chris Martin (2nd from the right) went on to win.

Serena Williams plays at the Pacific Life Open 2001.

Desert Inn's Mashie Course the No. 7 green circa 1930s.

THE GLORIOUS GAME OF GOLF

Palm Spring's first golf course was a nine-hole course built by Prescott Stevens, the builder and first owner of the El Mirador Hotel (before it was bought by Walter Pinney) in 1928. But in the aftermath of the 1929 stock market crash, Stevens was forced to close the course in 1932.

Golf re-emerged in Palm Springs in the 1940s when Tom O'Donnell, a wealthy visitor and frequent guest at The Desert Inn, built a large house overlooking the hotel and purchased land near it for a private course. His guests played by invitation only. When his health began to fail in 1944, O'Donnell invited 25 friends to form a club with himself as president. O'Donnell eventually deeded the course to the City of Palm Springs and the city's first continuously operating golf course, the O'Donnell, still operates today.

The electric golf cart was developed and first used at the Thunderbird Country Club in Rancho Mirage.

Landmark Golf 2000 Skins Game (L to R) Joe Walser, Jr. Executive V.P. and Ernie Vossler, President Landmark Golf Co., Robert Wagner Chairman Landmark's Advisory Board, Judy Vossler, Tournament Director, Colin Montgomerie, 2000 Skins Game Champion.

But the real golf course boom began when the Thunderbird Dude Ranch in Rancho Mirage was converted into the Thunderbird Country Club. The course was financed by selling lots along the fairway to people looking for second homes in the desert.

The following year, Tamarisk Country Club opened for play with Ben Hogan, the world's best-known golfer at the time, as pro. Golf course country clubs soon became the vogue, attracting those entranced by the prospect of owning a second home with fairway and mountain views, drenched in an atmosphere of luxury and leisure. Early country clubs like Morningside, Canyon, The Vintage, Eldorado, The Springs and Cathedral Canyon all copied the successful formula of Thunderbird.

Ernie Vossler's Landmark Golf Company built many of the desert's golf courses from the 1950s on. When asked about his early vision of the golf community growth and development in the Coachella Valley, he replied, "I consider what's now called 'my vision' to have been merely a good guess. As a PGA Touring professional and while playing in a golf tournament at Thunderbird Country Club in 1955, I recognized that there seemed to be unlimited land and an affordable, plentiful water supply here. I also knew that land and water for development were becoming scarce in the Los Angeles/Orange County areas of Southern California. That, combined with the natural beauty of the desert and the affluent people who were coming to the area, led me to believe that our golf course developments would be successful. That's the guess I made, and it just happened to be right."

Bill Bone was another pioneer in the building of the first desert golf communities, founding the Sunrise Company in 1963 and gradually earning a reputation as a national expert on residential/recreational development. Today the Sunrise Company

Battle at BIGHORN 2002 golfers Tiger Woods and Arnold Palmer.

continues to develop country clubs throughout the western United States, with the much-anticipated Toscana Country Club about to begin construction in Indian Wells.

Today the Coachella Valley claims the title of "Golf Capital of the World," with more golf courses per capita (113) than anywhere in the world. It hosts several nationally televised golf tournaments including the The Skins Game, The Battle at BIGHORN, The Nabisco Tournament, the Bob Hope Chrysler Classic, the Frank Sinatra Celebrity Invitational and the Kraft Nabisco Championship, among others.

Looking to the future, Vossler comments that, "Due to the land mass and the desire for a quieter, more secure quality of life, growth here will continue for decades. Proportionately, there will be more high-end projects with the service industry following. Growth here will double faster than anyone can project; environmental issues can be solved here while it's nearly impossible in the Los Angeles area. I'm one who looks to the future…and from where I sit, it looks exciting."

Bob Hope early '80s at the Bob Hope Classic.

An early breakfast for the Desert Riders circa 1940s.

DESERT RIDERS

Horseback riding has always been a popular pastime in the Coachella Valley. Guests who stayed at Palm Springs very first hotels took guided horseback rides into the nearby Indian Canyons. In the 1920s, Smoke Tree Stables opened in Palm Springs, and in the 1930s a group called the Desert Riders formed, organizing rides into the local mountains and canyons.

About the same time, people began playing polo in the desert. Today Indio is known in polo circuits as "The Winter Polo Capital of the West," where English royalty and celebrities from the world of polo come to test their skills. Along with West Palm Beach, Florida, Indio is considered America's polo epicenter, and owes much of its success to its dry climate, ideal conditions for growing the Bermuda grass upon which the game is played.

Wild horses, a legacy of the Valley's early settlers, could be spotted in the Indian Canyons as recently as 1992.

Desert Riders circa 1931.

Prince Charles plays polo at the Eldorado Polo Club circa 1986.

Alex Jacoy, General Manager of the Eldorado Polo Club, comments that "We stable over 1,200 head of horses and stage 1,000 games every season. We're active in the community, having given money to a number of local organizations such as Pegasus Riding Academy, the Bob Hope Cultural Center, Desert Junior Golf and the Barbara Sinatra Children's Center. We've been in the Valley for 46 years."

Eldorado Polo players visiting from Mexico.

THE CONVENTION BUSINESS

Beginning in the 1950s, business interests began cultivating a new kind of tourist, the conventioneer. As the convention business grew it sparked a new wave of hotel construction. Eventually it spawned the 100,000-sq. ft. Palm Springs Convention Center, and today – according to the Palm Springs Desert Resorts Convention and Visitors Authority (PSDRCVA) – convention attendees account for nearly 30 percent of all visitors to the Coachella Valley.

"The convention visitor is critical to our tourism industry," says Doug Small, vice president of sales and marketing at the PSDRCVA, "because the leisure traveler is generally here on the weekends only, and so the conventioneer helps to fill in those gaps. The convention hotels like the Desert Springs JW Marriott Resort and Spa wouldn't survive without the convention visitors. Group business accounts for about 70 percent of the business at the larger hotels. While only 32 out of our 200 hotels handle group business, those 32 hotels have a majority of the Valley's rooms. We look at the convention business as our base business."

Westin Mission Hills Resort & Golf Club, list as one of the "Top 75 Golf Resorts in America", Golf Digest Magazine, March 2002.

With the Valley spreading eastward, ranking destination hotels in the new resorts east of Palm Springs began to absorb some of the convention business. The Hyatt Grand Champions and Miramonte Hotels in Indian Wells, the Desert Springs JW Marriott Resort and Spa in Palm Desert and the Westin Mission Hills Resort & Golf Club in Rancho Mirage became destinations of choice for organizations looking to reward their most valuable employees. Today many top hotels are enlarging their facilities to accommodate even more conventioneers. The Hyatt Grand Champions is presently adding 60,000 square feet of convention space, while plans are underway in Palm Springs to double their Convention Center to over 200,000 square feet of meeting space.

Palm Springs Convention Center.

The Hyatt Grand Champions Resort and Spa - Indian Wells.

Hot air balloon ride showing the Valley.

Concert in Palm Desert with fireworks.

A PRIME DESTINATION

In addition to the traditional favorites of golf, horseback riding, and tennis, tourists who come to the Valley have many other options of entertainment and diversion. There are a jeep tours and hot air balloon rides; guided bicycle and hiking tours; Knott's Berry Water Park; the Palm Springs Aerial Tramway; rock climbing adventures on an outdoor climbing wall; strolls through the 1,200-acre Living Desert Wildlife Preserve or along El Paseo, with its world class stores; gambling at one of the local Indian Casinos … the list goes on and on.

Local concerts and festivals also draw crowds to the Valley. The La Quinta Arts Festival™, the gay-oriented White Party and the Pride Parade, the Coachella Music Fest held on the Empire Polo grounds, the dozen or so film festivals, the Riverside County Fair and National Date Festival and more, combine to draw hundreds of thousands of visitors to the desert each year.

According to Tim Sullivan, General Manager of the Desert Springs JW Marriott Resort and Spa, the desert's real attraction lies less in what there is to do than in its magical atmosphere. "This is a place that gives visitors a glorious sense of disconnect," he says. "It's a relief you just don't get in Las Vegas or other destinations where there's a city close by. This place still has a small-town atmosphere and small-town values, despite all the recent development. There's a certain 'zeitgeist,' a spirit in the air. People come here and their cares just fall away when they relax and luxuriate in the warmth."

Mark Graves, Media Relations Manager for the Palm Springs Desert Resorts Convention and Visitors Authority, says the number one appeal of the desert is to "Rest, relax and rejuvenate. People leave here feeling a heck of a lot better."

The geography, along with the weather, has a lot to do with its therapeutic effects. "The mountains that surround the Valley are a physical barrier that separate us from the rest of the world," Graves notes.

With proper planning, Graves sees no end in sight to Palm Springs appeal. "We know there is going to be growth and that is fine. We have to temper that growth to preserve the area's natural appeal and scenery. Many of our large resorts these days are adding on to their existing properties, instead of building one 600-room resort after another.

"We're always going to be a prime destination, as long as we maintain the magic and the way of life."

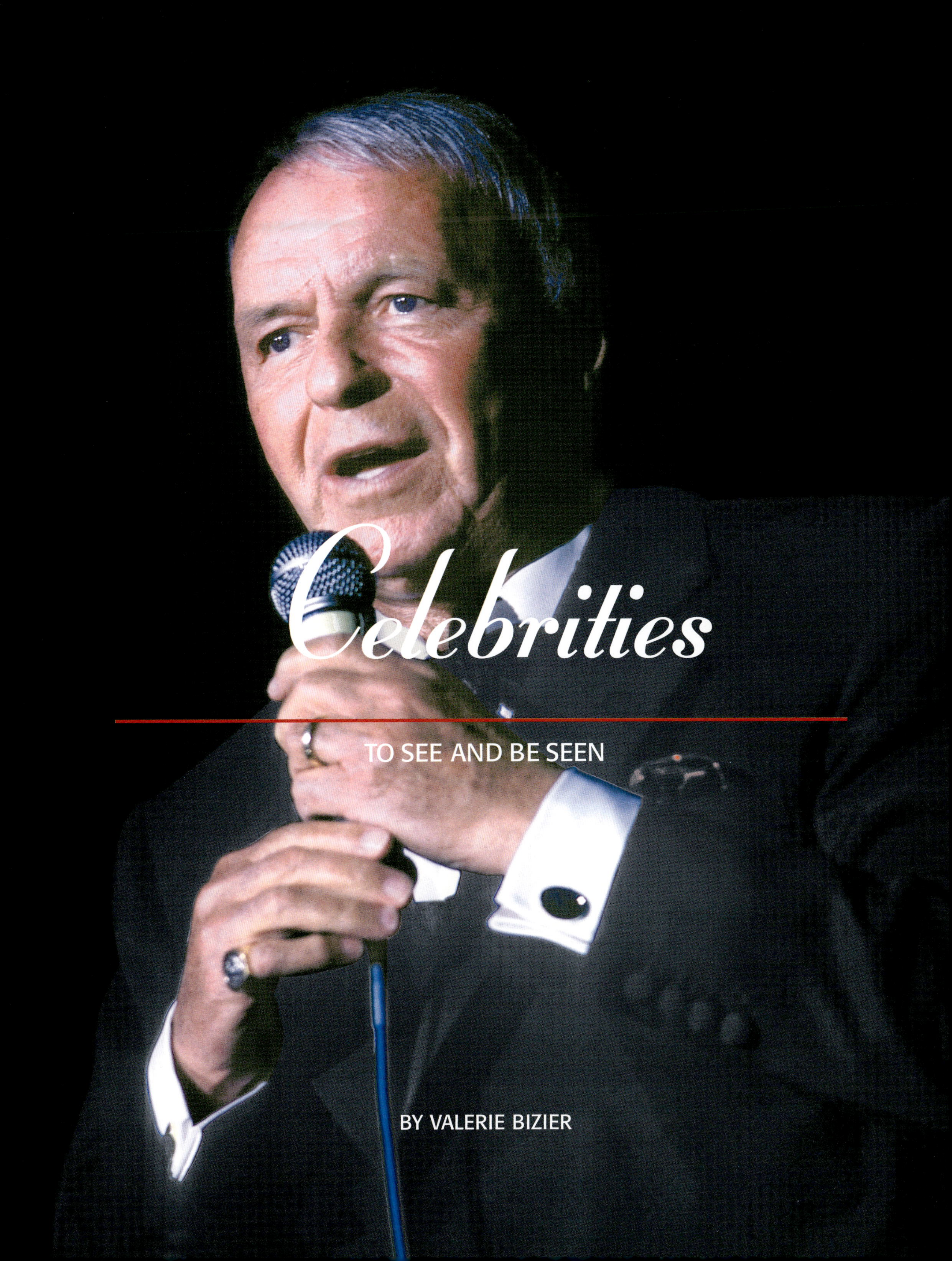

Celebrities

TO SEE AND BE SEEN

BY VALERIE BIZIER

Walt Disney riding in the Desert Circus Parade, circa 1955.

Courtesy of Palm Springs Historical Society

TO SEE AND BE SEEN

Whenever stories are told about the legendary Palm Springs, Hollywood celebrities are a part of it.

The earliest visits by Hollywood royalty happened early in the 20th century, when the desert was used as a backdrop for silent movies. Movies set in desert-like locations — movies like "Salome" with Theda Bara and "Desert Gold" with William Powell, not to mention the ubiquitous Hollywood Westerns — often went on location. When the location was Palm Springs, the leading men and women of these films would be put up at The Desert Inn or some other hostelry, often staying for days or weeks. They got comfortable in the desert, becoming a natural part of the local scene.

Residents soon took them for granted and stopped noticing that they were stars. This easy harmony between stars and residents created an atmosphere that would last for decades, many say until the early 1960s. A kind of "Camelot" era ensued, in which stars could let down their hair and act like normal people, socializing, doing business and playing sports with locals, and blending into the desert scene. For the stars, it was a luxury they'd given up in their search for fame and fortune — the luxury of public anonymity.

The first Desert Circus was held in Palm Springs in 1934 to raise money for the church rectory on the Indian Reservation.

Shirley Temple was a frequent guest at The Desert Inn. She is seen here greeting the owner Nellie Coffman and christening her cottage with a bottle of milk, circa 1930s.

WHERE THEY STAYED

The La Quinta Hotel opened in 1926 and the El Mirador in Palm Springs in 1928, both attracting a Hollywood set looking for freedom, privacy and fun. Writers and directors especially appreciated the solitude of La Quinta to work on scripts. Three-time Oscar-winning director Frank Capra liked it so much he eventually moved into the hotel, where he is said to have written "It's a Wonderful Life," among other Oscar-winning movies.

But the most legendary hangouts for the Hollywood set would center in Palm Springs. The El Mirador Hotel actively courted celebrities as part of its marketing strategy. It sent flyers to the studios in Los Angeles and advertised in the movie industry's trade papers. Whenever a star of some magnitude showed up at the El Mirador, photos would be taken and distributed to newspapers. Gradually, the El Mirador became "the" place to go for Hollywood's elite.

Jack Benny often stayed there, bringing along his colleague Eddie Anderson, who played Rochester on Benny's radio and television programs. It is said that Anderson, despite his fame, encountered racism and was turned away from a number of downtown hotels in Palm Springs. The El Mirador's manager, Walter Pinney, was the only hotelier sophisticated enough to grant him entrance.

Frank Bogert, first Elected Mayor of Palm Springs 1958-1966 and 1982-1988, early photo 1927.

Lucy at the El Mirador in 1938 when she was a young starlet.

Stars like Bing Crosby used to cruise the Valley looking for night spots, hitting the bars and nightclubs where a variety of Western bands played authentic country music. Hollywood was so enamored of the village's Western culture that it started a charity fundraiser in 1934 called the Desert Circus. Honorary sheriffs were appointed, and empowered to arrest anyone not dressed in Western attire. The fines went to fund local charities and civic causes.

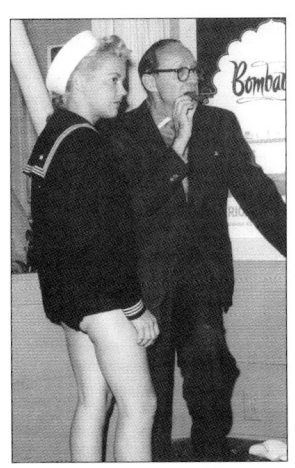

Photo By John Miller

Racquet Club, 1939. Jackie Cooper greets newlyweds Lana Turner & Artie Shaw.

Tracy, Ginger Rogers and the original crooner, Rudy Vallee, were among the first guests. Dietrich eventually stayed there, too, until she bought a house in Palm Springs and became a desert resident, sending her daughter to Palm Springs High School. Daughter Marie Riva and her son Paul still live in Palm Springs. Paul's wife, Marilee, is the leader of a Playwright's Circle that performs readings of new plays by authors from around the United States.

The Racquet Club became the place to see and be seen, and it developed a reputation for exclusivity. "We refused a lot of people admittance," Farrell admits. "It was a private club and you had to have a card." Even Mickey Rooney – a top box office attraction of the late 1930s – was once turned away.

THE RACQUET CLUB

In 1934 the Palm Springs Racquet Club opened. How it came into being is one of the legendary stories of Palm Springs.

Charlie Farrell, a silent movie star who often played opposite Janet Gaynor, was a tennis buff. He and pal Ralph Bellamy often played at the El Mirador Hotel. Once when they were enjoying a long match, Marlene Dietrich decided she wanted to play and had hotel manager Walter Pinney kick the two buddies off the courts (as a bigger star than either Farrell or Bellamy, Dietrich got to be king – or in this case queen – of the hill). The tennis buddies were so incensed they vowed to build their own tennis courts.

Farrell claims the Racquet Club was an afterthought. "There was no place to play tennis," he claimed, "so Ralph Bellamy and I decided to build some tennis courts. We built too many and had to make it a club."

Farrell and Bellamy invited their friends to play and stay at the Racquet Club, and it became an overnight success. Celebrities like Clark Gable, Spencer

Jack Benny watches a performance at the Bombay Club inside the Racquet Club.

Celebrating at the Racquet Club: Charlie Farrell, Rudy Vallee, (center) and Ralph Bellamy, circa 1930s.

Marlene Dietrich & Leslie Howard at the El Mirador (he played Ashley in Gone With The Wind) circa 1940s.

55

VISITORS BECOME RESIDENTS

The Racquet Club introduced scores of celebrity personalities to Palm Springs, inspiring both stars and moguls to build homes in the area. Charlie Chaplin and Paulette Goddard set up house in Palm Springs, where they enjoyed playing charades with William and Diana "Mousie" Powell. (Imagine competing against Chaplin in charades.) Darryl Zanuck of 20th Century Fox, Joe Schenk of MGM, Howard Hughes of RKO and Jack Warner of Warner Bros. bought land and built some of the biggest homes in Palm Springs.

Harold Lloyd owned a large estate in the old movie star colony, close to the home of heavyweight boxing champion Jack Dempsey. Al Jolson and Eddie Cantor, the highest paid stage performers of the 1920s, played golf and cards in the desert with other great vaudevillians such as the Marx Brothers and Milton Berle.

Bing Crosby invested heavily in land in the Coachella Valley, including a trailer park in Rancho Mirage. He convinced bandleader Phil Harris and his wife — 20th Century-Fox's top female star, Alice Faye — to buy land, too. Harris built a home in Rancho Mirage in 1933 that was so remote it didn't have a phone, and he had to drive down dirt roads to get there. Harris often said life in the desert was like "a game of pretend." Its distance from the "real" world of Hollywood gave it a dream-like quality — a dream you got to share with all of your best friends!

Depression-era directors Busby Berkeley, John Ford and Clarence Brown all had homes in the desert, as did Greta Garbo, Clara Bow, Cary Grant and, a little later, Kirk Douglas, Red Skelton and William Holden.

Mary Pickford (married to Buddy Rogers) in the 1930s.

All American Girls Professional Baseball League (1943-1954.) Seven of the original players who now call the desert their home got together at Big League Dreams Sports Park, 2003. (L to R) Shirley Burkovich, Marge Wenzell, Dottie Kamenshek, Lee Delmonico, Thelma "Tiby" Eisen, Pauline Crawley, Dorthoy Harrell Doyle. Front row Kim Kirmss and Victoria Bailey, Publisher, Desert Springs Publishing.

William Holden was a resident of Southridge. A permanent collection of his memorabilia may be seen at the Desert Museum in Palm Springs.

SALAD DAYS
THE BEST TIMES

Jack Benny and comedians Freeman Gosden and Charles Correll, who played the radio characters Amos & Andy, were among the few desert celebrities to ever broadcast their radio show from Palm Springs (they broadcast from The Plaza Theatre on Palm Canyon Drive). Many locals found it easier to see the duo in person than to hear them on the radio. Large antenna had to be installed in order to receive a Los Angeles station carrying the program, so why not simply drive down over to the Plaza Theatre to watch them perform?

Merv Griffin was introduced to the Coachella Valley through the old Palm Springs scene that included the "Amos & Andy Show." He ended up owning the glamorous Merv Griffin Resort in Palm Springs from 1998 until 2002. Griffin still lives in the Valley on a large, tree-lined horse ranch in La Quinta. He serves as honorary chairman of the La Quinta Arts Festival, entertaining crowds at the outdoor festival every year.

"We used to go to Charlie Farrell's Racquet Club of Palm Springs and the Doll House," recalled Griffin in 1999. "And one time my uncle took me out to show me Charlie Correll's place way out in La Quinta. I said to myself, 'Who the hell would ever come out here? And here I am. That was when there was no Rancho Mirage, no Palm Desert, nothing.'"

By the time it was incorporated in 1938, Palm Springs was hopping. With all the nightlife in the village, no one needed to travel for entertainment. There was Western music at Rogers Ranch (at a venue dubbed the Mink and Manure Club) and major music and comedy acts at the raging Chi Chi Club, which opened in 1936.

Palm Springs Aerial Tramway attracts celebrities Prince Rainer and Princess Grace of Monaco, their 3 children and a friend.

Howard Hughes became a familiar face in the desert around that time. "He used to come in the Racquet Club all the time when I was there," long-time resident Frank Bogert recalls. "Always had old tweed pants on and a white shirt, never a coat. We used to kid him about being deaf. You know, when you talked to him, he was deaf. But he said he could hear a girl whisper a mile away." He owned several homes in the Palm Springs area.

Buddy Rogers began staying in the desert after marrying his long-time friend, Mary Pickford, in 1937. He was a supporter of several causes associated with his golfing buddy, Bob Hope, and Hope's wife, Dolores, whom he had known in New York before she married Bob. But Rogers really stepped up his philanthropy in the desert after Pickford's death in 1979, when he took a managing interest in the Mary Pickford Foundation. He contributed to a number of local causes, but was particularly generous to the Variety Club of the Desert, Tent 66, which provides funding and services to local Boys & Girls clubs, and the Coachella Valley Symphony.

With an endowment from the Pickford Foundation, the Buddy Rogers Youth Symphony was formed, which today unites young musicians from all over the Valley. Shortly before his death in 1999, Rogers was named Good Samaritan of the Year by the Good Samaritans of the Desert for his support for the elderly. A street in

Kirk Douglas and family are long-time residents of Palm Springs. Some of the Douglas children have attended Palm Springs schools.

Courtesy of Palm Springs Historical Society

Audrey Hepburn.

James Dean after a car race in Palm Springs.

Ingleside Inn owner Mel Haber with Lucy.

THE BOB HOPE INFLUENCE

Many celebrities owned multiple homes in the desert, among them Bob Hope. He first visited the area in 1938 and would later be named the most popular celebrity in Palm Springs.

Hope had two recreational passions: golf and walking. Some say his enthusiasm for golf is what turned the sport into a major Coachella Valley industry. Hope's love of walking certainly helped him become the most visible major celebrity in the desert. "Hope used to walk through town with a golf driver over his shoulder and come in and see a lot of our shows at the Chi Chi," says band leader Bill Alexander. Hope's sociable meandering kept him in touch with a range of people around the desert, making him a reliable staple of Palm Springs life.

Bing and Bob in Palm Springs making one of their "Road Show" pictures, priest unidentified.

Cathedral City was named in his honor after a campaign spearheaded by the late Variety Club Tent 66 executive director, Irene Austin.

Mary Pickford spent time in the desert, too, but was not as active in philanthropic activities as her husband. Rogers and his next wife, Beverly Rogers (who still has a home in the desert), arranged through the Pickford Foundation to build a small museum in memory of Mary Pickford in the Cathedral City Town Square. Buddy Rogers Drive runs right by the Mary Pickford Theatre, where the museum is housed.

THE INGLESIDE INN

No discussion of celebrities in the desert would be complete without mention of The Ingleside Inn, the quaint 30-room resort close to downtown Palm Springs. It was a mainstay of visiting Hollywood royalty from the 1930s through the 1960s, and it continues to attract a select Hollywood crowd in search of the "real" desert scene.

First owned by Ruth Hardy from 1935 to 1965, it had been converted from a private home originally built in 1925. For over 30 years, Hardy somehow managed to attract to this charming resort the top tier of celebrities (including Howard Hughes and Elizabeth Taylor), as well as America's captains of industry (such as the presidents of Bank of America and the Hoover vacuum cleaner empire). "How she attracted these celebrities and captains of industry I'll never know," remarks Mel Haber, who bought the place in 1975, 10 years after Hardy's death. Haber inherited Hardy's luck in attracting the rarefied echelons of the Hollywood elite. Regular patrons have included John Travolta, Sylvester Stallone, George Hamilton, Liza Minnelli and Arnold Schwarzenegger.

He built his first home in the old movie star colony near Lloyd and Dempsey, and his last on a hilltop overlooking the Indian Canyons on one side and the entire Valley on the other. He still owns all three of his Palm Springs homes. His wife of more than 60 years, the former singer Dolores Reade, says, "Bob never sells a property."

He does, however, donate property. He donated the Rancho Mirage property that became the site for a number of venerable local institutions: Eisenhower Medical Center, the Betty Ford Center for chemical dependency, the Barbara Sinatra Children's Center for abused youngsters and adults, and the Gene Autry Tower. Later he hosted the famous Bob Hope Chrysler Classic and the Bob Hope Ball, the primary fundraisers for the Medical Center.

Hope's list of honors received in the Valley, including honorary mayor of Palm Springs, could fill several pages. His only rival for the title of the Coachella Valley's most popular resident was Frank Sinatra.

THE GOLDEN VOICE

Frank Sinatra was not only an icon of late 20th century American pop music, he was also a skilled actor, painter, movie producer and record company owner. For all of his talents, however, Sinatra's greatest work of art, like Oscar Wilde's, was his own life. All kinds of people gravitated to him. Remarkably, many picked up their lives and businesses to be near him in the desert.

Frank Sinatra and Governor Jimmy Davis of Louisiana, promoting the local radio station KCMJ broadcasting from the Plaza Theater in Palm Springs, circa 1945.

Sinatra first came to the desert at the invitation of his songwriter friend, Jimmy Van Heusen (who would go on to win five Academy Awards). Shortly after his first visit, Sinatra fell in love with the place and moved into a house close to Van Heusen's.

An entourage of favorite pals followed: Rat Pack buddy Dean Martin, restaurateur Mike Romanoff, preferred clothier Sy Devore, Las Vegas casino manager Jack Entratter, comic Pat Henry, drummer Irv Cottler, Paramount producer Howard Koch, and, of course, beloved New York saloon keeper, Jilly Rizzo. Each moved to within a few blocks of Sinatra's and Van Heusen's homes in Rancho Mirage.

In 1947 Sinatra built a house on Alejo Road in Palm Springs. There were no paved roads from Palm Canyon Drive to the house, so Sinatra kept an Army Jeep in his garage for trips to the store. The house was initially a family getaway for the Sinatras, but stories abound that once Sinatra met sultry film star Ava Gardner at the Chi Chi, the Alejo house became their love nest.

Celebrities mixed so comfortably with residents in those days that all of the stars – even Sinatra – listed their addresses and telephone numbers in the local directory.

Frank Sinatra, first honorary mayor of Cathedral City, circa 1967.

GOLF TRANSFORMS THE CELEBRITY SCENE

The only thing still missing in Palm Springs was an 18-hole golf course. Bogert and some friends set out to remedy that in 1948 by turning plans for a dude ranch into plans for a championship golf course. The course opened three years later and became Thunderbird Country Club, where the rich and wealthy snatched up prime fairway sites. Early investors were Hope, Crosby, Harris, Benny, Harpo Marx, songwriter Hoagy Carmichael, tire magnate Leonard Firestone, and Lucy and Desi Arnaz. Subsequent residents included Ginger Rogers, Gordon and Sheila MacRae, silent film star Billie Dove and, in 1977, former President and First Lady Gerald and Betty Ford.

At her fairway home, Lucille Ball cultivated the image of "Little Ricky's" mom to the hilt, publicly appearing as the contented, conservative housewife. Music publisher Howie Richmond joined the club in the '50s and invited fellow publisher Abe Olman to move in next door. One day, when songwriter Johnny Mercer was visiting from Palm Springs, the three men conceived the idea for the Songwriters Hall of Fame in New York.

Bob Hope Desert Golf Classic 1963: Bob Hope, Frank Sinatra, and Dean Martin.

Bing and Bob with friends for a round of golf at Thunderbird Country Club.

In 1960 Arnold Palmer wins the first Classic, with added victories in 1962 and 1968.

The 2003 Bob Hope Chrysler Classic winner was Mike Weir.

Lucy & Desi anniversary dinner at Thunderbird Country Club, circa 1950s.

It wasn't too long after Thunderbird's opening that Benny and Marx, who were Jewish, sold their properties when they perceived the club to be anti-Semitic. One year later, they joined other Jewish celebrities and supporters to form an even more star-studded country club a few blocks away, Tamarisk Country Club. Harpo, Zeppo and Groucho Marx (the comedian who said that he'd never dream of joining a club that would have him as a member) immediately signed up at Tamarisk, along with producer Hal Wallis, comedians Danny Kaye and Red Skelton, oil man Marvin Davis and, in 1954, Sinatra. Golfing great Ben Hogan was brought on as the golf pro and Charlie Farrell, then starring in the TV series "My Little Margie," became board vice president. Walter Annenberg, Milton Berle and Dinah Shore also joined.

Courtesy of Palm Springs Historical Society.

President Eisenhower and friends golfing at Indian Palms Country Club in Indio, circa 1950s.

THE PLAYGROUND OF THE PRESIDENTS

Courtesy of Electric Car Distributors

President George Bush playing golf at Sunnylands, the late Walter Annenberg's estate.

President Eisenhower and his caddy in what is believed to be the first electric golf cart, circa 1950s.

While trying to enjoy a round of golf on the Tamarisk course several years later, Annenberg complained about the long wait for a tee-time. Someone suggested Annenberg "build his own golf course." So, in the early '60s, Annenberg did just that. In 1966 he and his wife, Lenore, settled into a 32,000-square-foot home right next to their own 9-hole golf course. Dubbed "Sunnylands," the pink-walled property at the corner of Bob Hope and Frank Sinatra drives in Rancho Mirage became internationally renowned for the number of American presidents who stayed there, including Nixon, Ford, Reagan, George Bush and Bill Clinton. (It is also the place where Frank Sinatra married Barbara Sinatra.) With former Vice President Spiro Agnew living up the street at The Springs Country Club, Rancho Mirage came to be known as the "Playground of the Presidents."

President John F. Kennedy visiting Palm Springs, greeted by Mayor Frank Bogert, circa 1962.

Courtesy of Electric Car Distributors

Actually, though, U.S. Presidents had long been coming to the Valley. Harry Truman and Herbert Hoover visited after their terms in office, Truman staying at a Tamarisk residence and Hoover at The Desert Inn in Palm Springs. But no presidential visit quite equaled the sensation caused by Dwight D. Eisenhower's 1954 Palm Springs vacation. Bogert recalls 2,000 people coming out to greet Ike and Mamie Eisenhower. For six days, Paul Helm's Smoke Tree Ranch home became the "Western White House," as the president played golf day after day at Tamarisk and Thunderbird country clubs.

GOLFING FOR CHARITIES

Photographer Ned Redway

Bob Hope Classic 1995: Presidents George Bush, Gerald Ford, and Bill Clinton.

The 15th annual Frank Sinatra Celebrity Golf Tournament was held February 2003 at the Renaissance Esmeralda Resort. The golf tournament benefits the non-profit Barbara Sinatra Children's Center founded in 1986.

Photographer Tom Brewster

Bob Hope Classic 2002: Richard Dreyfuss, President Gerald Ford, and Leslie Neilson.

While Arnold Palmer was popularizing golf across the country, he made a dramatic impact on the Coachella Valley by participating in a tournament that came to be known as the Bob Hope Chrysler Classic. It began in 1952 as a private event called the Thunderbird Invitational, at Thunderbird Country Club. The two-day tournament grew to four days, but by 1959 both the event and the golf course proved to be inadequate to the caliber of the Invitational's participants. Organizers — including Milton Hicks, Jimmy Hines, Eddie Susalla and Ernie Dunlevie — relocated the tournament to courses considered more challenging, among them Tamarisk, Indian Wells and Bermuda Dunes country clubs. They also had the tournament added to the Professional Golf Association's schedule as the Palm Springs Golf Classic.

By 1963, celebrity golf was popular enough to prompt Frank Sinatra, at the height of his Rat Pack days, to start his own pro-am. But it only lasted one season.

"We did the program for the first Sinatra tournament in 1963 at Canyon Country Club," said Milt Jones, publisher of one of the Valley's most venerable media institutions, *Palm Springs Life* magazine. "But it was in November and up against football season. Besides that, I think he hit someone in a parking lot around that time and all hell broke loose."

When Jones says Sinatra "hit" someone he's not referring to a traffic incident. "That was in the days when he was hitting people," Jones remarks.

It was a tough couple of years all around for Sinatra. His friend, President John F. Kennedy, had been assassinated in 1962; The Nevada Gaming Control Board threatened to revoke his license to operate his Cal-Neva Lodge in Lake Tahoe due to reports of mob ties; and his son was kidnapped from Cal-Neva and held for several days by extortionists.

Planning a follow-up golf tournament was probably the furthest thing from Sinatra's mind.

Bob Hope took it upon himself to carry on the Palm Springs celebrity golf tradition. In 1965, organizers of the Palm Springs Golf Classic asked him to host their tournament, which they would rename in his honor. The tournament became a success as much for the vaudeville on the green as for the championship golf. Players like Jackie Gleason and Mickey Rooney could crack up a gallery with their body language and quips.

The success of Bob Hope's pro-am tournament inspired a dozen other celebrity pro-ams in the desert, led by stars like Andy William and game show host Dennis James whose pro-am golf tournament the "Dennis James Celebrity Golf Classic" benefits United Cerebral Palsy.

Sinatra finally got another pro-am going in 1989 to benefit Palm Springs Desert Regional Medical Center, which had named a building in honor of his father. It was perhaps the most star-studded golf tournament of the '90s. Its gala was a social highlight, featuring guest stars like Julio Iglesias, Willie Nelson and Vic Damone performing alongside Sinatra. The event also supported the Barbara Sinatra Children's Center when that facility was in its planning stages. It later became a benefit exclusively for Eisenhower Medical Center when Desert Regional Medical Center was bought by a for-profit corporation. Frank Sinatra gave his last musical performance in 1995, at the black tie gala to conclude that tournament.

A WOMEN'S GOLF TOURNAMENT

Only one other celebrity pro-am provided the championship golf action that the Bob Hope offered. That was the Colgate-Dinah Shore Winners Circle, started in 1972 by the much-loved singer and television personality. The event received national television coverage from the very beginning, elevating the Ladies' Professional Golf Association from a golf footnote to a headliner attraction. It started with just 40 pros and a $110,000 purse. Shore's love for golf was contagious, though, and the pro-am kept growing in stature and star power. It was taken over by the Nabisco Corporation in 1982. The tournament's name has changed several times since then (it is now the Kraft Nabisco Championship) but the respect and admiration between players and Dinah Shore has remained constant.

Dinah Shore and Amy Alcott jumping into lake at the Colgate-Dinah Shore LPGA Tournament.

Colgate-Dinah Shore Winners Circle Amy Alcott winning the LPGA presented by Dinah Shore.

In 1988, after winning the tournament, Amy Alcott initiated a tradition at the LPGA event by spontaneously jumping into a golf course lake. Dinah told her, "If you do it next time you win, I'll jump in with you."

The following year, Alcott headed to the 18th hole with her second win in sight and noticed Dinah wearing a black outfit instead of her traditional white. Alcott expressed concern to her caddy, Bill Curry, about the prospect of Dinah's possible dive. "I said to Bill, 'You might want to say something to her. She's gonna slip and kill herself,'" Alcott recalled later. "But Dinah said she wanted to do it. And she did."

Dinah Shore was arguably the desert's most influential female celebrity during the '80s and '90s. She was one of Palm Springs Life's Big Three cover icons — Bob Hope for January, Frank Sinatra for February and Dinah Shore for March. "Celebrities sell magazines," remarks publisher Milt Jones, and Dinah Shore "was on the March cover for over 20 years. It was always our biggest seller. People never got tired of her."

A major figure in the desert for decades, Dinah Shore's death left a huge void for many.

MUSICIANS IN LOVE WITH THE DESERT

Elvis Presley first leased a home in Palm Springs in the mid 1960s. His manager, Colonel Tom Parker, had made the area his primary residence earlier in the decade, and Presley visited several times before making the commitment. Elvis and Priscilla Presley spent their 1967 honeymoon in a Palm Springs house now rented for special events as "The Honeymoon House."

Liberace with his brother George in the Desert Circus, 1965. Liberace is wearing his custom cowboy boots with candelabras on them.

Liberace came to the Valley in 1952 and bought several homes. He was a devoted son and lived with his mother in Palm Springs. Liberace was the second major American celebrity (after Rock Hudson) to die of AIDS, thus helping to publicize the disease's menace at a time when much of American society was either ignorant or in denial about it. Liberace died on February 4, 1987.

Sonny Bono relaxing by the pool at the Palm Springs Riviera Hotel.

Courtesy of Riviera Resort-Palm Springs

Desi Arnaz entertaining at the Palm Springs Riviera Hotel, circa 1950s.

Several members of the Rock 'N' Roll Hall of Fame developed a fondness for the desert, including the late John Phillips of the Mama and the Papas, Eric Burdon of the Animals and Glenn Frey of the Eagles. Burdon moved to Palm Springs in the '60s on the advice of his motorcycle-riding buddy Steve McQueen, who loved to ride his Harley-Davidson on the open desert roads.

Many ranking songwriters, too, have made the desert their home. Michael Masser, who penned Whitney Houston's "The Greatest Love of All," Diana Ross's "Touch Me In the Morning" and Peabo Bryson's "If Ever You're In My Arms Again," moved to Thunderbird Country Club in 2001. He began performing with local talent at charity fundraisers the following year. Billy Steinberg, who wrote Madonna's "Like A Virgin," Cyndi Lauper's "True Colors" and the Divynls' "I Touch Myself," is a graduate of Palm Springs High School.

FROM ROCKER TO REPUBLICAN

The only rocker to become a true "desert celebrity" was the late Sonny Bono, who had to become a politician to rise to that level. Sonny and Cher frequented Palm Springs and the Salton Sea in the '60s when they were recording songs like "I Got You Babe," "The Beat Goes On" and "Bang Bang." Bono continued visiting the desert after his divorce from Cher, and in the mid-1980s he and his fourth wife, Mary, decided to open a restaurant called Bonos in Palm Springs and make the city their full-time home.

For the grand opening of Bonos, they held a reception for the local media at the Racquet Club. Bono seemed as out of date there as the fabled but faded club itself. Fortunately for him, *Palm Springs Life* gave his image a boost when it ran a shot of the couple on its cover.

"It was a fluke," admits publisher Milt Jones today. "The cover we were planning that month didn't work out, and we had photos of Sonny and Mary our photographer had taken earlier in Los Angeles. When we lost the other cover, we thought, 'We've still got those photos of Sonny and Mary,' so it ran. I got all kinds of heat. Later, Sonny came back to me and said 'You have no idea what that's done for me.'"

Courtesy of Palm Springs Life magazine

Palm Springs Life Cover of Sonny and Mary Bono.

Initially, The Palm Springs International Film Festival honored local celebrities like Kirk Douglas, Lucille Ball, Frank Capra and Ruby Keeler. But by the time Bono had been elected to the U.S. Congress in the mid-'90s, it began importing younger stars. Among them were Richard Dreyfuss, Susan Sarandon, Sylvester Stallone and John Travolta.

When Bono died in a tragic skiing accident in 1998, his fame ascended to another level and propelled his widow, current Congresswoman Mary Bono, into national politics. A stretch of Interstate 10 has been named the "Sonny Bono Memorial Highway," and the Palm Springs International Airport has named a terminal after Bono.

In a move that would have amused the self-effacing singer-songwriter, the federal government named the Intellectual Property Rights Act in his honor.

Sonny Bono elected Mayor of Palm Springs.

Photographer Ned Redway

Bono was elected mayor of Palm Springs the same night Cher won an Oscar for "Moonstruck." The former hippie became a Republican, eventually leaving behind a legacy that includes the founding of the Palm Springs International Film Festival (today called the Nortel Networks Palm Springs International Film Festival).

Photographer Ned Redway

President Gerald R. Ford, Mayor Sonny Bono, Mary Bono, and Senator Bob Dole.

THE SPIRIT OF CHARITY

By the 1990s there was a distinct feeling that Palm Springs' glory days as a movie star haven were fading. It seemed as though the biggest stars coming to town were checking into the Betty Ford Center for rehab: names like Elizabeth Taylor, Liza Minnelli, Mary Tyler Moore, Kelsey Grammer, Johnny Cash and even Ozzy Osbourne.

Certain celebrity residents, however, continue to receive tribute locally from the McCallum Theatre in Palm Desert. The Valley's leading performing arts center manages to find a few nights every season to highlight its own: well-known singers such as Kaye Ballard, Jack Jones, Keely Smith, Peter Marshall and Ralph Young of Sandler & Young. These shows inevitably sell out, amidst a party atmosphere that infects everyone in the audience.

Today Barry Manilow is one of the few entertainment industry heavyweights who chooses to be as active publicly as the stars of yesteryear. For years, the one who "writes the songs" denied that he lived in Palm Springs at all. Then he came forward after reading about a theft of musical instruments from College of the Desert in Palm Desert. He and fellow Palm Springs resident, Suzanne Somers, each donated $5,000 to the college. After that, Manilow performed benefit concerts for the college, the Palm Springs Desert Museum, Desert Regional Medical Center and the Barbara Sinatra Children's Center.

The capper was a benefit performance at the McCallum Theatre for victims of the September 11 attack. Manilow, Somers, Jones, Marshall, Smith, Young, Hal Linden and Herb Jeffries gathered for a memorable musical revue. It was reminiscent of the days when Sinatra and friends would stage an impromptu benefit concert for a worthy cause.

CAMELOT

What's next for the Coachella Valley celebrity scene?

Stars and big-time movie producers continue to visit the desert, but they are secretive about where they stay. Rumor has it the action has moved north to the Two Bunch Palms in Desert Hot Springs, where Hollywood royalty go to relax. Two Bunch Palms maintains a celebrity section separate from the lodgings where ordinary folks stay.

Plenty of stars still buy second homes in the desert, too, but no one knows just where. Since this is their place of retreat, they make sure it stays that way.

In short, today's celebrities are as invisible in the Coachella Valley as they'd be in Los Angeles, New York or anywhere else. Camelot has ended – but the memories still live on.

Attractions

EVERYTHING UNDER THE SUN

BY PAMELA BIERI

EVERYTHING UNDER THE SUN

Imagine warm days and velvet nights, lavender mountains and turquoise skies. Natural beauty and a perfect winter climate are the Desert Resort Cities first and perhaps most compelling attraction.

Into this superb natural setting have come creature comforts, entertaining pastimes and aesthetic delights. Today's visitors and residents can enjoy all of the diversions of civilized life while submerging themselves in the desert's unique scenic majesty.

NATURAL ATTRACTIONS PARK PRESERVES AND GARDENS

The breathtaking Indian Canyons and Joshua Tree National Park have been preserved in their pristine state, while The Living Desert is a man-made celebration of desert forms and features. The Palm Springs Aerial Tramway, one of the desert's most famous attractions, highlights the Coachella Valley's sweeping geographical diversity as it scales the San Jacinto Mountains.

Indian Canyons

Centuries ago, ancestors of the Agua Caliente Cahuilla Indians settled in the Palm Springs area and developed extensive communities in the Canyons. Trace their ancient footsteps in the Palm, Andreas, Murray, and Tahquitz Canyons with hiking trails that offer a variety of flora, fauna, and unforgettable scenery.

Visit the Trading Post for native jewelry, crafts, plants and Native American exhibits. Re-opened for the first time since 1971, visit Tahquitz Canyon's spectacular 60-foot waterfalls, rock art, ancient irrigation systems and native wildlife and plants, just minutes from downtown Palm Springs. Entrance to the 15-mile long Palm Canyon, Murray and Andreas Canyons is on South Palm Canyon Drive. Guided hiking tours are available.

Joshua Tree National Park

The Mojave and Colorado deserts join to form this wondrous place with its awesome rock formations that attract hikers and rock climbers from all over the world. The Joshua Tree Park Center, located at the west entrance to the village of Joshua Tree, offers maps,

Photographer Tom Brewster

Indian Canyons.

Tahquitz Canyon.

souvenirs, guidebooks, handcrafted desert-inspired gifts, a fine art and sculpture gallery, and café.

Founded in 1962, Joshua Tree National Park is especially picturesque during wildflower season in springtime. Visitors can take leisurely strolls through this magnificent nature park to observe the striking Joshua Tree and many other desert plants and animals. Campgrounds and hiking trails are available.

Palm Springs Aerial Tramway

The Palm Springs Aerial Tramway provides a breathtaking view of the desert as 360-degree revolving cable cars rise from the desert floor and ascend 10,000 feet, all in about 12 minutes. Tram riders pass through four separate ecosystems during the climb.

The project was conceived one sweltering summer day in 1935, when electrical engineer Francis Crocker was driving to Banning. He looked up at the soaring San Jacintos and was struck with the idea of whisking people from the desert floor up to the cool mountain air. The notion of building a cable car to the wilderness peaks was born.

While many scoffed at Crocker's idea, he refused to give up and led a 28-year battle with state and local legislatures to clear the way for construction.

"Crocker's Folly" became "Crocker's Dream" when The Palm Springs Aerial Tramway opened to the public on September 14, 1963, heralded as the "Eighth Wonder of the World." Then Governor Edmund G. Brown and his wife Bernice christened the first car up with a bottle of champagne.

Today the Palm Springs Aerial Tramway boasts the world's largest rotating cable cars — two 80-passenger tramcars that carry visitors two and a half miles up to the San Jacinto Mountain preserve. The 13,000-acre preserve includes 54 miles of hiking trails and 11 campgrounds. Some 400,000 annual visitors reach the summit's peak.

Palm Springs Aerial Tramway.

The Living Desert

The Living Desert was the brainchild of several prominent citizens who, anticipating what resort development would do to the Coachella Valley, wished to create a sense of the desert in its pristine state. Philip L. Boyd and other trustees of the Palm Springs Desert Museum decided to establish an interpretive native trail and preserve on 360 acres in the then "remote" community of Palm Desert.

A young naturalist, Karen Sausman — an experienced zookeeper and park ranger with graduate work in wildlife biology — was hired to direct the project in 1970. Her canvas was raw desert strewn with trash and overgrown trails.

Giraffes at the Living Desert.

The Living Desert today is an exotic 1,200-acre wildlife zoo, botanical park, and scenic wilderness all in one facility. More than 325,000 visitors enjoy its rare exhibits, that include the world's smallest fox, the majestic bighorn sheep, coyotes and mountain lions, birds of prey, reptiles and insects, the Grevy's zebra, Mexican wolves, hyenas, camels and dozens more animal and bird species.

The botanical gardens replicate 10 major North American desert regions, as well as Africa, and eventually Australia. The Living Desert pioneered the immersion concept in garden and animal exhibits, allowing visitors to walk into gardens and seemingly come face to face with wildlife in natural settings. This is the only zoological and botanical park in the country that specializes in just one entire ecosystem, interpreting and conserving deserts of the world.

Tram tours carry visitors throughout the developed 200-acre site, starting at the upper patio with stops at Eagle Canyon and the African Village Watutu. The newest exhibit is the African Savannah with giraffes and ostriches. Membership provides free entrance while supporting wildlife conservation efforts.

Cheetah at the Living Desert.

Andreas Canyons.

Salton Sea migratory birds.

Moorten's Botanical Garden

In 1938, Patricia and the late "Slim" Moorten established this internationally famous living museum. Originally located in downtown Palm Springs, it moved to its present location on South Palm Canyon Drive in the mid-1950s. Moorten's Botanical Gardens fully represents the diversity of desert plants, with more than 3,000 varieties including giant cacti, agaves, and prickly pears in a magical private setting. Moorten's is available for weddings, meetings, and art exhibits. Wildlife thrives among the plants along this self-guided tour.

Coachella Valley Preserve

This 13,000-acre preserve contains clear springs, mesas, bluffs, dunes, and the spectacular Thousand Palms Oasis, all inhabited by rare and abundant wildlife. There are hiking and riding trails, picnic areas, and a visitor center, located 10 miles east of Palm Springs on Thousand Palms Road.

Coachella Valley Wild Bird Center

This is a bird watchers' haven with some 116 migratory species that make this wetlands their Southern California stopover. The center offers a full service medical facility for sick or injured birds. Visitors can walk several miles or sit and watch the birds. Located at 4600 Van Buren in Indio.

Salton Sea

In 1905, during the construction of the All-American Canal, a dike broke accidentally and the Colorado River overflowed its banks. This filled the sink of an ancient seabed, creating the Salton Sea.

Today it is one of the world's largest inland seas. This 360 square-mile basin is a popular site for boaters, water-skiers and anglers. Catches include ocean corvine, gulf croaker, tilapia and sargo. Swimmers, birdwatchers and other visitors enjoy the site's many recreations. Peak bird populations can be seen in December and January. Endangered species include the Yuma clapper rail, California brown pelican, desert pupfish, Aleutian Canada goose, Southwest willow flycatcher and bald eagle.

Visit the Salton Sea State Recreation Area or the Sonny Bono Salton Sea National Wildlife Refuge. Located 30 miles southeast of Indio on Highway 111, the park is located between Highway 10 on the North and Highway 8 on the South.

Lake Cahuilla

Surrounded by the stark beauty of the Santa Rosa Mountains in La Quinta, Lake Cahuilla is a favorite recreation area for camping, fishing, picnics, swimming, hiking and equestrian trails, and special events. The 153-acre park with a concrete-lined lake was built by the Coachella Valley Water District in 1969 as a reservoir for the area and today is a Riverside County park.

OUTDOOR SPORTS AND ADVENTURES

Horseback Riding

Horseback riding was among the first sport activities for visitors to the desert. People rode into the canyons, across open desert, up mountain trails, and through palm oases.

Harriet Cody opened the first stable in 1919 on South Palm Canyon Drive, followed by Norman Farra who had 200 horses and a dozen wagons at his ranch at Tachevah. By 1934 there were nine riding stables including Smoke Tree Ranch, Deep Well Ranch, Desert Inn Stable, and several on Avenida Caballeros.

The Desert Riders, a horseback-riding club organized in 1930, has built hundreds of miles of trails in the mountains and canyons. Prestigious pioneers have included Earl Coffman (Desert Riders' first president), Pearl McManus, Boo Hoff (president in the 1960s), Zaddie Bunker, and Frank Bogert. Still riding the trails, the organization has more than 100 members.

On what was once the edge of town, Smoke Tree Stables is now lodged near one of Palm Springs posh neighborhoods in the Canyon area. Riders trek over the water channel into the wash. Los Compadres Stables, one of the oldest riding clubs in Palm Springs on El Cielo near the Palm Springs International Airport, takes routes along the wash to reach trails into the mountains.

Eldorado Polo Club.

Vandenburg Stables in Cathedral City, Clancy Lane South in Rancho Mirage, Equestrian Centers International and Shadow Valley Equestrian Park in Palm Desert are in neighborhoods close to estates and private homes.

Additional stables in the area are the Jack Ivey Equestrian Center in Thousand Palms and the Willowbrook Riding Club in Desert Hot Springs.

The Desert Circuit and Polo

The equestrian lifestyle is evident in Indio and La Quinta, where private ranches and polo fields still abound.

Today the Indio Desert Circuit Horse Show at the Eldorado Polo Club features the top hunters and jumpers in the world, competing for more than $1 million in prize money in a six-week event, January through March. This has become the largest horse show in America.

The Eldorado Polo Club and Empire Polo Club offer local and international, amateur and professional polo competitions, horse jumping circuits, as well as rodeos, balloon festivals, concerts and other outdoor events.

Polo was first played at Smoke Tree Ranch in 1927, but ended with the onset of WW II. Later, polo at Thunderbird Country Club became a regular Sunday event that brought several respected polo players to the area, including Walt Disney.

Empire Polo Club.

Desert Adventures Jeep Tour.

Jeep travel has made it easier to traverse the desert quickly, and makes the rugged mountain terrain more accessible. Journey by jeep to a hidden palm oasis and explore an authentic replica of an ancient Cahuilla Indian Village. Take remote backcountry roads to climb high into the Santa Rosa Mountains National Scenic Area, surrounded by snow-capped mountains. Ride deep into the Colorado Desert to see how the forces of nature have shaped this spectacular landscape. Hike along the San Andreas Fault, explore historic gold mines, and travel through one of the world's riches agricultural areas on the way to Painted Canyon, a maze of steep-walled canyons, colorful pinnacles and fantastic rock formations. Among the top jeep tours are AAA Five Star Adventures, Canyon Jeep Tours, and Desert Adventures.

Hiking

Ancient trails and footpaths, carved by horses and humans, networked Cahuilla villages from the desert floor to the mountains.

Today, dozens of trails traverse throughout the mountains and valleys, monitored by the U.S. Bureau of Land Management (BLM), a federal agency that protects a number of endangered species including the bighorn sheep. While most trails are open year round, new lambing season closures may prohibit hikers in some of the desert's most popular areas.

Trail names hint at some of the adventurous places. Bear Ridge, one of the most popular in La Quinta's "The Cove" area, meanders above Bear Creek with spectacular views of the desert below. The trail ends in the foothills of Sheep Mountain at a small fan palm oasis.

Jeep Tours

Touring the canyons, mountain trails and palm oasis preserves are adventures one should not miss. Jeep tours may have gotten their start during World War II, when General Patton's troops were stationed in the desert to train for North African combat.

Photographer Tom Brewster

McCallum Trail, an easy two-mile trek, traverses the Coachella Valley Preserve between Thousand Palms and Sky Valley.

Indian Potrero Loop is a moderate hike in the Indian Canyons to a flat, grassy area where the Cahuilla once kept cattle or horses. "Potrero" means pasture in Spanish.

Lost Palms Oasis trail in Cottonwood Springs at Joshua Tree National Park contains the largest group of fan palms in the world, irrigated by water from a fault.

Sawmill Trail in the Santa Rosa Wilderness leads up the north side of the Santa Rosa Mountain with panoramic views of Pinyon Flats and Asbestos Mountain.

Fanciful ancient petroglyphs cover a patch of boulders in the middle of the desert along an old Indian trail from the Salton Sea near Travertine Rock. While the petroglyphs are hard to find, the hike offers colorful vistas of vineyards, the Salton Sea, and Chocolate Mountains.

The hike to Wellman's Cabin in Idyllwild leads to the ruins of this cattleman's cabin in a lovely meadow surrounded by mountains. Take the Devil's Slide Trail to Saddle junction and head toward San Jacinto Peak for this strenuous 12-mile hike.

Hiking clubs are a great way to explore the area with seasoned experts.

Balloon Flights

If some trails are off limits, the sky's the limit when it comes to hot air ballooning. Float above it all and see the tapestry of green golf courses, topaz swimming pools, and red clay rooftops. Hot air balloon companies take you to their launch sites in the east valley near Indio and La Quinta, fete you with champagne picnics, then take you aloft, suspended in the quiet atmosphere, and let you gently down in an open field.

Experienced balloon flight operators include Balloons Above the Desert, Dream Flights, and Fantasy Balloon Flights. Ballooning season is from September through June. Takeoff locations depend on wind direction, but four typical launch sites are from Cook Street and Frank Sinatra, Palm Desert; Washington and Darby in Bermuda Dunes; Monroe at Airport Boulevard and Madison at Highway 52 in Indio.

Balloon companies pick up and return guests from hotels, resorts and country clubs to the launch site, or return guests to their cars. Flights are generally one hour and balloons travel an average of 15 miles.

Guided and Self-Guided Tours

For some, it's the vicarious thrill of visiting the movie colony, spotting celebrity homes, and hearing the local history from knowledgeable guides. Whether it's a bicycle self tour through sleepy neighborhoods, an airplane tour, bus or limousine tour of stars' homes, a ride in a covered wagon, a camel ride through a date garden, or scenic tour to outlying rustic areas, the desert has a tour company for your every wish.

Bicycling through desert landscapes.

Dozens of bicycle paths across the Valley's cities meander through parks, neighborhoods, shopping areas, past golf courses, and through desert landscapes. Visitors can rent bikes at local bike shops or opt for a real guided adventure.

For self-guided tours, maps, or information, contact the local Chambers of Commerce.

Knott's Soak City

The woodies are cruising to Palm Springs since Knott's Berry Farm, California's oldest theme park operator, opened the newly renovated and expanded Knott's Soak City USA. This latest theme was inspired by the beach and surf towns of the 1950s Southern California coast.

A deluxe, family-oriented water playground in a private beach club atmosphere, Knott's Soak City features 13 waterslides including the Tidal Wave Tower, two seven-story-tall, high-speed slides, the Sea Snake, an enclosed slithering tube slide, the Kahuna's Beach House, a 4-story interactive water playhouse, and three 70-foot-tall body slides.

There's a wave pool for body and board surfing, a circular river for floating on inner tubes called the Sunset River, wade pool and fountains for splashing in the Gremmie Lagoon, or a misted cabana for relaxing out of the sun. Knott's Soak City is a great place to soak up the sun and water.

Photographer Tom Brewster

Knott's Soak City.

Food and beverage outlets offer favorite beach food, and a Surf Shop has everything you forgot and more. Knott's is located on Gene Autry Trail between East Palm Canyon and Ramon Road.

MUSEUMS

Palm Springs Desert Museum

Discover a cultural oasis in the desert at the Palm Springs Desert Museum. This landmark has been a cultural showplace for more than 60 years. It is a prestigious art, performing arts, and natural science facility. Classes and field trips are offered by the busy education department.

An outstanding permanent collection includes: 20th Century Art, Western American and Native American Art, Mesoamerica and Stars at Play a photo exhibit. In the Denney Western American Art Wing are works from the collections of George Montgomery, Kirk and Anne Douglas, Alexander and Sidney Sheldon, Ernest and Jean Hahn, and William Holden.

Seasonally changing exhibitions have included treasures from the Smithsonian, shows of renowned contemporary and native artists, and natural science exhibits of prehistoric animals and other deserts of the world.

The Annenberg Theater offers a full season of jazz, classical dance, Broadway and off-Broadway performances, lectures and seminars in an intimate 433-seat theatre located on the lower level of the museum. With nearly perfect acoustics, seating is configured continental style with no center aisle. Lovely sculpture gardens outside invite relaxation. The theatre was one of Ambassador Walter and Lenore Annenberg's many philanthropic gifts to the desert.

Photographer Tom Brewster

Palm Springs Air Museum.

Palm Springs Air Museum

Offering one of the world's largest collections of flying World War II airplanes displayed in bright, clean, spacious hangars, the Palm Springs Air Museum is a living tribute to American's veterans and the planes they flew. Visit bombers, fighters and training aircraft, including the famous Bob Pond Collection, and watch vintage footage in the Buddy Rogers Theatre. There are flying demonstrations of aircraft from the World War II collection and visiting aircraft.

Guided or self-guided tours bring back the days and heroism of World War II. Ideal family entertainment, the museum offers a comprehensive calendar of special programs, ceremonies and events, as well as continuous movies and videos.

Palm Springs Desert Museum.

Photographer Tom Brewster

Children's Discovery Museum.

Children's Discovery Museum

"Do touch" is the theme at the Children's Discovery Museum, where every child and the child in every adult has the delicious chance to play and explore hands-on. Children may choose to rock climb, splash paint on a Volkswagen, sort out a skeleton, create sculpture at a magnetic wall, dress up in the attic shop, shop at a grocery store or work with hand tools.

More than 50 exhibits are designed to stimulate the imagination and engage all the senses. Kids can dig it, paint it, fix it, and create it, all in serious fun. At a mock archaeological dig, children can uncover replicas of Cahuilla Indian artifacts.

Its beautifully landscaped campus offers an outdoor amphitheater, community gardens, covered picnic area, meeting rooms, and museum store filled with fun, educational gifts, toys and ideas.

Located at Gerald Ford Drive just west of Bob Hope Drive in Rancho Mirage.

Agua Caliente Cultural Museum

In November 2005, a new 96,000-square-foot Agua Caliente Cultural Museum will open on a 52-acre site at the entrance to the Indian Canyons. Destined to become a museum of national acclaim, the cultural center will feature a 22,000-square-foot permanent gallery, 3,700-square-foot changing exhibit gallery, five educational classrooms and meeting rooms, a 4,500-square-foot research library, 150-seat auditorium, plus café, museum store and curatorial facilities for artifacts and archives.

It is designed by nationally known American Indian architect John Paul Jones, a principal partner of Jones & Jones Architects and Landscape Architects, who designed the National Museum of the American Indian of the Smithsonian Institution in Washington, D.C., IQ Magic Exhibit Design, together with the museum's board of directors, staff and consultants, are developing interactive and innovative exhibits.

The building's multi-level concentric circle design, inspired by Cahuilla basket designs and the natural canyons setting, will be finished with native rock. Permanent and changing exhibits, classrooms, a state-of-the art library, recreation of a Cahuilla village and botanical garden, restaurant, picnic facilities and hiking trails incorporating archeological features are integrated into the museum's design.

The Agua Caliente Cultural Museum intends to inspire people to learn about the Cahuilla and other native cultures, keeping the ancient spirit alive through exhibitions, collections, research and educational programs.

The present Agua Caliente Cultural Museum is located in the Village Green Heritage Center in downtown Palm Springs. It traces the history of the Agua Caliente Band of Cahuilla Indians and other Cahuilla from their earliest days to the present time. Visit the Flora Patencio Basketry Exhibit, and the gift shop offering Native American jewelry, pottery, baskets, clothing, photography, crafts, music, books and videos. The museum also offers education programs and a research library.

Historical and Cultural Museums

The Cabazon Band of Mission Indians Cultural Museum, which opened in April 2002, is located across from the tribe's Fantasy Springs Casino in Indio. It traces the life and times of Chief Cabazon and early ancestors who lived in the central desert area. There is free admission, and groups are welcome Wednesday through Sunday.

Cabot's Old Indian Pueblo Museum, a 35-room, rustic, Hopi-style structure built by Cabot Yerxa in Desert Hot Springs, features collections of historic photos, baskets, and artifacts.

Indio's Coachella Valley Museum and Cultural Center is situated on the grounds of a 1926 adobe home on Miles Avenue, and features historical farming and railroad artifacts as well as the work of local artists.

The Palm Springs Historical Society located in the Village Green Heritage Center on Palm Canyon Drive features the McCallum Adobe Museum and Miss Cornelia White's "Little House" two of the oldest structures in Palm Springs, as well as Ruddy's General Store, a replica of a late 19th century general store.

Palm Desert's Historical Society Museum is in the original firehouse on El Paseo with tours, exhibits, archives, and a reference library.

The La Quinta Historical Society is housed in the city's oldest commercial building on Montezuma.

Homestead of Cabot Yerxa.

FESTIVALS AND GALLERY WALKS

Rancho Mirage Art Affaire.

La Quinta Arts Festival™.

Dozens of festivals, art events and gallery walks may be found throughout the season across the Valley. The La Quinta Arts Festival™ and the Palm Springs International Art Fair are held in March.

Indio is known as the City of Festivals, home of the International Tamale Festival, the Southwest Arts Festival, Spring and Fall, Indian PowWows, Riverside County Fair and National Date Festival.

Other art fairs include the Rancho Mirage Art Affaire and the Fine Arts & Crafts Fair in Palm Springs.

Monthly art walks throughout the gallery districts provide evening entertainment.

La Quinta Arts Festival™

This nationally acclaimed, juried fine art show features the works of more than 250 artists from around the world and includes painting, sculpture, photography, jewelry, fine crafts, printmaking and other design categories.

It was founded in 1982 by civic leaders Kay and Fred Wolff and John Klimkiewicz, then-chairman of La Quinta's Planning Commission. Sponsored by the La Quinta Arts Foundation, the four-day outdoor event in March is now held on the new La Quinta Arts Foundation site, a 28-acre site that will eventually house galleries, classrooms, a performing arts venue, amphitheater, offices, community meeting facilities and outdoor sculpture gardens. The full-service performing and visual arts center will be constructed in phases over the next several years.

Lifetime honorary chairman Merv Griffin, a La Quinta resident, hosts a number of events leading up to the Festival. Proceeds benefit the Foundation's outstanding education and arts scholarship programs.

The Foundation also presents the Plein Air Festival, a celebration of outdoor painting from the desert floor to the top of the Palm Springs Aerial Tramway. A Quick Draw competition, lecture at The Living Desert and exhibit of pieces for sale also benefit local arts programs.

International Tamale Festival

Held in early December, this is one of Indio's favorite festivals, featuring a holiday parade, carnival, and more than 300 booths of gourmet tamales, arts and crafts, entertainment, cooking demonstrations, a car show, 5K and 10K runs, as well as tamale judging and eating contests.

Riverside County Fair and National Date Festival

For more than 40 years, this Arabian-themed County Fair and Date Festival held in February at the Riverside County Fairgrounds in Indio has celebrated the date harvest and the area's rich agricultural heritage. In addition to livestock shows and auctions, young 4-H members bring their prized animals for sale. Live entertainment includes camel and ostrich races and a nightly Arabian Nights musical pageant. There are also carnival rides, food booths of all varieties, hundreds of arts, crafts, and souvenir vendors, as well as scientific and educational exhibits by area schools and various public and private organizations.

Riverside County Fair and National Date Festival.

Indio PowWows

Hosted by the Cabazon Band of Mission Indians, the Spring and Fall PowWows are American Indian Festivals where hundreds of dancers and singers gather from throughout the United States and Canada. They meet at the Cabazon Band reservation in Indio. PowWows provide an opportunity for the young to learn from their elders and carry on traditions. It is also an opportunity for non-Indians to learn about and appreciate Native American culture. The Grand Entry is a procession of color and sounds that brings spectators to their feet. A drum is played and high men's voices carry sound into the hearts of the dancers. Arts, crafts and traditional Native American foods are part of the festivities.

Indian PowWow.

Palm Springs International Art Fair

Paintings, sculpture, glass, functional art and objects are displayed at the Palm Springs Convention Center in March. Galleries from North America, Latin America, Europe and Asia gather to exhibit and sell museum quality original fine art.

The Convention Center is transformed into a huge contemporary art gallery with numerous sculptures placed in the lobby and outdoors on the grounds. The opening night preview is a benefit for a local charity organization.

Art Walks

Galleries across the Valley open their doors to the public during monthly Art Walks. The first Thursday of every month is Palm Desert's Art Walk on El Paseo, with more than 25 galleries, free parking, free shuttle service, entertainment and refreshments at many galleries. Acclaimed galleries such as Imago, Buschlen Mowatt, Denise Roberge and Richard Danskin offer arts, jewelry, functional and art objects that delight every sense.

The first Friday of each month during season, discover Palm Desert's unique art and interior design complex The Art Place, off Hovley Lane, with live music, hosted bar and hors d'oeuvres.

Palm Springs' eclectic North Palm Canyon features more than 50 antiques, furnishings, and art galleries and is open for a great evening out on the first Friday of each month. Adagio Gallery, Heusso Gallery, Desert Art Center, Carlan Gallery/Pedro Faille are among the top galleries here.

THE PERFORMING ARTS

The McCallum Theatre for the Performing Arts

The McCallum Theatre for the Performing Arts, Bob Hope Cultural Center opened in 1988. It offers an eclectic mix of drama, dance, music, concerts, and comedy during its season series.

Illustriously named for the McCallum family pioneers and beloved comedy icon Bob Hope, the McCallum Theatre has become the desert's premier cultural center, attracting major stars and touring companies from across the county and around the world.

The 1,129-seat theatre is venue for a stellar season that includes subscription packages for dance, concerts, drama, comedy, and children's theatre. Located on Fred Waring Drive at Monterey Avenue in Palm Desert, the

The McCallum Theatre for the Performing Arts.

McCallum Theatre is also home to a growing theatre education program for area teachers, principals, and children during the summer months.

The Fabulous Palm Springs Follies

Celebrate the music, dance, and comedy of the '30s and '40s with a cast old enough to have lived it. Open seasonally starting in November.

Located in the historic Plaza Theatre in downtown Palm Springs, this world-class vaudeville extravaganza features acts reminiscent of Flo Ziegfield's production numbers, plus hilarious vaudeville acts. Renowned guest stars appear regularly, along with the "Legendary Line of Long-Legged Lovelies," a chorus line of beauties from 54 to 87 years young.

Matinee and evening performances are available for the Holiday Show (November and December) and for the Spring Show (January through May). Shows change every season. Enjoy the Follies' special brand of patriotism in a star-spangled salute to members of the armed services.

Film Festivals

It's no coincidence that film festivals have flourished here. Palm Springs close proximity to Los Angeles and the fledgling movie industry of the 1920s helped put this exotic locale on the map.

When the late Sonny Bono, then Mayor of Palm Springs, launched the Palm Springs International Film Festival in 1989, it was his vision to rekindle dynamic synergy between the international film industry and Palm Springs.

This two-week long event each January attracts producers, filmmakers, corporate sponsors and film audiences from all over the world. The film festival is headquartered at the Camelot Theatre in Palm Springs.

An offshoot during July and August is the Palm Springs International Short Film Festival.

CASINO ENTERTAINMENT

Fantasy Springs Casino.

The New Spa Resort Casino will be completed in 2003.

Today, Indian-owned casinos offer 24-hour gaming and top name entertainers. World-class performers who have appeared at the casinos include Tony Bennett, Olivia Newton-John, Englebert Humperdink, Art Garfunkel, Wayne Newton, Waylon Jennings, Willie Nelson, Chaka Khan, Marc Anthony, the Beach Boys and Lee Ann Womack, among many others.

Agua Caliente Casino

The Agua Caliente Band of Cahuilla Indians successfully opened its second casino in April 2001 with over 30,000 square feet of gaming excitement and the latest and best machines, table games and progressives. You can play in style here at a real Vegas-style casino. There are over 1,000 slot machines – including reel slots, video poker and video Keno – 45 table games and 10 poker tables. You can play Texas Hold-Em, Omaha Hi'Lo and Seven-Card Stud.

Agua Caliente Casino.

For your dining pleasure, choose the Prime 10 Steakhouse, Maraskino Restaurant & Bar, or the Grand Palms Buffet. Canyons Lounge is a cabaret-style lounge with nightly live entertainment, comedy on Fridays, jazz on Sundays and a video poker bar. The Cahuilla showroom offers headline entertainment in an intimate setting with a state-of-the-art lighting and sound system.

The Agua Caliente Casino is located at the Bob Hope Drive exit off Interstate 10 in Rancho Mirage.

Augustine Casino

The newest Valley casino, owned by the Augustine Band of Cahuilla Mission Indians in Coachella, is a boutique casino reminiscent of early Las Vegas with great food, great prices and friendly service. Open 24 hours, seven days a week for a winning experience. Located off of 54th Avenue in Thermal.

Augustine Casino.

Spa Resort Casino

The Agua Caliente's original casino and world-class spa, the Spa Resort Casino is located in the heart of downtown Palm Springs. Try your luck with 1,000 slot machines and a variety of table games including blackjack, poker, Let-It-Ride and others. There are drawings, bonuses, and great prizes that make this casino exciting. Gaming, cocktails, food and valet service are available 24 hours. Dining options include casual dining at the Agua Bar & Grill and The Steakhouse, and a 24-hour Snack Bar service located inside the casino.

Fantasy Springs Casino

Voted "Best of the Valley" for eight straight years in a Desert Sun reader's poll, Fantasy Springs Casino is a Las Vegas-style casino featuring 1,300 slot machines, 40 gaming tables, daily bingo and satellite horse wagering.

The Amphitheater attracts stellar entertainment, and the theater stages ongoing revues like Joey & Maria's Comedy Italian Wedding. The 24-lane, state-of-the-art Fantasy Lanes Bowling offers family recreation. There's live entertainment at the Fantasy Lounge on weekends and special events midweek. Fantasy Springs is located in Indio, off the Golf Center Parkway near the I-10.

Trump 29 Casino

Trump 29 has come a long way since it was Spotlight 29 opening in 1996. After a multi-million dollar renovation and partnership with the Trump Organization, one of the largest hotel and casino operators in the United States, Trump 29 premiered in September 2002 with a 200,000-square-foot casino in retro Palm Springs style.

Trump 29 Casino.

Hot headliner Marc Anthony starred in the first concert in the new 2,500-seat Spotlight Showroom, and Donald Trump paid a visit to the Valley to tout his newest venture. With colorful neon glitz and high-tech gaming, Trump 29 is an entertainment hotspot.

DINING AROUND

During the 1930s, '40s and '50s, Palm Springs famous restaurants included the Racquet Club, The Doll House, and the Chi Chi, a glamorous nightclub on the present site of the Desert Fashion Plaza.

Las Casuelas Terraza.

Today's desert dining is a passionate pastime, with a dizzying array of restaurants located in every corner of the Valley. From chic bistros and exclusive European-style restaurants to family eateries, the dining options are endless. Choices range from American and California regional cuisines to Mexican, Mediterranean, Continental, French, Italian, Japanese, Chinese, Thai and Indian food.

Palm Springs has been the launching pad for a number of successful restaurants. The original Las Casuelas restaurant was started in 1958 by the Delgado family and has expanded into a string of family-owned restaurants across the Valley. In Palm Springs, Las Casuelas Terraza's long terrace and outdoor patio are favorite places for watching the action along Palm Canyon Drive.

Cornerstone Palm Springs establishments like Sorrentino's and Riccio's, where Frank Sinatra and the Rat Pack played, paved the way for other elite hangouts such as Melvyn's Ingleside Inn. Snuggled against the San Jacinto Mountains, Melvyn's is where Garbo once slept and where today's celebrities go for a true "Palm Springs experience." Lyon's English Grille serves classic English fare, La Shank House Persian Cuisine and Sherman's Deli & Bakery brings a real New York Delicatessen to the

Le Vallauris.

Kaiser Grille.

desert. For an awesome burger sensation don't forget Tyler's or Ruby's to experience the '50s era, or the critics choice and locals favorite the Kaiser Grille.

Outstanding boutique restaurants like Pomme Fritte, Johannes, Canyon Bistro, and St. James at the Vineyard definitely raise Palm Springs culinary stature.

Cathedral City's eclectic restaurants include The Wilde Goose, Red Tomato and House of Lamb, Maria's Italian Restaurant, La Casita Restaurant (which has two other locations in Palm Springs), and the locals' favorite, El Gallito.

Restaurant Row in Rancho Mirage has long been a destination for well-heeled diners. Wally's Desert Turtle, Kobe's Japanese Steak House, Las Casuelas Nuevas, the Beach House and Marie Callender's are among those that remain from the original Restaurant Row. Classics such as Bangkok Five, Roy's of Hawaii, and Massimo have been added to the fine dining mix. A little off the beaten path on Frank Sinatra Drive is the eclectic Shame on the Moon, which has a sister restaurant, Blame It On Midnight, in Palm Springs.

P.F. Chang's China Bistro.

The River at Rancho Mirage adds another dimension to the Valley's dining and entertainment. New stars in that constellation include P.F. Chang China Bistro, The Yard House, Babe's (whose owner founded Marie Callender's) Flemings Prime Steakhouse, and all magnets for an upscale dining experience.

La Quinta Cliffhouse.

The Nest.

Hotel dining at the Desert Springs JW Marriott includes, Mikado, Lake View, Tuscany's, the Sea Grille and Colibri Grille. And also on Country Club Drive a local favorite, Morton's of Chicago-The Steakhouse.

Stretching along Highway 111 are popular dining establishments such as Cucina Pasta, Las Casuelas Café, Omri & Boni, Tony Roma's, Cosmos's, Palomino, The Bella Luna, McGowan's Irish Inn, Kaiser Grille and Macaroni Grille.

Since 1965, Indian Wells' cozy, European bistro, The Nest, has been an institution to the golf and country club crowd, attracting celebrities to its piano bar. Le St. Germain, Vicky's of Santa Fe, Don Diego's, and dining at the Hyatt Grand Champions, Renaissance Esmeralda Resort, the Miramonte Resort, and Indian Wells Resort Hotel round out the constellation of choices.

La Quinta always has its share of intriguing restaurants. It is becoming the third point in a magic culinary triangle for the more successful family-owned restaurants such as L.G.'s Prime Steakhouse, Omri & Boni, The Falls and opening soon is Las Casuelas Quinta at the corner of Washington and Highway 111. Other intriguing dining spots are The Cliffhouse, Desert Sage, the Sand Bar, and Azur by Le Bernardin in the historic La Quinta Resort and Club.

Devane's.

Palm Desert hogs the spotlight for culinary excellence with a number of fine restaurants. Cuistot, one of the best California French restaurants in the region, and Jillian's, a romantic setting with eclectic gourmet American cuisine, join others on El Paseo such as The Bella Luna, Augusta, Le Paon, Pacifica in the Desert, City Wok, Café des Beaux-Arts, Tommy Bahama's, Sullivan's, and many more.

Indio's celebrity-owned William Devane's New York Style Italian Restaurant "Devane's" beckons from its inviting premises on Highway 111, surrounded by gardens. Ciro's Ristorante and Pizzeria has been serving the Valley in Indio since 1966, now also in La Quinta. Indio has a host of great family Mexican restaurants and taquerias such as Teresa's Café and Taqueria El Charro.

Enjoy all the attractions, dining and entertainment the desert has to offer under its bright, inviting sun — or soft moonlit nights. This winter playground is very busy in season, and weekend dining reservations are strongly recommended.

Photographer Tom Brewster

SHOPPING

At the turn of the 20th century, dry goods stores along Palm Canyon Drive provided just the bare essentials. If you were lucky enough to find a hammer on one trip, chances were you couldn't find nails. Ruddy's General Store, at the Village Green Historical Center in downtown Palm Springs, gives visitors the experience of shopping in the early days.

Today Desert Resort Cities offer shopping choices beyond the imagination, with districts across the entire Valley.

In Palm Springs' the famed Palm Canyon Drive is both vibrant and retro. Its hacienda-style buildings brim with collectibles, clothing, paintings, sculpture, jewelry, and antiques. You can find everything here from chandeliers dripping with crystals to kitschy collectibles from the '50s. Palm Springs has lately become the center of the Modernist maelstrom, with several stores dedicated exclusively to collecting and selling mid-century furniture, housewares and accessories.

The River at Rancho Mirage adds a whole new upscale dimension to the Valley, offering a variety of restaurants and exclusive retailers. A massive multi-plex theatre lies at the center of The River, across from an outdoor amphitheater. The whole area is surrounded by a meandering river water feature. The River creates a cultural and visual oasis along Highway 111, and raises the bar of retail development in the Valley.

Palm Desert's posh El Paseo, the Rodeo Drive of the desert, began as a line drawn in the sand by developer Cliff Henderson, who envisioned this two-mile stretch off Highway 111 for shops and businesses. He never imagined the couture shops, upscale restaurants, art galleries, and professional offices that would eventually make El Paseo one of the most exclusive retail areas in the Valley.

The two-level, open-air Gardens on El Paseo opened in 1998. It is anchored by Saks Fifth Avenue and decked out with top nationally known retailers such as Williams Sonoma, Ann Taylor, Banana Republic, The Pottery Barn, Talbot's, and many others. Additionally, there are cafes, terraced restaurants, and upscale dining offering the finest cuisine.

The late Ernest Hahn built the Palm Desert Town Center in 1983. Now called Westfield Shoppingtown, this regional mall is currently undergoing major renovation and expansion to be complete by 2004. It is anchored by Macys, Robinsons-May, JC Penney with over 140 specialty stores.

The Indio Fashion Mall at Highway 111 and Monroe, anchored by Sears and Harris Gottschalk's, features dozens of nationally known shops, boutiques and specialty stores. From bridal fashions and diamond rings to hardware and cell phones, Indio offers an eclectic blend of retail stores.

The Gardens on El Paseo.

Palm Springs VillageFest

Stroll under the stars, listen to music, savor international foods, shop the farmer's market and listen to children laughing – all this while shopping for the perfect handicraft at Palm Springs VillageFest. The New Orleans-style venue materializes every Thursday night from 6 – 10 p.m. in the heart of the village on Palm Canyon Drive between Baristo and Amado.

VillageFest.

College of the Desert Street Fair

Every Saturday and Sunday from 7 a.m. until 2 p.m. find hundreds of merchants, crafters, artists, food booths and a farmer's market at the College of the Desert campus. The Street Fair is open year round. Parking and admission are free. Located at Fred Waring and Monterey in Palm Desert.

College of the Desert Street Fair.

El Paseo Drive in Palm Desert.

Valley Cities

A FAMILY ALBUM

BY GAYL BIONDI

Desert Hot Springs Spa Hotel.

Natural hot water mineral springs.

Photographs by Betty Wallin

A FAMILY ALBUM

First they came by horseback and stagecoach. Then they came by Southern Pacific Railroad. They still come – by plane, train, automobile and luxury RV – to the verdant Coachella Valley in search of the desert lifestyle.

From the early years well into the 1970s, visitors to this desert destination used the blanket term "Palm Springs" to refer to the entire Valley, even though their final stopping place had a very good chance of being outside the Palm Springs city limits. Today the emphasis has shifted, and each of the nine cities lining the base of the San Jacinto and Santa Rosa mountains has acquired an identity all its own.

Like siblings in a modern family, the cities revel in their own character and style. They range in age from enthusiastic 20-somethings to active seniors, some of whom have reinvented themselves more than once. While there's a healthy sense of rivalry among them, like any family unit they know how to share their wealth and resources for the benefit of all concerned. Let's open the family album and look at a snapshot of each Valley city from west to east.

DESERT HOT SPRINGS

Higher in elevation and farther north than the rest of the Valley cities, Desert Hot Springs has a lot going for it. It enjoys commanding views of distant Mt. San Jacinto and a long-standing reputation as a spa city. The town rests on one of the world's finest sources of natural hot water mineral springs. It also boasts a supply of award-winning drinking water.

Its recorded history goes back to 1913 when Cabot Yerxa claimed a homestead of 160 acres near Two Bunch Palms. When he first arrived he slept in a cave and cooked over a campfire, later building a 10- by 12-foot cabin. One day while digging a well, he found water at 132 degrees Fahrenheit.

In the 1930s Yerxa was joined by L.W. Coffee, who built a spa and sold lots for $40 and up. In 1941, Desert Hot Springs first streets were laid out. Soon a café opened and more settlers started trickling in. On September 17, 1963 Desert Hot Springs voted for incorporation.

For all of its natural virtues, however, the city has never reached the sort of mach speed development other desert cities have reached. One reason may be the high winds that blow there almost constantly. (Some residents have dubbed the city "Little Chicago.") Today 80 percent of the land within the city's 23 square miles lies vacant.

Two Bunch Palms Spa and Resort in Desert Hot Springs.

Travel + Leisure cover featuring Sagewater Spa, fed by the area's celebrated hot springs. The mineral water is considered some of the best in America - 2001.

Photographer Tom Brewster

Festival of Lights, Palm Springs Christmas Parade on Palm Canyon Drive.

Ironically, this very quietude has resulted in Desert Hot Springs becoming one of the trendiest vacation spots in the country today. Its retro hotels — which were never torn down to make way for more ambitious buildings — have lately been lionized in fashionable magazines like *Vanity Fair, Vogue* and *Travel + Leisure*. These media powerhouses have declared Desert Hot Springs' mid-century modern architecture chic, and placed it high on the list of "secret" destinations for the savviest of travelers. More than 40 hotels and day spas now enjoy unprecedented status as they provide relaxation to stressed-out celebrities and everyday vacationers.

While Desert Hot Springs' small-town atmosphere is the delight of its 17,000 residents, city leaders would prefer to take part in the development that has prospered so much of the rest of the Coachella Valley. The city's aggressive economic development team is focusing on a master plan for worldwide promotion of Desert Hot Springs as a spa destination. They will be bringing in investors for planned communities and spearheading beautification projects for the old downtown and the city's main gateways.

New communities already in the planning stages include developments that will combine hotel accommodations with golf courses, single-family homes and condos. These mixed-use developments follow a model that has been astoundingly successful in other desert cities.

Desert Hot Springs vision for itself, however, goes far beyond mere resort planning. It includes ambitious civic goals such as setting energy standards and encouraging solar power and water conservation for new construction. The city plans to develop a municipal electric utility to provide lower rates and a stable power source for residents and businesses.

As the Coachella Valley grows, Desert Hot Springs will add its unique personality to the mix. It will afford yet another option to people enamored of the desert lifestyle.

PALM SPRINGS

The name evokes an image of fun in the sun. And rightly so. Palm Springs is the Big Daddy of desert resorts.

It gained prominence as a celebrity hangout back in the 1920s, and its reputation as an elite watering hole has thrived ever since. The name "Palm Springs" will probably always evoke the Hollywood Golden Era, when moguls ruled and luxurious excess was the name of the game. Celebrity photographs continue to adorn the walls of many local businesses, and stories are told and retold of the good old days when international stars mingled unselfconsciously with locals. The Movie Colony, a fashionable residential district built by the kings of the movie industry, continues to draw interest from real estate-savvy investors, eager to renovate these properties full of historic significance.

Palm Springs International Airport.

More than any other desert city, Palm Springs has successfully developed distinctive neighborhoods within close proximity to a true town center. By preserving its walking-neighborhood past, Palm Springs has laid claim to an ambience that can't be imitated by the newer cities to the east. It's an ambience that's appreciated more and more by people looking to get away from the suburban sprawl cities where they were raised.

Baby Boomers, young professionals and gay couples have "discovered" Palm Springs village-like intimacy, and are buying and restoring homes there. The city's famous mid-century modern homes are particularly prized. Stores have sprung up along Palm Canyon Drive catering specifically to new homeowners furnishing their sleek modern homes with retro finesse.

Gays and lesbians, who have been vacationing in Palm Springs for decades, are now putting down roots and renovating entire enclaves into private resorts or luxurious vacation homes. Some estimates place the gay presence in Palm Springs at 40 percent of the overall population. The result is a Palm Springs with a bit of a Greenwich Village feeling to it, where sophisticated bohemian pleasures thrive in the easy atmosphere of a small town.

With a vibrant downtown shopping district and uptown gallery walks full of fine art, furniture and flea market treasures, Palm Springs is a magnet for collectors, renovators, designers and shoppers in general. City leaders are well aware of Palm Springs' unique ambience, and they are banking on it to attract new residents for the future. Home/studio loft spaces are being planned for the heart of downtown and elsewhere. This urbanizing touch will only add to Palm Springs' uniqueness among the desert resort cities.

Spa Hotel - Casino and The Agua Caliente Women (Sculpture) Commemorating The Agua Caliente Band of Cahuilla Indians.

CATHEDRAL CITY

An urban-inspired housing development has already been permitted on the old reservoir site at the corner of Stevens Road and North Palm Canyon Drive. There, a master planned community will soon arrive with live/work condominiums mixed in with retail space.

Other housing development includes Palm Springs East, being developed by the Burnett Companies north of Vista Chino around the Palm Springs Country Club. Homes in the $200 to $300 thousand range are planned.

Commercial development is also in the pipeline, with a Class A office/commercial complex due at Mid-Valley Center. It is part of a 273-acre master planned development that will include hotel and timeshare units as well as a championship golf course.

Nearly 50 years after Palm Springs incorporated, its next-door neighbor, Cathedral City, gained cityhood. During those five decades Cathedral City morphed from a rural, Western-style town into a blue-collar bedroom community.

Civic Center in Cathedral City.

Photographer Tom Brewster

A view from the Palm Springs Aerial Tram.

Other commercial space has been made available for development, with the city's Business Retention and Expansion Program assisting businesses with their plans. Across from the Palm Springs International Airport stands a 40-acre industrial/business park with lot sizes up to five acres. Adjacent to Interstate 10 are two areas for light to heavy manufacturing and distribution, with office/warehouse space available too.

Much of Palm Springs is still owned by the Agua Caliente Band of Cahuilla Indians, whose ancestor's settled centuries ago in Palm, Murray, Andreas, Tahquitz and Chino Canyons. Of the Tribe's 32,000 acres, 6,200 lie within the Palm Springs city limits.

Today, although much has changed, much has stayed the same. The creative energy, resourcefulness and profound sense of honor that defined the Tribe's ancestors are still evident. Palm Springs has been a prime melting pot of two cultures working together. This has been very beneficial for tribal members and for the community. With the building of the new $90 million Agua Caliente Casino and the proposed 50-acre museum development bring both jobs and revenue to the community. These projects and others result in a boost to Palm Springs and Coachella Valley's economies.

In the 1990s the city experienced an unprecedented spurt of commercial growth. Officials saw the opportunity to create a Civic Center from a blighted stretch of storefronts along Highway 111. Using creative redevelopment strategies and public/private partnerships, Cathedral City planted the seeds for a pedestrian-friendly town square, siting a new City Hall next to a multiplex movie theatre and multi-level parking structure.

The design of the town square is colorful and inviting, with a whimsical fountain as the centerpiece. The fountain has become a gathering spot for families and a backdrop for civic events. The Mary Pickford Theatre is a state-of-the-art movie complex that also houses a museum of Mary Pickford memorabilia. Street-level boutiques and specialty shops have begun sprouting along Highway 111 nearby.

Mary Pickford Theater in Cathedral City.

Palm Springs Riviera Resort & Racquet Club.

Big League Dreams Field in Cathedral City.

IMAX Theater in Cathedral City.

A whimsical fountain in the Town Square in Cathedral City.

Cathedral City is sowing its seeds wide and deep to capture a fair share of the retail and commercial enterprises that will inevitably come to the growing Coachella Valley. The Civic Center is poised to welcome new hotels and eateries, an ecologically sensitive golf course, as well as new retail, commercial and office tenants in the greater downtown area.

New housing has mushroomed in the area between Ramon Road and Interstate 10, while Cathedral City Cove has become a desirable area for homeowners intent on fashionable renovation. Rio Vista Village has been mapped out and will attract those who long for a more traditional lifestyle: with front porches and tree-lined streets, the approved tract of 1,350 proposed homes brings the New Urbanist architectural trend to the Valley. A master planned community, it will contain apartments, neighborhood shopping, a recreation center and an elementary school.

Unlike many other cities in the Coachella Valley, Cathedral City is not positioning itself only for upscale development. It wants to build a rich social fabric that will appeal to a wide range of residents who enjoy sharing their cultures and backgrounds through community activities.

RANCHO MIRAGE

Before the manicured country clubs and the well-known Betty Ford Center, there were ranches.

Da Vall's Wonder Palms Date Ranch begat Eleven Mile Ranch, so named because it was located exactly 11 miles from both Palm Springs and Indio. The historic property then became the White Sun Guest Ranch, which thrived for another 40 years as a private ranch and later a resort.

By 1934, the area was attracting attention from land developers who bought up acreage with the intention of building a community. The town-to-be needed a name. It wasn't the first time, and certainly won't be the last, that a California land salesman placed "Rancho" in front of another word to create a destination with cachet.

Nowadays, Rancho Mirage is best known for exclusive country clubs and famous residents behind guarded gates. It started in the 1940s with the Valley's first 18-hole golf course at Thunderbird Country Club. Early members included Ambassador Leonard Firestone, Phil Harris and Alice Faye, Desi Arnez and Lucille Ball, Bob Hope and Bing Crosby. Shortly thereafter, Ford Motor Company named an automobile after the exclusive enclave. In 1966, Bob and Dolores Hope donated 80 acres of land for what is now the campus of Eisenhower Medical Center.

Sunnylands, the late Walter Annenberg's estate at the corner of Bob Hope and Frank Sinatra drives, is the lasting legacy of a great businessman and ambassador. The 205-acre property contains 12 ponds and a nine-hole golf course. It is here that Annenberg regularly entertained presidents and heads of state. The Palm Springs Tourism office estimated in 1987 that each annual visit by then President Ronald Reagan on New Year's Eve was worth $500,000 in advertising to the area. At one point, Annenberg announced he was offering political asylum to the Shah of Iran's mother and sister at his estate.

Cancer Survivor Park located in Rancho Mirage.

The River at Rancho Mirage.

The Lodge at Rancho Mirage.

> By 1915, the rutted wagon trails of the stagecoach line had been completely plowed over and graded, creating the "Bradshaw Highway," later known as "Highway 111."

Highway 111 as it winds through Rancho Mirage is often referred to as Restaurant Row. There you can take a culinary journey from Mexico (at Las Casuelas Nuevas) to Hawaii (at Roy's) and the Far East (at Bangkok Five). New hotels and entertainment complexes hug the highway, beckoning you to stop in and enjoy a stroll or a tasty meal.

The River at Rancho Mirage is more than simply a shopping and entertainment center. It is a destination, which provides a park-like waterfront with an entertainment amphitheater, live music, fountains and cascading waterfalls.

Another recent addition is the Agua Caliente Casino off Rte. 10 at the Bob Hope Drive exit, boasting world-class entertainment and the best of Indian gaming.

In a move toward economic balance, city officials have planned a complex of affordable housing for seniors called Santa Rosa Villas. The city purchased a former mobile home park in 1994 and hired architects to design a community of 33 single-story, two-bedroom, garden-style residences with private outdoor space. The gated community will offer a clubhouse, pool and spa.

The civic spirit doesn't end there. Plans for an $8.5 million library are underway, with the building set to open in late 2004.

PALM DESERT

El Paseo Drive at night in Palm Desert.

Palm Desert is perhaps best known as the shopping mecca of the Coachella Valley. Dozens of national chain and department stores, popular name brand shops and elegant boutiques can be found there.

Two men at different times set the template for Palm Desert to become the Valley's retail juggernaut. Cliff Henderson was a man with a vision who saw El Paseo Drive as a street of dreams, and kick-started development there in the 1960s. Things were humming along nicely when, 20 years later, Ernie Hahn chose a prime piece of Highway 111 real estate for a regional shopping center. Today Westfield Shoppingtown is a magnet for commerce from all over the Valley.

Commerce mixes comfortably with art in Palm Desert, which is the first "museum without walls" city in Riverside County. Its Art in Public Places program has received national attention, with approximately 96 sculptures placed throughout the city in parks, street medians, public facilities and private businesses.

The Palm Desert Civic Park is the most comprehensive and beautiful public park in the Valley, with an amphitheater, picnic/barbecue pavilions, tennis courts, baseball fields, playground, volleyball courts, dog park, skateboard park and walking trails. It has become a gathering place for families, a well-managed and spacious public place in an otherwise highly privatized Valley.

Culture and leisure travel are also on the menu in this mid-Valley city. The McCallum Theatre for the Performing Arts is a jewel box of a venue that brings fine entertainment to the desert from across the country. International tourists flock to the Desert Springs JW Marriott Resort and Spa, a deluxe resort hotel surrounded by lush landscaping and waterscapes where regal swans and pink flamingos glide. In the multi-storied lobby, a huge man-made lake connects the indoors to the outdoors. At an indoor dock gondolas pick up guests and whisk them away to dining establishments on the property.

Palm Desert prides itself on its financial stability and pro-business attitude. A progressive community, Palm Desert was a pioneer in the use of drought-tolerant landscaping to save water. Its municipal golf course, Desert Willow, is a stunning example of the program's success. A pilot project to make golf carts street legal for neighborhood convenience and fuel economy received rave reviews and has kept Palm Desert in the forefront of 21st century thinking.

Palm Desert's bold civic thinking has resulted in a new claim to fame. It will soon become the Valley's educational vortex, with plans afoot for bringing quality higher education to the northern sector. When the new institutions are up and running, they will establish the Coachella Valley as an important player in the world of academia.

College of the Desert has been turning out graduates since 1968. It is a highly regarded member of the California Community College system, the largest educational organization in the world. Its role is to offer two-year degree and certificate programs to recent high school graduates as well as adults pursuing new career challenges. The Coachella Valley campus of California State University, San Bernardino has also had a presence in Palm Desert, providing a seamless transition to four-year degree programs and graduate studies. In addition, Chapman College has offered targeted degree programs aimed at busy professionals.

Photographers John and Jeannie Henebry

Desert Willow, palm oasis scene is of the 8th hole on the Firecliff course.

On the horizon is an exciting new center for higher education called the Heckmann Center for Entrepreneurial Management. Affiliated with University of California, Riverside, it will expand the Valley's educational opportunities by offering degrees and certificates in such areas as the electronic economy and international finance.

The Heckmann Center, on Cook Street near Interstate 10, has already become a magnet for new housing, retail and recreational amenities. This type of development is expected to accelerate as the Center nears completion.

"The Dreamer" by bronze artist David Phelps, located in the Civic Center Park.

Desert Springs JW Marriott Resort and Spa presents a paradise of pools.

INDIAN WELLS

In Indian Wells, it's all about quality, not quantity. Since its incorporation in 1967, this decidedly blue chip community has spent years on the Top Ten List of highest per-capita income cities in California. While the median age hovers near 60, the town is being recharged with younger urban escapees looking for sophisticated solace. With little raw land yet to be developed, Indian Wells' future is more about maintaining the high expectations of its residents.

During the Gold Rush, this spot was an Indian village with a well that provided respite for stagecoaches and wagons traversing the Bradshaw Trail to stake claims along the Colorado River. The "Indian Well" remained a familiar namesake through the 1950s, when Desi Arnez christened his new Indian Wells Country Club and golf course. It was exclusive enough to become former President Dwight D. Eisenhower's winter home and the site of the first Bob Hope Desert Classic golf tournament.

Hyatt Grand Champions Resort and Spa in Indian Wells.

Indian Wells Desert Symphony.

Not a big proponent of retail, Indian Wells is instead a resort destination and ultra high-end country club community. Its stellar hotels include The Hyatt Grand Champions Resort and Spa, the Miramonte Resort, the Indian Wells Resort Hotel and the Renaissance Esmeralda Resort & Spa. Residents benefit from perks including discounts at the city-owned Golf Resort at Indian Wells and Indian Wells Tennis Garden. The Tennis Garden is home to nationally-televised world-class tennis competitions featuring top names like Pete Sampras and the Williams sisters. The sparkling stadium and grounds are also a luxurious

As early as 1823 the name "Indian Wells" was documented in the expedition diaries of Captain Jose Romero, who had been sent to find a route through the San Gorgonio Pass to Tucson.

Indian Wells Tennis Garden.

Photographer Tom Brewster

Eisenhower Walk of Honor Memorial in Indian Wells.

performing arts and entertainment venue that has hosted artists such as Luciano Pavarotti.

Dozens of captains of industry – including Bill Gates – make their part-time homes behind the gates of private clubs like The Reserve, Desert Horizons and The Vintage. The city is also active in local philanthropy, supporting symphony and museum programs as well as lecture series presenting world leaders and newsmakers. City government has given issues like highway safety, street maintenance and household hazardous waste disposal its top priority.

LA QUINTA

Legend has it that early Spanish explorers, anxious to conquer as much virgin territory as possible, were known to ride for days at a time. After forging ahead from dawn to dusk for four days straight, they stopped to rest on "la quinta," or, "the fifth" day. Eventually, La Quinta became the term used for a resting place or a small country estate. Point Happy, the rock outcropping at Highway 111 and Washington Street, was once such a resting place and watering hole.

In the early 1920s, a wealthy gentleman from San Francisco built an exclusive hotel in a cove of the Santa Rosa Mountains west of Indio and named it the La Quinta Hotel. When the city of La Quinta incorporated in 1982, it was said to be the first recorded city to be named after a hotel.

Cahuilla Indian history reports that the ancient tribes called what is now La Quinta "The Garden of Eden," believing it was here human life began on Earth. A lot of residents still think La Quinta is the cradle of civilization, at least for them. And why not? With its protected cove,

La Quinta Art Festival™ 2002.

historic village and strong sense of community, La Quinta inspires a fierce loyalty among its residents.

The inspiration was certainly there for Hollywood legend Frank Capra, best known for his Christmas classic, "It's a Wonderful Life," starring Jimmy Stewart. Capra wrote the screenplays for "It Happened One Night" and other classics while staying at the La Quinta Hotel. (Tom Capra has kept his father's memory alive with his Palm Springs eatery It's A Wonderful Deli.)

In 2002 La Quinta was named the fastest-growing community in all of Riverside County. Retirees and baby boomers have been buying homes in its upscale communities (such as PGA West, Tradition Country Club, Lake La Quinta and The Citrus), while "The Cove" is being transformed by fashionable new homes.

Adding to its cachet is the La Quinta Arts Festival™, which happens every March. This long-running outdoor art show is known today as one of America's most important art fairs, with juried artists and artisans displaying paintings, sculpture, jewelry and crafts.

Lake Cahuilla, at the city's southern end, is a county campground and day use facility for swimming, fishing and picnicking. Hiking and biking trails abound, affording enthusiasts both no-incline and mountainous terrain. Miles of landscaped and improved trails transport hikers and mountain bikers from the top of "The Cove" to the base of the rugged mountains that frame this city's dramatic backdrop.

The Famous 17th hole, also known as Alcatraz on PGA West.

Outdoor recreation and entertainment options will continue to bring people to the La Quinta Civic Center campus and 18-acre La Quinta Park in the downtown village area. Civic leaders are working to expand the choices of hotels, shops, restaurants and services. Even resident Arnold Palmer is getting in the act with a golf-themed restaurant near his Tradition Country Club. La Quinta may signify a resting place, but this up and coming desert community is not resting on its laurels. It's moving full speed ahead.

INDIO

Landmark Golf Course #1 South Course, "Rocky Peak," 382 yards, par 4.

Photographer Paul Ames

In 1886, C.P. Huntington, president of Southern Pacific Railroad, brought back date shoots from an Algerian vacation and gave them to Pat Gale, the first agriculturist in Indio.

Bunches of dates bagged to protect from moisture and pests.

Where else can you watch an international polo match while drinking a date shake before returning to the private boat dock of your estate home to go water-skiing in the desert? Only in Indio.

The Valley's oldest and most populated city, Indio began as an agricultural city that soon became world-famous as the date capital of the world. Today more than 80 percent of America's date crop – over 27 million pounds annually – is grown in and around Indio. The Riverside County Fair & National Date Festival – complete with Arabian Nights Pageant has been held here every year since 1947. Another agricultural crop for which Indio is famous is table grapes. Indio's table grapes are shipped everywhere in the United States.

Indio has come to be known as the "City of Festivals," home to numerous festivals celebrating everything from tamales to techno-rock music. More than 600,000 visitors attend the various events. It hosts virtually every U.S. polo tournament, and is known as as "The Polo Capital of the Western United States." Fifteen contiguous polo fields span the Eldorado and Empire Polo clubs, with stable facilities for more than 1,200 horses.

Downtown Indio is where you'll find the Riverside County government administrative center and Larson Justice Center court complex, as well as College of the Desert's East Valley Education Center.

A variety of housing opportunities crosses all buyer spectrums. Starter homes co-exist alongside sprawling ranches and country estate properties. The population is, quite simply, exploding. An estimated 12,000 to 14,000 new residents are expected to fill the 1,750 new single-family detached homes now under construction. Another 2,500 homes are in the process of being approved.

In addition to affordable housing, Indio offers its residents and businesses affordable electricity through the Imperial Irrigation District, and inexpensive water through the Indio Water Authority.

Retail opportunities abound in Indio, and city officials are working with a Los Angeles consulting firm to bring in the right mix of businesses to service its growing population. They have targeted four main areas for commercial development, including a Hospitality Corridor, the Fashion Mall, Old Town and the I-10 Corridor.

Indio is fortunate to have an ace in the hole for luring new companies to these locations. The city is located within the Coachella Valley Enterprise Zone, one of 39 zones in California designated to receive

Larson Justice Center in Indio.

economic stimulus programs for new businesses. Business owners are eligible for tax credits that can save more than $30,000 per employee over a five-year period, along with other incentives.

Indio has already made a name for itself as a destination for the growing population of luxury RV owners. Six resorts cater to this crowd of well-to-do snowbirds, and two of them have been awarded national recognition for their quality: Outdoor Resorts, a national chain catering to million dollar motor coaches and Fiesta RV, a family-oriented resort.

One of the reasons Indio came into being was its location at a vital transportation hub – it was a stop along the Southern Pacific Railroad. Today three corridors converge in Indio: Interstate 10 shadows the cross-country rail route and carries passengers from Los Angeles to points east; State Highway 111 connects most of the Coachella Valley cities; and State Highway 86 – known as the NAFTA Highway – serves as a direct link to Mexico. From a logistical standpoint alone, Indio seems destined to be a major player in the Coachella Valley's growth.

COACHELLA

Cabazon Band Of Mission Indians Tribal Chairman, John James stands in front of a mural depicting a Cahuilla Indian Village. Mural shown here is in the Cabazon Cultural Museum which is across from the Fantasy Springs Casino.

Hundreds of farms and over 70,000 acres of irrigated land drive the economy of the eastern Coachella Valley and its closest city, Coachella. A significant portion of California's citrus fruit, vegetables and dates are grown here, thanks to an intricate canal system bringing in water from the Colorado River. Over the years, family farm operations have created a diverse community of Japanese, Armenian, Italian, Croatian and other nationalities making their livelihoods here. Today a major innovator in fruit and vegetable varieties, Sun World International, has its world headquarters in Coachella.

The word "Coachella" is thought to be a mapmaker's misspelling of the Spanish "conchella," meaning little seashell. The tiny shells were reportedly left behind when ancient Lake Cahuilla receded from the Valley over 500 years ago. Although Coachella is one of the oldest incorporated Valley cities (it was incorporated in 1946), it is one of the youngest in the median age of its overwhelmingly Hispanic residents. Many residents are associated with the agriculture industry, and the employment mix is growing for commercial and residential development.

Photographer Paul Ames

Grape vineyard.

The City of Coachella is not leaving future development to chance. It is busy planning for an entertainment corridor along Interstate 10 to complement two existing Indian casinos – one of them Trump 29 Casino, co-managed by Donald Trump. The new district is set to include hotels, golf courses, shopping centers and other attractions. Coachella also welcomes the new luxury RV class of snowbirds, with an upscale RV community called The Vineyards setting the tone. With a host of amenities usually associated with elite country clubs, The Vineyards will attract the ultra-high-end class of RV travelers.

Coachella is a community of contrasts that's committed to staying true to its past while pursuing a vibrant future.

The Vineyards–a Luxury Motor Coach Country Club where each pad has a Casita.

Bermuda Dunes Airport is a privately owned "Public Used General Aviation, Utility Category Airport." There are some fifty thousand operations (landing and takeoffs) per year.

In 1893, the State Legislature created Riverside County, removing 590 square miles from San Bernardino and 6,410 square miles from San Diego.

THRIVING COMMUNITIES

There are a number of thriving communities sprinkled here and there and still governed by Riverside County that, nevertheless, play an important role in the future of the Coachella Valley.

Thousand Palms is perched directly north of Rancho Mirage and Palm Desert along Interstate 10, making it easy to get to from anywhere in the Valley. It is already the location of an impressive light industry center with excellent freeway access.

Bermuda Dunes is a little gem tucked away between Palm Desert and La Quinta. Mostly residential, it has a strip of attractive light industrial commercial development poised between Interstate 10 and Bermuda Dunes Airport. The airport is a small fixed based operation facility that caters to private planes and corporate jets.

Thermal and Mecca grace the eastern-most end of the Valley and remain largely rural. Agriculture is a career and a lifestyle on farming operations cultivating field crops, table grapes, turf grass and date palms. Expansive ranches afford residents plenty of elbow room and the opportunity to raise horses and livestock. The Desert Resorts Regional Airport has untapped cargo and passenger capacity well into the future, and provides easy access for private and corporate jets flying into the eastern Coachella Valley.

Mecca – Fish Farm at St. Anthony's.

Photographer Paul Ames

SAND IN YOUR SHOES

The Desert Resort communities of the Coachella Valley are uniquely separate, yet unified by geography and a love of the desert lifestyle. A Native American expression handed down through the ages says that once you've experienced a deep purple sunset and a clear desert night with a gentle, warm breeze, you'll have "sand in your shoes." Translation: wherever you go, a little piece of this desert paradise will stay with you.

Commerce

IN PARADISE

BY GAYL BIONDI

Women's Club of Indio, 1925. President was Clara Boyer (3rd from the left) and one of the valley's first resident doctors who had retired was Dr. June McCarroll in the white dress, (8th from the left).

Courtesy of Coachella Valley Water District

PARADISE FOUND

Forces of nature laid the foundation for the dynamic economic opportunity that has grown steadily in the Coachella Valley. Earthquakes formed the mountains, creating a series of sheltered coves protected from coastal weather conditions. Ancient Lake Cahuilla receded, leaving hundreds of square miles of dry but promising land flat enough to travel over and build upon. The Cahuilla people developed a rich culture in this once remote paradise blessed with an "A List" of economic development amenities – mild weather, abundant natural resources and hundreds of square miles of space in which to plant one's entrepreneurial flag.

By the mid-1800s, government mapmakers had discovered an overland route to connect the Mississippi River with the Pacific Ocean. First a stagecoach trail was blazed. Later, Southern Pacific Railroad tracks forged their way through the Coachella Valley and the San Gorgonio Pass, creating a passage to the West Coast. The new trade route brought with it fortune seekers, explorers, farmers, land speculators and immigrants chasing the American Dream. In 1873, gold was discovered nearby in the high desert area of Joshua Tree at mines with names like Lost Horse, Desert Queen and Golden Bee.

By 1880, white settlers had discovered the possibilities waiting in the virgin Coachella Valley. They were quick to learn what the native people already knew – that dry air and mineral waters could soothe a multitude of ills.

The federal government gave 10 miles of land in a checkerboard pattern to the railroad to induce them to expand through the region. The first trains were scheduled out of Indio to Los Angeles on May 29, 1876. By the 1930s, Hollywood's matinee idols and producers were flocking to Palm Springs to escape the glare of the spotlights. When air travel finally became practical in the 1950s, the Valley, known collectively as Palm Springs, was already a well-established celebrity hangout and tourist destination.

Courtesy of Coachella Valley Historical Society

The first landing of an airplane in the valley was in Mecca in 1911. The pilot, Robert Fowler, was flying a Wright biplane made of wood, wire and muslin.

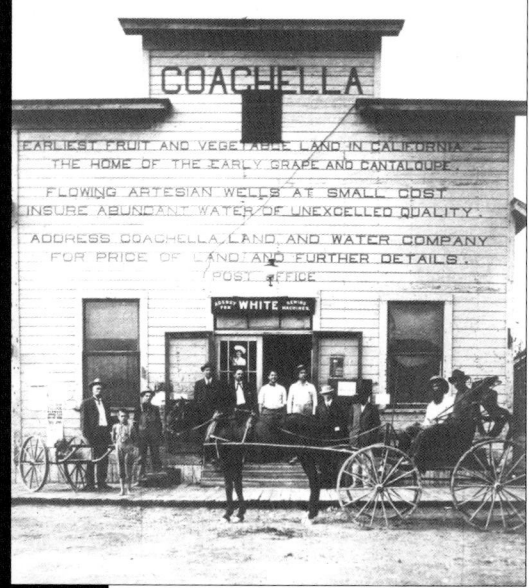

Huntington & Smythe Store, Coachella's 1st post office. From left, Bill Bethal, Willie Huntington (little boy), A.L. Peaarson, C.B. Estel, Deputy Unkn, C.B. Jones, J. L. Smythe, Frank McCarroll, Pancho Rameriz, (Indian) from Cabazon Reservation. David Thomas and his brother Issac Thomas sit in the buggy, circa 1909.

Jacqueline Cochran was America's leading female pilot. In 1950 she set a new speed record for propeller-driven aircraft and in 1953 she became the first woman to break the sound barrier.

Richard Milanovich, Tribal Council Chairman, Agua Caliente Band of Cahuilla Indians.

BUZZING WITH BUSINESS

Fast-forward to the present, as international television audiences watch the Bob Hope Chrysler Classic Golf Tournament or the Tennis Masters Series of Indian Wells, bringing major media coverage to the desert resorts. Millions of dollars of real estate changes hands each time a sporting or entertainment event broadcasts images of clear blue desert skies in February, when most of the country is in the deep freeze. Guests who visit in person can enjoy a gamut of experiences ranging from serene minimalist mineral water spas in quiet Desert Hot Springs to the Vegas-style glitz of a 60-foot wall of fire inside Trump 29 Casino.

Since passage of the Indian Gaming Compact, local tribes have come into their own with revenues from casino interests. As Tribal Council Chairman Richard Milanovich reports, "The Agua Caliente have created more than 2,000 jobs with the development of the Spa Resort Casino, Spa Hotel, Agua Caliente Casino, Tribal Administration and other Tribal entities." These local descendants of the ancient Cahuilla are among the most successful Native American business people in the country, managing diverse investments and participating in a variety of community projects including the Indian Health Program, an economic development corporation and a cultural museum.

It's no surprise that the desert resort communities continue to be a favorite haunt of Hollywood's elite as well as vacationers from around the country and across the globe. The Valley's permanent population of just under 350,000 swells to nearly half a million during the winter season to include part-time residents, seasonal visitors and tourists. Nearly 40 percent of the local workforce is employed in either the retail trade or hotel and amusement activities. The desert lifestyle with its 100+ golf courses, 600 tennis courts, 30,000 swimming pools and five Indian Casinos fuels the area's prime industry – tourism.

Technicians at work in the DISC Network Operations Center. The Valley's first dedicated business-class communications facility.

While the desert resorts cultivate their get-away-from-it-all attitude, there's more than just fun in the sun going on around here. The once sleepy towns are now buzzing with business and residential activity. The Coachella Valley Economic Partnership (CVEP) reports some 10,000 jobs were created in the last 18 months by new or expanding business entities in such diverse sectors as custom cabinetry and ornamental hardware, golf cart assembly and medical equipment manufacturing. Says one CVEP official, "Historically, the Coachella Valley has been less affected by economic ups and downs than the rest of the state. People who move here generally have the financial resources to succeed. That causes the local economy to be much more self-sufficient."

One vital California industry – high tech – has found the Coachella Valley to be a perfect fit. Citing labor costs 35 percent below those of the Silicon Valley, communications companies are making the Valley home. According to Rod Vandenbos, COO of Digital Internet Services Corporation, "People ask us why we would place a leading edge technology company in the desert. One of the most exciting advances with technology is that we no longer have to be in a big city to do business. The Coachella Valley offers businesses fiber optic high speed connections that make our connectivity to the Internet just as good as it would be in San Francisco, Los Angeles or New York."

Pete Sampras playing in the Tennis Master Series.

Photographer Tom Brewster

GREEN IS MY VALLEY

Visitors can't help but be seduced by the Valley's charms. But few get to fully appreciate the Valley's other industry – agriculture. This place may be a desert by geology but it's a cornucopia by irrigation design. The list of crops grown here is staggering and includes artichokes, broccoli, lettuce, citrus fruits, table grapes, herbs, palm trees and turf grass. The Coachella Valley's unique soil and climate conditions make it the ideal place to produce more than 80 percent of the dates grown in the United States.

Agriculture employs just over 12 percent of the local workforce. Farming and ranching is still a way of life for plenty of east Valley dwellers. Family and corporate farms feed their own economy of pickers, packers and shippers. James Wallace, Agricultural Commissioner for Riverside County, provides the annual crop report. The value of agricultural crops grown in the Coachella Valley in 2001 was nearly half a billion dollars. A total of 51,000 harvested acres is divided into five categories. From most acreage to least acreage the categories are 1) Vegetable, Melon and Miscellaneous 2) Tree and Vine Crops 3) Citrus 4) Nursery Stock and 5) Field and Seed Crops.

HOMES ON THE RANGE

Building permit valuation continues to be a strong economic indicator along with demographics, population, assessed property valuation, retail sales and hotel room sales. The Coachella Valley portion of the Inland Empire region out-paces growth in population and job creation throughout the state. The city of La Quinta's annual increase in assessed property values has often topped every other city in Riverside County. Land sales in Coachella have tripled in recent years.

While the nine cities of the Coachella Valley make up less than 20 percent of Riverside County's population, they account for some 30 percent of its total assessed property values. In the decade between 1990 and 2001, assessed valuation grew over 82 percent or $12.3 billion. Building permit valuation during the same period totaled more than $5 billion. New home sales grew from just over 2,100 homes sold in 12 months during the year 2000 to more than 2,000 homes sold in just the first six months of 2001.

At the same time, Palm Springs is enjoying a strong residential resale market fueled by a strong interest in 1950s mid-century modern homes by architecture buffs from New York, Los Angeles and San Francisco. General contractors, remodeling specialists, period artisans and vintage resale furniture folks are keeping busy giving facelifts to mature neighborhoods until everything old becomes new again. The stark desertscapes of Palm Springs in the 1950s were a clean slate for modernist architects like Richard Neutra, William Cody, John Leutner and Albert Frey. Today's collectors and devotees come from around the world to pay homage to the relaxed desert lifestyle.

THE SPORTING LIFE

Equestrians make up a significant population in the eastern Coachella Valley. Six hundred forty acres of polo grounds and related services in the Indio Ranchos area are a magnet for the horsey set, who contribute hundreds of millions of dollars to Valley coffers. Polo is an international sport and the Coachella Valley is a widely recognized destination for the sport of kings.

Alex Haagen III, principal of Empire Polo Club, sees potential for the expansive park-like setting as a corporate and special event venue. "We sell the image to Fortune 1000 companies who might not otherwise bring their business to the Coachella Valley. We can stage rodeos, polo matches with golf cart polo at the breaks and fireworks displays after dark. We once hosted a corporate group of 1,800 people that flew Don Henley of the Eagles in for a private concert."

During the winter horse-jumping season alone, some $130 million is infused into the local economy by horse owners, trainers, riders and spectators, who buy everything from feed and grooming supplies to meals, lodging and even housewares for their elaborate on-site stables or luxury motor homes.

Private hangars at Bermuda Dunes Airport make it easy for breeders and owners to fly in for an afternoon's matches and be back in the city by dinnertime. It's not uncommon for dignitaries to land by helicopter directly on the polo field. In 2001, Riverside County's Economic Development Agency completed $8 million of improvements to the Desert Resorts Regional Airport in Thermal. A fixed based operation with a main runway of 8,500 feet, it has untapped cargo and passenger capabilities for well into the future.

Sarah Ferguson, Prince Andrew and Sarah's father Ronald Ferguson at the Eldorado Polo Club.

BEYOND THE BLUE HORIZON

Clear, blue skies are characteristic of the Coachella Valley and critical to its future as a place of wellness and relaxation. You might be surprised to learn that one of the Valley's biggest proponents of clean air is its local public transit provider. SunLine Transit Agency became the nation's first public transit authority to switch entirely to alternative fuel buses in 1994. Since then, it has branched out into hydrogen fuel cell vehicles, alternative fuel taxis, golf carts and vans, paratransit service, regional street sweeping and a whole lot more. Open 24 hours a day, an innovative fueling station allows anyone with a vehicle that runs on compressed natural gas, liquefied natural gas, hydrogen or Hythane to top off their tank.

SunLine's Thousand Palms campus is a tourist attraction in itself. To date, over 6,000 hotel room nights have been booked by transportation or government representatives from 29 countries who came to see for themselves the innovative alternative energy incubator SunLine has created. The visitors who come are less likely to be Shriners from Peoria than scientists from Beijing. The Coachella Valley is recognized worldwide as the destination of choice for advanced transportation technologies, alternate fuels testing, energy research and development and new technologies job training and job creation.

Without real world applications for such space age products as hydrogen fuel cells, SunLine's efforts would be little more than show-and-tell. Thanks to forward-thinking economic development partners like Southern California Gas Company and ENRG, the valley has created public fueling stations and demonstration projects that serve as community models for the future. A steady stream of trainees in alternative fuel technologies matriculates through College of the Desert, the Palm Desert-based institution that developed the first U.S. curriculum for studying alternate fuel vehicles.

A fluke of nature makes the Valley an ideal place to produce renewable power from wind energy. The San Gorgonio Pass connects the warm desert to cooler valleys and coastal areas to the West. According to the Desert Wind Energy Association, as desert air heats up, it rises and creates a pocket of low pressure that acts like a vacuum pulling in the cooler air. An annual average wind of around 20 miles per hour feeds state-of-the-art wind turbines that generate electricity like a conventional power plant with one major difference – the fuel is free, inexhaustible and non-polluting.

Coachella Valley wind farms are privately owned and operated. The turbines generate close to 600 million kilowatt hours of power annually – enough to supply the city of Palm Springs energy needs. The wind farms themselves are an economic development magnet for the valley. They are also a cost-effective investment. It costs one cent per kilowatt to operate and maintain modern wind power plants. By comparison, it costs twice as much to operate, maintain and fuel nuclear-powered and coal-fired plants, and three times as much to operate gas and oil-fired power plants.

The first transit agency in the world to offer the public compressed natural gas, liquefied natural gas, Hythane (a blend of CNG and hydrogen), and hydrogen in one location.

ThunderPower hydrogen hybrid fuel cell bus refueling at SunLine Transit Agency, Thousand Palms, California. ThunderPower is the world's first hybrid fuel cell bus to be placed into revenue-generating service.

Palm Springs Chamber CEO David K. Aaker uses the Chambers Global Electric Motorcar (GEM) to promote business.

A line thru history, Dr. June McCarroll, a pioneer physician of the Coachella Valley, came up with the idea in 1917 to put a white safety line down the middle of the road.

Dr. June McCarroll said in a 1939 interview, "I wanted to be a housewife, but under the conditions, I couldn't refuse to share my medical training, so only a few weeks after arriving in Indio I became Coachella Valley's only doctor."

TAKING CARE OF BUSINESS

The Coachella Valley Economic Partnership helps innovative companies expand or relocate to the Coachella Valley. One of the area's real selling points is its proximity to Los Angeles, Phoenix, San Diego and Las Vegas – all major western markets. Former CEO of U.S. Filter, a division of Vivendi, Richard Heckmann puts it this way about doing business in the Valley: "Of all the places we considered for locating our worldwide headquarters, the Coachella Valley won hands down. The low cost of living combined with affordable housing and top quality schools creates a quality of life that helps us attract key employees and top executives from around the world. The Coachella Valley has proven to be a great place for families and businesses alike."

Among the clients CVEP has brought to or kept in the Coachella Valley are Palm Desert's Guthy-Renker, the world's largest infomercial company with more than $700 million in annual sales, and Palm Springs Bird Products, a subsidiary of VIASYS Healthcare, Critical Care Division, a world leader in the manufacturing of respiratory devices. Sino CTB Company, a golf bag and equipment manufacturer and distributor, has its U.S. headquarters in the desert. Guy Evans Inc., with over 500 employees and a 50,000 square foot showroom in Thousand Palms, is one of the West Coast's largest suppliers of designer doors, windows, hardware and plumbing accessories.

Thane International is a La Quinta based company with $100 million in annual gross revenue that develops and markets products through infomercials and direct marketing. The Coachella Valley is a great fit for Thane's business, says President and CEO Bill Hay, because the company deals in relationships. Says Hay, "Our business is made up of the people who work here and the people who we work with – our allies in the marketplace throughout the world. This is a global business. Barriers between countries don't exist any more. I don't think of Thane as a U.S. business with an international arm but as a business that before too long will be doing more business around the world than we do in the United States."

The Coachella Valley is the only region in the nation that offers companies a Federal Empowerment Zone, a Federal Foreign Trade Zone and a State Enterprise Zone. The incentives collectively available through these three programs provide businesses with up to $53,000 per employee in hiring tax credits over a five to eight year period, below market financing options and a reduction and/or elimination of import tariffs and duties.

Specifically, the Empowerment Zone provides tax-exempt financing for business facilities and equipment at two-thirds the prime lending rate. The Foreign Trade Zone reduces or eliminates duty for companies involved in adding value to products before export. Preferential treatment is given by U.S. Customs to products destined for a Foreign Trade Zone.

The bottom line for businesses relocating to the Coachella Valley is cost savings through incentives, an abundant supply of inexpensive land, low labor costs, affordable housing, a low cost of living and a lifestyle second to none. The Valley's business climate helps companies operate within California to meet market demands without a heavy tax burden. "Our system of permitting and localized private and public sector incentives that reduce land and utility costs, which are already among the lowest in California, helps explain why over 850 companies have moved to the Coachella Valley in the last two years," says Kristie Porter of the Coachella Valley Economic Partnership.

The Valley's transportation assets are also formidable. Interstate 10 connects the Coachella Valley west to Los Angeles and east to Phoenix and beyond. Highway 86 is Southern California's "NAFTA Highway," linking our region to Mexicali, Mexico. Union Pacific Railroad offers companies rail access to both West Coast harbors and middle America through the Valley. The City of Indio is capitalizing on its location where Interstate 10, Highway 111, Highway 86 and railroad lines meet to create a multi-modal transportation center. Within the Valley, 4.1 million riders annually are served by SunLine Transit Agency.

THE WORKFORCE OF TOMORROW

In order to train and keep professional talent, the Valley supports a variety of educational institutions and programs. College of the Desert is one of 107 California Community Colleges – the largest educational organization in the world – and is recognized as a pioneer in curriculum development for new business and industry applications. College of the Desert has worked diligently with the three local K-12 school districts, private career and vocational institutions and four-year colleges to create a seamless transition for students throughout their school years that can efficiently test student performance and guide individuals into programs that best suit their needs. Enrollment at College of the Desert has reached as high as 12,000 students – some of whom are high school graduates while a significant portion are working adults re-entering the job market.

Education in high tech industries is reshaping the desert resorts economy by providing a trained workforce and business infrastructure for higher paying jobs and the kinds of clean industries a tourism-based region can sustain. On land provided by the City of Palm Desert near the Cook Street off-ramp of Interstate 10, a new university park is underway.

College of the Desert's new campus-wide outdoor light posts were installed to brighten the campus at night.

The new Palm Desert University Park complex, shares land with California State University off Cook Street.

California State University, San Bernardino broke ground in 2001 on a Coachella Valley satellite campus financed by local donors who rose to the challenge of adding value to the area's economic development potential with undergraduate studies in areas such as business, nursing and education. Community boosters intend to keep young talent here and attract businesses that demand workers with up-to-date skills.

The University of California, Riverside is no stranger to the Coachella Valley. It has a nearly 100-year history in providing and applying research that helped establish agriculture as the region's first economy. The institution has plans to further develop its Valley offerings including both academic and research initiatives in such diverse fields as Energy Technology, Information Systems, Media Technology, Fine and Performing Arts and Ethnic Studies. "UCR looks forward to adding these other dimensions to our portfolio of work in order to assist the future economic growth of the region while being sensitive to the critical environmental characteristics of the desert," explains Terry Green, Assistant Dean of Desert Programs.

The university has broken ground on its portion of the Palm Desert University Park complex with the identification of the Heckmann International Center for Entrepreneurial Management, named after retired CEO of U.S. Filter, Dick Heckmann. The concept of the center is to draw upon the considerable local talent available among retired CEOs and Fortune 500 business people who frequent the Valley. Through the Heckmann Center, they will have a chance to mentor the next generation of entrepreneurs.

A QUILT OF MANY COLORS

Native Americans play a high-profile role in the future of the Coachella Valley. To date, five Indian Casinos are prospering on the tribal lands of four separate tribes. Donald Trump has attached his name and management expertise to one of the splashiest entries, Trump 29 Casino, which serves as an anchor for what the City of Coachella hopes will be a mini-Las Vegas-style entertainment corridor along Interstate 10, complete with hotels, shopping centers and golf courses.

Meanwhile, gaming revenues from Fantasy Springs Casino allow the Cabazon Band of Mission Indians to branch out into new business ventures on tribal land in the remote east valley. The Cabazons recognize the need for well-conceived and environmentally sound industries that preserve, recycle or transform waste streams. To that end, they designated 640 acres of their reservation for a resource recovery park. The planned mix of projects within the park is intended to create a synergy that will increase efficiency and improve the economic and environmental benefits of each business.

Currently operating at the site are Colmac Energy, Inc., a 48-megawatt biomass waste energy facility and Cabazon Resource Recovery Park, a crumb rubber recycling facility. Future projects proposed include metals reclamation, biomass gasification and soils and fertilizer production. The Revenue Reconciliation Act of 1993 outlines several tax advantages for businesses on Indian land, including accelerated depreciation schedules and incremental wage credits and insurance costs. The land planning and project review process is handled entirely by a tribal planning department. Land use approval occurs prior to investing in expensive environmental impact reports, which saves applicants time and money.

The gay and lesbian community represents a significant economic indicator to the Coachella Valley, both as a vacation destination and place to own real estate. Desert Business Association is the voice of up to 500 gay or gay-friendly businesses in the valley and serves as a gay Chamber of Commerce with monthly business and networking meetings dedicated to providing the best service possible to gay and lesbian patrons and access to customers for gay and gay-friendly business enterprises. Likewise, the Desert Gay Tourism Guild represents up to 100 hotels and hospitality firms that cater to the gay population.

Colmac Energy Plant, and Cabazon Resource Recovery Park, which includes the tribe's First Nation Recovery Inc. tire-recycling operation.

John F. Kennedy Memorial Hospital.

YOUR HEALTH

The Annenberg Center for Health Sciences is an educational partner at Eisenhower Medical Center.

Eisenhower Medical Center in Rancho Mirage.

Since 1951, Desert Regional Medical Center has been providing medical care and services to the desert resort communities from a complex located on the site of the former El Mirador Hotel, one of Palm Springs most successful early health resorts. Part of Tenet HealthSystem, a provider of nationwide health care, Desert Regional Medical Center is a busy 393-bed acute care facility, as well as home to the Valley's only designated trauma center. An impressive array of services is offered through the Nabisco Dinah Shore Wellness Center, Comprehensive Cancer Centers of the Desert, the Women and Infants Center, Arthritis Institute and International Heart Institute of Palm Springs. Other specialty services offered include the Asthma Management Program, Diabetes Service, Hospice, Neonatal Intensive Care and Transfusion-Free Medicine and Surgery.

Another Tenet hospital serves the central and eastern Coachella Valley. John F. Kennedy Memorial Hospital in Indio has provided medical care and related services for more than 30 years. To meet the needs of the east Valley's younger population, JFK offers an extensive pediatric unit and a family-oriented obstetric department. To serve its senior population, the hospital features an Arthritis Institute, rehabilitation services, diabetes management and a Cardiac Catheterization Lab.

Half way between the two Tenet medical centers is the Valley's only not-for-profit health care institution, Eisenhower Medical Center in Rancho Mirage. For more than 30 years, EMC has been at the forefront of treatment and clinical research in areas such as cardiology, orthopedics and cancer care. Health care services are extended beyond the walls of the Rancho Mirage campus with Immediate Care Centers in Cathedral City and La Quinta.

Eisenhower Medical Center is the first hospital in California to use barcode technology to act as a safety net at the bedside before medications or blood products are administered to patients. It is also the only hospital in the Valley to offer digital image checking of mammograms, which can detect tumors that may not otherwise be visible to even the most highly trained radiologist. Studies show use of the technology could result in earlier detection of up to 23.4 percent of breast cancers.

The tower at Desert Regional Medical Center, once the famous El Mirador Hotel.

A FUTURE OF LIMITLESS OPPORTUNITY

After the glory days of the 1950s and '60s when Palm Springs reveled in a hip Rat Pack image, the desert resort communities took on an identity as a retirement enclave for older, predominantly white residents. Census 2000 showed us that in today's Coachella Valley, nearly 50 percent of the population is under 35 and nearly 53 percent is non-Anglo. Eighty percent of local residents surveyed say they chose to live in the Coachella Valley and plan to stay at least five years.

From wireless and digital Internet service providers, film and video production companies and food processing plants to sports equipment and apparel manufacturers, the Desert Resort communities are humming. The new Valley economy includes growth in business services, financial and banking services, health care, government, light manufacturing technology, gaming and education. The Coachella Valley is the corporate home of high technology specialty manufacturing, assembly, communications, finance and much more. Proximity to markets is vital to any business. The Coachella Valley offers cost-effective access to over 25 million consumers within a 250-mile radius, at a commercial space cost of less than half that of many major markets.

The vision for the future of the Coachella Valley is one of limitless opportunity in new economy lines of business. The profile of the future Coachella Valley businessperson is one of high energy with high expectations for a rich quality of life. Bob Smith of Mainiero, Smith and Associates puts it this way, "If the Valley continues to grow as it has in the past four years, we'll have to concentrate on how to sustain the quality of life that we all moved here to enjoy. It's likely that the new 'urban' desert residents will live, shop, dine and even work in their own 'villages,' with less dependence on automobiles."

Photographer Tom Brewster

Dates being cleaned before packing at Oasis Date Gardens in Thermal.

The qualities that first enticed people to this rugged landscape – mild winters and room to grow – are still largely responsible for the influx of residents and visitors who come from all over the world to soak up the desert sun or invest in the local economy. Tourism and agriculture rule our business model today as they have since the first settlers landed in the Valley and proclaimed it the Shangri-La of its time. But the outside world is no longer a dusty day's stagecoach ride away. Tomorrow's Coachella Valley is the best of both worlds – close to the creature comforts of the 21st century and full of the pioneer spirit that has made this a desert paradise.

Photographer Tom Brewster

Coachella Valley's Businessmen attending a luncheon invitation from Desert Springs Publishing which was held at Desert Willow's Country Club, October 2002. (Left to Right Front Row) Milt Jones, Publisher Palm Springs Life, Frank Bogert, Former Mayor of Palm Springs, Ernie Vossler, President, Landmark Golf Co. (Second Row Left to Right) Bill Powers, President/CEO, Pacific Western Bank, Joe Walser, Executive Vice President Landmark Golf Co., Carl Sam Maggio, Managing Member, Prime Time International, Paul Ames, President, The Ames Group, Dave Erwin, Partner; Best Best and Krieger LLP, Steve Hoffmann, President/CEO Canyon National Bank.

(Above)
Manuel Abarca
and Rick Morris

Photo By
Tom Brewster

A & M Construction

For nearly two decades, A&M Construction has played a significant role in the Coachella Valley's development.

Owners Rick Morris and Manuel Abarca first met on a framing project in Orange County. At the time, Morris was an electrical contractor and Abarca was an accomplished carpenter. They respected each others' work, struck up a friendship and eventually began a partnership that is still going strong today.

Their company's first project was Regency Homes in Rancho Mirage. Soon they were hired to work on some of the most prestigious multiple-residence framing projects in the valley, including Rancho La Quinta, Calif., Victoria Falls, The Tradition and The Summit at PGA WEST.

A&M Construction employs at any time between 200 and 400 people. Many have been with the company for more than 15 years. This loyalty stems from the company's long-standing reputation as an organization founded on integrity, honesty and a hands-on willingness to work together toward mutual goals.

The company specializes in custom homes, building between five and 10 pre-sold custom homes each year. In addition to its general contractor work, A&M Construction is also a framing subcontractor for high-end, unique homes.

"Although the major part of our business is providing support to other contractors, custom projects give us the most satisfaction," Morris explains.

Both Morris and Abarca relish the personal relationships that develop during the creative process and continue long after the client has taken up residence. They feel they earn their customers' friendship by going far beyond the basic architectural blueprint. Blending the talents of a team of seasoned professionals, they are able to provide unparalleled strength, craftsmanship and expertise, resulting in very special homes for very special clients.

> "...They are able to provide unparalleled strength, craftsmanship and expertise..."

"Our clients appreciate our accessibility and our get-it-done attitude. They know we're there for them and that we are uncompromising in our commitment to quality. When you're building someone's dream home, it is essential that you listen and are totally dedicated to making the experience an enjoyable one," Morris says.

A&M Construction is also dedicated to the village of La Quinta, where it has been headquartered since it began. The owners take great pride in their community, which they feel is the ideal place to work and raise a family. Their pride is evidenced in their commitment to community service. Organizations benefiting from their assistance include La Quinta Sports & Youth Association, La Quinta High School Blackhawks Football Team, La Quinta Boys & Girls Club, La Quinta Historical Society, La Quinta Chamber of Commerce, Main Street Marketplace, YMCA of the Desert, and Leadership Coachella Valley.

For more information: 760-564-4832.

Aaker & Associates

David Aaker has made a business out of customer service. He speaks nationally on the subject, and is invited to instruct corporations, hotels, casinos and municipal government about what good customer service entails.

One of Aaker's maxims is, "Every telephone call has a future." Because someone has chosen to call your business for whatever reason, it is your responsibility to make the most out of each and every opportunity.

Aaker & Associates is a firm dedicated to providing audiences with up to date information on business-to-business and business-to-customer relationships. "There are many choices for the consumer to make on a daily basis," Aaker says. "Every 24 hours we read or are exposed to over 4,000 advertisements. Because of all that competition, everyone in business must make the most of every customer inquiry they get.

"People will forget what you did and people will forget what you said," he continues, "but people will never forget how you made them feel. That simple fact will bring them back to you."

> "...People will never forget how you made them feel. That simple fact will bring them back to you."

Consider these seven simple customer service rules for success: 1. Know your customers by their first names, and repeat their name in the first seven seconds of the conversation. You will be surprised how their attention span will broaden. 2. Listen twice as much as you talk. 3. Always tell the truth because that way you'll never forget what you said. 4. Never argue with customers. 5. Under-promise and over-perform. 6. Follow up, follow up, follow up. 7. Be thankful for customers who complain because you still have the opportunity to make them happy.

A graduate of the U. S. Chamber of Commerce's Institute for Organizational Management at the University of Colorado at Boulder, Aaker has been C.E.O. of the Palm Springs Chamber of Commerce since 1995. He was appointed by the U.S. Chamber of Commerce Board of Trustees to serve on the Board of Regents for Colorado Institute at Colorado College.

Aaker practices what he preaches. With over 20 years in Chamber of Commerce management, he sees each day as a new opportunity to apply his principles of customer service with deft and style. Call the Palm Springs Chamber and you will hear "the Aaker touch."

"The future of Aaker and Associates looks very bright," says Aaker. "Over 80 percent of new clients for my Customer Service Workshops and keynote speeches come from audiences after a presentation." For more information: www.davidkaaker.com or 760-323-4600.

(Above) Photo by Eathan Kaminsky

Palm Springs is often associated with glamour, and few have done more to perpetuate this connection than Board Certified Plastic and Reconstructive Surgeon Scott Aaronson, M.D., F.A.C.S.

Aaronson has been "beautifying the desert since 1984" by practicing at the cutting edge of cosmetic surgery procedures and technology. His patients praise him. His staff revels in his professionalism, and his state-of-the-art Aaronson Plastic Surgery Center is a welcome enhancement to the medical community — a tribute to all that he has accomplished since launching his practice in Palm Springs, Calif.

> **"What sets us apart is that our patients are extremely happy with not only their results but the entire experience."**

At the University of Miami in Florida, Aaronson was a member of the Phi Kappa Phi Honor Society and graduated magna cum laude. The recipient of a Trustee Scholarship, he continued his postgraduate studies at the University of Miami Medical School. During this time, a lecture by Dr. Ralph Millard — a renowned plastic surgeon who is now retired — was to inspire his career path.

Dr. Milliard would not be the only one to make an impression on the young doctor. After completing his general surgery residency at the University of California at Irvine, Aaronson went on to a plastic surgery residency at St. Joseph's Hospital in Houston. It was here that he met Dr. Thomas Biggs, an aesthetic plastic surgeon and instructor with whom he still maintains contact. Aaronson considers Biggs one of the greatest influences on his career.

Just as these surgeons have impacted Aaronson, so has he changed the lives of many.

"What sets us apart is that our patients are extremely happy with not only their results but the entire experience. From making an appointment, to a thorough consultation, to getting acquainted with the staff, to the procedure itself and through to the post-op care, we have refined what we do and do it right," Aaronson explains.

Patients range in age from 17 to 92. Intensely patient-conscious, Aaronson listens to what each patient is seeking and explains the various methods he feels would be appropriate. He is thorough and leans toward the conservative when counseling patients, to ensure realistic expectations and optimum results. He and his staff carefully educate patients on pre- and post-operative instructions.

Those wishing for a glimpse of how they will look after surgery can take advantage of the MIRROR™ 2000 Aesthetic Imaging System, which allows Aaronson to transform the patient's "before" picture into an after-surgery likeness.

Another technological marvel utilized at the Aaronson Plastic Surgery Center is the Vasculight™ IPL™, which uses an intense pulsed light to treat sun-damaged skin, small facial veins, larger veins in

Aaronson Plastic Surgery Center

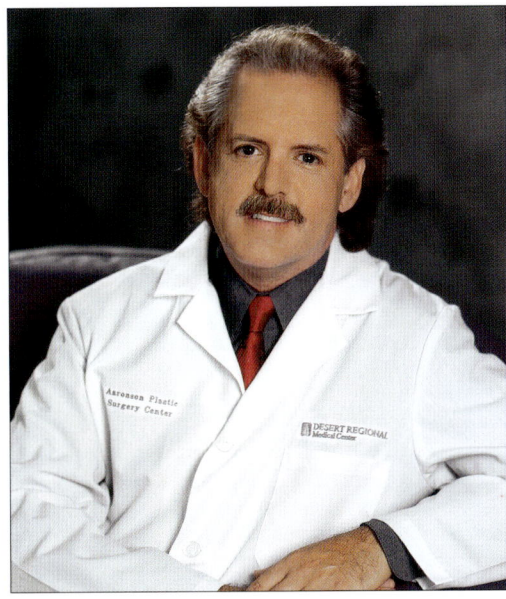

the legs, as well as remove hair and soften wrinkles.

Aaronson was the first plastic surgeon in the area to purchase the Coherent UltraPulse Laser that resurfaces the skin and concentrates on deeper wrinkles. In most cases, patients are healed and ready to use make-up in just two weeks.

Among the many specialties performed by Aaronson on a regular basis are facelifts, brow lifts, abdominoplasty (tummy tuck), liposuction, blepharoplasty (upper and lower eyelid surgery), and breast enlargements, reductions and reconstructions.

Popular non-invasive procedures include collagen and botox injections as well as microdermabrasion, often referred to as a Parisian Peel, a treatment that lightly sands the facial skin, producing a smoother, younger-looking complexion.

Scott M. Aaronson, M.D., F.A.C.S.
Diplomate of the American Board of Plastic Surgery

Just as his practice has expanded since 1984, so has his office space, growing from 2,000 square feet to a modern 6,000-square-foot out patient surgery facility located across Indian Canyon Drive from the Desert Regional Medical Center. The impressive Aaronson Plastic Surgery Center was designed by Narendra Patel, AIA, of Design Development Corporation.

"It is a state-licensed and Medicare-certified facility that enables us to offer total excellence from the initial consultation to post-surgical care. Patients benefit from spacious offices, a second operating room and more exam rooms. Most significantly, the Center offers overnight observation under the care of a private duty nurse. It is an added measure of control which helps ensure the final results will be everything patients desire."

The launch of the center in 1998 was a crowning point in the doctor's career. It was such a joyous occasion that at the opening party, Aaronson, a jazz flute aficionado, delighted staff and friends by joining his musician brother for a few sets.

Aaronson is a member of the American Society of Plastic and Reconstructive Surgeons, the American Society for Aesthetic Plastic Surgery, the California Society of Plastic Surgeons, the Lipoplasty Society of North America, and the American Society for Laser Medicine and Surgery.

He and his wife, Sandi, are the proud parents of Peyton and Chase.

For more information: www.saaronson.com or 760-325-5255.

(Left)
Photo by
Eathan Kaminsky

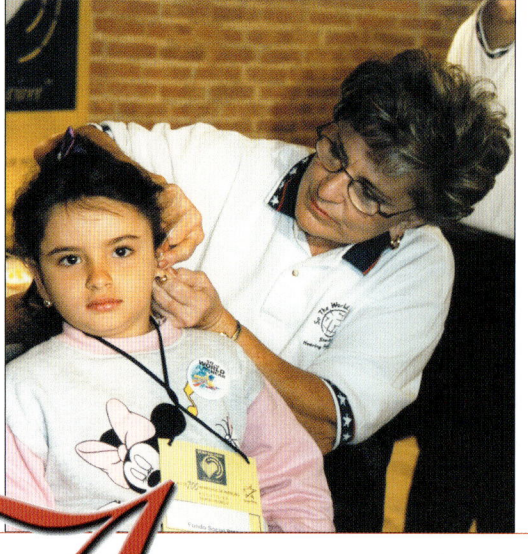

(Above) Brazil Mission, fitting a child

Advanced Hearing Systems

(Above) Joe and Pat Manhart
Photo by Allison McBee

According to the U.S. Department of Health, 28 million Americans, or one out of every 10 people, have a treatable hearing loss. Yet millions of these sufferers are let vanity and denial get in the way of buying a hearing aid, a simple step that could significantly improve the quality of their lives.

With more than 40 years of combined experience, Pat and Joe Manhart, owners of Advanced Hearing Systems, are ready to combat hearing problems with early detection reinforced with the latest technology. Advanced Hearing Systems is the largest, state-of-the-art hearing aid office in the Coachella Valley.

Patient satisfaction is directly related to the hearing professionals' expertise. Advanced Hearing Systems accurately evaluates, corrects, and programs the hearing aids to the unique lifestyle and needs of the patient. Advanced Hearing Systems' comprehensive evaluation techniques, specialized fitting, programming flexibility, and world-class post-fitting care will ensure your complete satisfaction.

"Hearing loss can have an intimidating effect on people," says Pat Manhart. "What we strive for is an evaluation of the individual's needs and an understanding of what makes them comfortable."

Many people who come to Advanced Hearing Systems' offices do not require hearing aids. Often, earwax may be the only problem. Advanced Hearing Systems' trained professionals utilize a miniature video camera to scan the ear, ear canal, and eardrum to identify common problems such as earwax blockage.

> "...the largest, state-of-the-art hearing aid office in the Coachella Valley."

Today's digital hearing aids are far and away the best hearing aids ever made. You will be amazed at the significant improvement in the comfort and the clarity of digital sound. Digital "Completely-in-the-Canal" (CIC) hearing aids are so small, no one can tell you're wearing them.

Restoring hearing is more than just a local mission with the Manharts, who regularly venture to places like Ecuador, Brazil, Puerto Rico, and Bahamas, where they have helped fit hearing aids to more than 1,400 underprivileged children through the Starkey Hearing Foundation. The next mission for the Manhart's will be in San Salvador November 2002, fitting underpriviledged children.

"We want to convey to people that this is a non-threatening, no pressure environment designed to contribute to their hearing health," the Manharts say. "We want to make better hearing available to everyone. Our motto is, "Better hearing, not just a hearing aid."

For more information: 760-341-9619.

All About Massage

Mention "massage" in the desert and most locals will point you in the direction of All About Massage. This unique Spa Therapy Center in Palm Desert, Calif. offers what locals and visitors most want: "serious therapy with exceptional value."

All About Massage and Desert Massage Associates have built their reputation by providing experienced therapists to treat specific needs. The group's excellence was recently recognized in the book "100 Best Spas in the World," which named All About Massage in its directory.

Masaru & Kelly Yamada started Desert Massage Associates in 1992, providing massage services in their clients' homes, businesses, resorts and clubs. They have built strong cooperative relationships with concierges and spas at major resorts in the valley, where their massage therapists regularly travel to provide in-room massages to guests. They provide Seated Massage for convention groups and Sports Massage for contestants at the Indian Wells Tennis Tournament each year.

The Spa Therapy Center (All About Massage) opened in 1997. It has grown to 13 treatment areas providing an array of services from Massage to Skincare, Spa Treatments, Hot Stone Treatments, and Spa Manicures & Pedicures. The casual, peaceful atmosphere is attractive to men and women of all ages, with special packages for teens and children. At the Spa Shop, guests can choose from a large selection of massage-and relaxation-related supplies, gifts and home spa items.

The "Target Massage" is perfect for those with chronic aches, pains and specific conditions. This emphasis on "serious massage" is what sets All About Massage apart from most other day spas, salons and resort spas. Acupuncture will soon be added to All About Massage's repertoire, as Masaru completes his four-year training to acquire a state license in Oriental Medicine.

> "They have built strong cooperative relationships with concierges and spas at major resorts in the valley."

Masaru & Kelly have been active in the community as well. They worked closely with the City of Palm Desert to update the city's Massage Ordinance in 1997, then continued with the help of the Coachella Valley Spa Directors' Association and the Coachella Valley Association of Governments (CVAG) to create a Model Massage Ordinance in 2001. The Model Massage Ordinance is now in effect in almost all of the valley cities. This was a major step toward making local licensing more affordable, consistent and relevant to today's spa environment.

"The Coachella Valley has one of the largest concentrations of spas per capita in the country," says Kelly. "The spas provide a perfect addition to golf, tennis, and the beauty and tranquility that have drawn people to this area for years. We are proud to be an integral part of this community and its future."

For more information: www.AllAboutMassage.com or 760-346-7949.

The New Spa Resort Casino which will replace the existing structure. Completion in late 2003.

It began centuries ago when ancestors of the Agua Caliente Band of Cahuilla Indians settled in the Palm, Murray, Andreas, Tahquitz and Chino Canyons. There they developed complex, thriving communities, thanks to an abundant water supply and the industriousness of the Tribe itself.

In 1876, the U.S. Federal Government deeded in trust 32,000 acres to the Tribe for their homeland, including 10 miles of odd sections of land adjacent to the Southern California Railroad. Of the Tribe's 32,000 acres, 6,200 lie within the Palm Springs city limits.

Today, although much has changed, much has stayed the same. The creative energy, resourcefulness and profound sense of honor that defined the Tribe's ancestors are still very much in evidence.

"From our humble beginnings we had an interaction with non-Indian forces," explains Richard Milanovich, chairman of the Tribal Council. "Palm Springs has been a prime melting pot of two cultures. This has been very beneficial for tribal members and for the community. We have accumulated knowledge from a business perspective and have been blessed with great working relationships with our employees and the community."

In 1992, the Tribal Council acquired the 230-room Spa Hotel, which boasts 6,000 square feet of meeting space and a world famous spa. The Spa Casino was added in 1995. The Spa Casino features 1,000 slot, video poker and progressive games and 21 table games. In 2001, the Agua Caliente Casino was built in Rancho Mirage, setting a historic precedent for the Tribe when it became the first Native American group to own and operate two gaming facilities in California.

The $90 million Agua Caliente Casino features 1,000 slot, video poker and progressive games, 32 gaming tables and the Primrose Room for high-limit gaming. There are also six restaurants offering a variety of cuisines and the 1,000-seat Cahuilla Showroom with headline entertainment.

More than 2,000 jobs have been created by the development of these projects and other enterprises, resulting in much-needed boosts to the Palm Springs and Coachella Valley economies.

And most importantly, the money from these enterprises has allowed the Tribe to provide the vital resources needed to fund education, economic development, cultural preservation, housing and health care programs for Tribal members.

Construction is currently underway for a new $90 million Spa Resort Casino, which will replace the existing structure. The 119,000-square-foot casino is slated for completion in late 2003. It will feature three restaurants, including a 300-seat buffet, a casual restaurant with terrace dining and a sports bar. There will also be a 150-seat entertainment

Agua Caliente Band of Cahuilla Indians

Left: AGUA CALIENTE CASINO which is on the corner of Bob Hope and Ramon in Rancho Mirage.

Right: Tahquiz Canyon which is located in Palm Springs.

lounge. Parking will be plentiful, with 1,303 spaces. "The luxury and ambiance will be breathtaking," says Milanovich. "And it will mark the beginning of what we anticipate to be a premier centerpiece in downtown Palm Springs, located on the same site

where the Agua Caliente Band of Cahuilla Indians discovered 'Se-Khi' (boiling waters), the hot mineral springs that gave our city its name."

Another major accomplishment of the Tribe has been the reopening of Tahquitz Canyon, a sacred site that had been closed to the public for some 30 years. The Canyon was depicted as Shangri-La in the 1937 film classic, "Lost Horizon." Today visitors can view a spectacular 60-foot waterfall, rock art, ancient irrigation systems and native wildlife and plants through ranger-led tours of the area.

At the entrance to the canyon is the Tahquitz Visitor Center, complete with cultural exhibits, a display of Cahuilla pottery and tools, an observation deck and a theater where a video depicting the legend of the Tahquitz Canyon is shown.

Keeping the spirit of the legends and native cultures alive will be the mission of the new Agua Caliente Cultural Museum. Currently housed in the Village Green Heritage Center in the heart of downtown Palm Springs, the proposed 50-acre museum complex's slogan is, "The Spirit Lives." The spirit will be kept alive through exhibitions, collections, research and educational programs housed in a 96,000-square-foot structure located adjacent to the Indian Canyons.

It is projected that the museum's extensive facilities will annually welcome approximately 150,000 national and international visitors of diverse backgrounds, ages, and interests.

"It will be yet another way for our members to give back to the community as part of our long-standing tradition to be good neighbors and to share our blessings with everyone fortunate enough to call this area home," Milanovich says.

Over the past six years, the Agua Caliente Band of Cahuilla Indians has donated more than $8 million to local community, civic and non-profit organizations.

"We will continue progressing and developing our parcels of land, either singly or jointly with others. And we will continue to have a great time putting together projects that, when completed, will have a panache second to none," Milanovich concludes.

For more information:
www.aguacaliente.org or 760-325-3400;
www.sparesortcasino.com or 760-325-1461;
www.hotwatercasino.com or 760-321-2000.

"Palm Springs has been a prime melting pot of two cultures. This has been very beneficial for tribal members and for the community."

Michael G. Allen "Special Agent"

He has been putting the "HO, HO, HO" into holidays for the City of Palm Springs for more than 30 years. Mike Allen is the city's official Santa — and so very much more.

An insurance agent, consultant and senior advisor affiliated with Weingarten & Hough for the past 25 years, Allen has been involved in his community in a profound way.

"My involvement in the community has been a true love affair. By proclamation of city council I am the official Santa for the City of Palm Springs. Two of my favorite sayings are: 'When Palm Springs has bad weather, we have the BEST bad weather,' and 'I live and breathe Palm Springs no matter where I go.'"

His past civic contributions include involvement with the Elks, Kiwanis Club, United Way, Guide Dogs of the Desert, Palm Springs Jaycees; Tourist Commission, and state president of the JCI (Junior Chamber International) Senators.

For more than 20 years he has been a proud board member of the Palm Springs Chamber of Commerce and also served as president.

Currently he is a member of the City of Palm Springs Recycling Committee, serves on the board of the Mizell Senior Center and is vice president of the Palm Springs 4th of July Fireworks, Inc.

> **"My involvement in the community has been a true love affair."**

Allen is a recipient of the 1980 Jaycees Humanitarian Award for the Desert and in 1986 was honored with the organization's Distinguished Service Award.

As one might expect, his boundless enthusiasm extends to his family and work.

"Lenore and I have raised five beautiful children. I call them the 'Dillon Gang' (Sam, Julie, Marie, Jennifer and Joe.) When we got married, we made a deal. I would take care of my community and she would take care of sick people. Today Lenore is a trauma nurse at Desert Regional Medical Center in Palm Springs. Although she retired two years ago they still keep calling her back."

Allen loves his work, which as a "Special Agent" is to determine the special needs of his clients and then find the right product for their situation. Products include all types of insurance for individuals, families and groups, i.e., life, health, disability, medicare supplements and long term care insurance, (ltci) may provide coverage for home care, assisted living and nursing home care.

In 2001 Allen received his CSA (Certified Senior Advisor), which allows him to educate the 50+ market on appropriate products. He is a member of the Health & Life Underwriter Association and the Society of Certified Senior Advisors.

"I am here to help. I can't help everyone but I can certainly try." Few have tried harder.

For more information: www.allenltc.com or 760-325-2526.

(Above)
Paul Ames
Photo by
Allison Mc Bee

The Ames Group

As a farmer and real estate developer with more than 50 years of ups and downs, Paul Ames still believes in the Coachella Valley.

Born and raised on a farm near Mecca, in 1942 he left to become a pilot in WWII. When the War was over he attended college, majoring in engineering and plant sciences. Then he felt the need to return to the Coachella Valley, and in 1949, coinciding with the opening of the All-American Canal, he moved back to Mecca.

During the next 15 years, through hard work, training and luck, Ames managed to make his acreage in Mecca bloom with vegetables and citrus trees. But when the Bracero program was terminated during the 1960s (the program allowed contracted Hispanic workers to cross the border, receive good wages and housing and then return to Mexico after the harvest) conditions got tougher. Many small farmers were forced out of the business. Ames was able to stay afloat by changing crops and pursuing other ventures.

One of his ventures was a business based on his own invention. Paul Ames is credited with inventing a durable plastic liner with waterproof seams that makes it possible to store water in manmade lakes and reservoirs. His PALCO liners have gained acceptance worldwide, and virtually all lakes and water features in the desert still use this product.

Currently, The Ames Group is involved in land development and real estate. Projects have included the Landmark Golf Club (which features the nationally televised Skins Game) Shadow Lake Estates, Desert Shores Motor Coach Resort and the Desert River Ranch.

"Our water supply is secure and development has not absorbed a great deal of the real farm land..."

As a leader, Ames has served on many boards, including the State Board of Agriculture. He was selected by the U.S. Junior Chamber of Commerce as one of America's four outstanding young farmers in 1958.

Today, Ames juggles his activities as farmer and developer. He's happy with the way the Valley is being developed and doesn't have any major concerns about current growth, which he calls "well planned and executed." He observes that, "Our water supply is secure and development has not absorbed a great deal of the real farm land, which is still located in the Mecca and Oasis areas, at the lower east end of the Valley."

As a 78-year-old, third-generation resident, Paul Ames still works hard. Now residing in Palm Desert, Calif. with his wife Johna, he lives by an old saying: "If you desire to leave footprints in the sands of time, wear work shoes."

For more information: 760-345-2555.

(Above) Pete and Ginny Becker

Becker & Becker Realty

When Pete and Ginny Becker moved to the Coachella Valley 23 years ago, they hadn't a clue that one day they would be proud owners of one of the most prominent real estate agencies in the area.

Pete, who had been co-owner of seven automotive agencies in Orange County, purchased a local dealership while Ginny opted to study for a real estate license.

Today Becker & Becker Realty is celebrating 19 years as one of the largest and oldest independent real estate companies in the desert. It began with six agents in a tiny office and has successfully expanded to 120 agents and six offices. The corporate and rental departments are headquartered in Palm Desert, Calif., while other branches are located in Palm Springs and La Quinta. There are satellite offices at the Deep Canyon Tennis Club, Cathedral Springs and Monterey Country Club.

"As a company we strive to accommodate a variety of clients from first time buyers to multi-million dollar transactions. With our state-of-the-art technology and an exceptional support staff we are available to our agents and clients at all times, as they come first," Ginny says.

Ginny's sales, marketing expertise and extraordinary service standards have been her entrée into premier country club developments including Morningside, Indian Ridge and Big Horn.

Pete brings to the team superb management

> "...One of the largest and oldest independent real estate companies in the desert."

and financial skills that have allowed them to grow at a steady pace while providing in-house training to keep agents current in all areas of the business.

"Pete is so supportive of everything I do. He's really the wind beneath my wings. We each have our own expertise. He runs the office and we still maintain the warmth of a small company."

Ginny and Pete complement each other in many ways including their interest in tennis and golf. In fact, they met playing tennis and it was love at first sight. Prior to her real estate career, Ginny owned and operated two tennis boutiques in Orange County.

She is the mother of four children. Her daughter was a Miss California and runner-up in the Miss U.S.A. competition. Her youngest son, Michael, has joined Becker & Becker Realty and brings to the operation 18 years of sales, marketing and financial management skills.

The company is active in the American Cancer Society's annual "Relay For Life." Its team of agents participates in the fund-raiser, which involves 24 hours of constant sponsor-financed walking.

Both Ginny and Pete are members of the presti-

gious Who's Who in Luxury Real Estate. Ginny is recognized in the national register's Who's Who in Executives & Professionals.

For more information:
www.palmspringsdeserthomes.com or
760-346-5593.

(Above) "MESQUITE SUNRISE" Palm Springs.

Tom Brewster Photography

Tom Brewster, Photographer

It is one thing to be an environmentalist, someone who reveres nature and wishes to protect it. Tom Brewster is that and more. He is a talented photographer who has been capturing the world around him and sharing it with the rest of us for more than 25 years.

"I listen with my eyes," explains Brewster, whose breathtaking desert landscape photography has been showcased in Palm Springs Life, Next magazine and Rangefinder, a national photography publication.

The article in Rangefinder showcasing Brewster's work was written by Lou Jacobs, Jr., a Coachella Valley resident who is the author of 23 how-to photography books. Brewster was reading Jacobs' books when he was starting out.

Brewster's association with stellar colleagues is a long one. He studied photography at the University of Missouri School of Journalism, where photojournalist Angus McDougal was a renowned instructor. After college, sports specialist Lew Portnoy hired Brewster to cover many of the pro teams in St. Louis.

> "From my personal fine art work, I'm able to transfer that sensitivity as well as technique to my commercial work..."

Brewster came to Palm Springs in 1977 to work as a staff photographer for Palm Springs Life. In no time at all his sensitivity and propensity toward strong composition and vivid color caught on, and Tom Brewster Photography opened for business.

Today he owns one of the largest collections of desert stock images in the world. He has covered many of the area's top social and corporate events. In addition to his commercial work, he has developed a body of fine art that includes stunning landscapes of the Southwest, Greece, Ireland and India. Locally, he has exhibited at Palapas Art Gardens in Palm Springs.

Of his 1998 exhibit at Palapas, Desert Sun art writer Jean McKig wrote: "Thomas Brewster's fine art photography is classically beautiful, celebrating the wonders of nature and fixing forever those transitory moments that celebrate beauty in all its natural forms."

"I'm very much an environmentalist and have to have the resource of nature to renew," says Brewster. "From my personal fine art work, I'm able to transfer that sensitivity as well as technique to my commercial work, as one might best see in my golf course and landscape photography."

Although his Fuji 617 panoramic camera has freed him to capture what he sees, much of his work today is done with a digital camera.

For Brewster, it's all about staying fresh, keeping things creative and not being afraid to have a beginner's mind.

For more information:
www.tombrewsterphotography.com
or 760-320-3684.

Canyon National Bank

Back row, from left to right:
Michael Harris, Esq.
Stephen G. Hoffmann,
President & CEO
Kipp I. Lyons, Esq.
Robert M. Fey, Vice Chairman
Richard Shalhoub

Front row, from left to right:
Marshall M. Gelfand
Tom Suitt, Chairman
Milton W. Jones

In 1998, with no commercial bank headquartered in Palm Springs, Calif., an opportunity presented itself to create a commercial banking institution with community appeal. A triumvirate formed, consisting of the Agua Caliente Band of Cahuilla Indians, 350 community shareholders and an eight-person board of directors. Together, they formed Canyon National Bank.

Today Canyon National Bank serves the banking needs of the Coachella Valley while proudly catering to Native American tribes throughout the state of California.

Stephen G. Hoffmann, president and CEO, offers insight into the triad: "Canyon National Bank's unique ownership consists of three groups of owners, and it's worked out extremely well." The eight founding board members are experienced business-persons, five of whom were previous bank directors.

Customer service is at the center of Canyon National Bank's mission. Prompt, personal assistance is expected – and provided – every hour of the day. It has made Canyon National Bank so popular that its total asset size has grown from zero to more than $125 million in just four years. Further signifying the bank's progress, a five percent stock dividend was declared in March 2002.

Hoffmann notes that Canyon's financial success, including profitability, was attained after only 12 months in business: The bank has done so well because we possess the technology, including on-line banking and bill pay, and provide highly personalized service. Our success demonstrates the huge need for a community-based financial institution.

Staff members at the Palm Springs and Palm Desert locations listen to their clients' needs. December 2000 witnessed the opening of a mortgage department that offers permanent mortgages, in addition to construction, business and consumer loans. We started this operation to serve the needs and desires of our customers. Our customers get great rates and deal directly with a local representative, Hoffmann explains.

In addition to customer service, Canyon National Bank is dedicated to community outreach. Canyon works with groups such as Palm Springs Desert Museum, Frank Sinatra Celebrity Golf Tournament, Coachella Valley Economic Partnership, Palm Springs Economic Development Corporation, Desert Health Care Foundation and the Chambers of Commerce.

With its focus on customer service and community outreach, Canyon National Bank's first CRA rating was outstanding, the highest award.

We are very pleased with the progress the bank has experienced, and also fortunate to be in an area with positive growth, Hoffmann says. We foresee that growth continuing throughout the Coachella Valley. An 8,000-square-foot full-service branch will open in Palm Desert in Fall 2003.

For more information: www.canyonnational.com or 760-325-4442.

Stephen Hoffmann, President and CEO, Canyon National Bank

> "The bank has done so well because we possess the technology...and provide highly personal service."

Cathedral City Chamber of Commerce

(Above) Photo by Taylor Sherrill Photography

Cathedral City is in perpetual motion, thanks to its proactive Chamber. "Cathedral City is a community in constant transition," said Cathedral City Chamber of Commerce CEO Patti Drusky. "We are relentlessly on the go, meeting the demands of the day; always growing and trying to be on the cutting edge."

While the Chamber offers maps and information common to most chambers, that is only a fraction of what it provides. The real work of this Chamber is to function as an advocate on behalf of local business.

The Chamber recognizes that for a business to do well, it must tend to the business at hand. But for the community to continue to thrive, someone must be watching the backs of business owners, protecting them from legislation that could make doing business difficult.

So, the Cathedral City Chamber of Commerce has become the voice of business.

A political candidate who wants Cathedral City's vote must pass muster with the Chamber, whose political action committee interviews each candidate to determine whether they are business-friendly. Chosen candidates will receive Chamber endorsement and financial support.

The legislative affairs committee tracks legislation and represents the city from Sacramento to Washington, D.C.

"We designed our Chamber to be relevant to our specific and diverse business community," explains Drusky.

"We are not just a means for networking and a visitor's resource center, we represent Cathedral City to the nation."

Such "hands-on" economic development strategies have contributed to the city having become one of the most diverse communities in the desert. Cathedral City's population is approximately 49 percent Hispanic and approximately 30 percent gay or lesbian. Over 20 percent of its businesses are female owned/operated.

"We designed our Chamber to be relevant to our specific and diverse business community..."

"Everything in the Coachella Valley is new, but our growth is unique," Drusky says. "We offer a comfort level for just about any population segment. That makes Cathedral City very appealing."

Recognizing diversity as a valuable marketing tool, the Chamber set out to ensure itself a stable business population that would allow for business retention and attraction.

The Chamber is encouraged by its City Council. The Council, for example, was determined to see an active city center.

"They wanted to create a heart for the city – not just a place that houses City Hall and the police station, but a center for entertainment and shopping, where people can spend time and enjoy themselves."

As a result, the downtown core of the city is now a people-friendly complex combining City Hall, an IMAX theatre, the Mary Pickford Theater, shopping and restaurants.

The latest focus has been on developing a cluster industry on Perez Road, getting the existing businesses to collaborate and position the area as a design center.

"Cathedral City drew me in with its futuristic thinking," Drusky says. "The daily question is always: 'How do we meet the needs of today and plan for the future?'"

For more information: www.cathedralcitycc.com or 760-328-1213.

Carole, Serge & Toni

*I*n this valley, drop the name "Frank" and most folks think of the great Frank Sinatra. He's a name, a personality. Like Frank, Carole, Serge and Toni never really need to use their last names. Their success awards them this recognition and their recent professional happenings would have had Frank serenading this dynamic team with the song "It Was a Very Good Year."

It has been just a year since this trio from Fred Sands Desert Realty formed the partnership they refer to as "The Combination That Really Works." Toni and Serge are broker associates and have scored among the top 10 percent in production at Fred Sands in the past five years. Toni, who has 25 years experience in mortgage banking, enjoys the administrative aspects of the business. Her husband, Serge, loves the challenge of matching the right people to the right houses. Carole, the consummate professional, has been a member of Thunderbird Country Club for more than 20 years and has a large and loyal clientele. This past year the trio moved into the Directors Circle, a prestigious designation for sales producers in the top 5 percent. No small feat, considering Fred Sands Desert Realty has more than 300 agents.

Together, Carole, Serge and Toni bring more than 50 years of real estate, marketing sales and mortgage banking experience to their clients.

> "Clients never have to worry because one of us is always available to meet with them."

The three agree that it is a combination of experience and service that is the key to their success. Real estate is a business that has a reputation for being driven by sales. These three share a refreshing attitude that truly puts the customer first.

As Serge puts it, "We don't really sell homes. We sell service, and it just happens that in the process of doing our job and looking after our clients' needs, we end up selling homes as well."

For this unique band of personalities, service and integrity are the principles that they live by, and that is what their business is all about. Each feels very fortunate to have the other two on the team.

"You don't select partners in a cavalier manner," says Toni. "We are professionals, and we feel very fortunate to have one another. Clients never have to worry because one of us is always available to them."

They have experience in all aspects of real estate, residential, new home developments, residential re-sales, income and commercial property. Their experience is not expensive; it is priceless!

"We have everything in the world going for us. We love this beautiful Valley. We have a great respect for each other, and we love what we do," say Carole, Serge and Toni.

For more information: www.sergeandtoni.com or (760) 779-4393.

The Classic Touch Fine Jewelry

(Above)
Kathy and Gary Miller
Photo by Tom Brewster

The name says it all – The Classic Touch Fine Jewelry. Kathy and Gary Miller, owners of the popular boutique, located since 1987 at Marriott's Desert Springs Resort & Spa, impart a classic touch in almost everything they do.

"I spent most of my 20s living in Italy and Europe," says Kathy. "It taught me that classic elegance never goes out of style. It's a mixture of quality, creative spirit and timeless beauty. We want our jewelry to be thoroughly modern and utterly timeless."

"When you invest in an engagement ring, a watch, a strand of Tahitian pearls – any 18k and platinum jewelry – buy quality. It will always endure the test of time. Purchase from someone who will listen to your needs and offer outstanding service. Select a company that is established and will be there for your future needs."

The Classic Touch Fine Jewelry's collection includes gold, platinum and sterling silver as well as multi-colored gemstones, South Sea and cultured pearls, exquisite watches, custom and designer jewelry. It specializes in the sale of Gemology Institute of America (GIA) certified diamonds in all cuts and sizes.

Kathy believes one of the keys to the jewelry store's success is their terrific partnership. Her husband, Gary, is a skilled artist who designs custom jewelry, often incorporating large diamonds.

> "It taught me that Classic elegance never goes out of style. It's a mixture of quality, creative spirit and timeless beauty."

"We have worked great together for 15 years. We balance each other," Kathy explains.

Being located in a four-star hotel provides a unique mix of customers from throughout the world.

Kathy and Gary know that whatever is purchased will be taken home and scrutinized by the local jeweler. Therefore they have opted to sell only the finest quality as well as unique designs that can't be found back home. Aware of customers' mindset that hotel purchases must be expensive, they decided early on that it was essential to offer great value.

"When a guest enters our store they are usually on vacation or celebrating a special event in their lives. The gifts they purchase link us to them forever. We receive such joy and happiness from sharing a part of people's lives this way. It really is one of the most magical parts of our business. We believe the success of our store is based on our relationships. We want our customers to feel they are part of our family."

For more information: 760-341-9331.

Since 1990, the Comprehensive Cancer Center has been providing programs and services for the detection, diagnosis, treatment, support and follow-up care for people with cancer.

All services are provided on an outpatient basis seven days a week. The center is located in the El Mirador Medical Plaza adjacent to the Desert Regional Medical Center. It is the premise of the center that hospitalization for many diagnostic and treatment services may not be necessary or desirable.

The 49,000-square-feet facility represents a collaboration between two leading health care organizations, Desert Regional Medical Center, a multi-specialty, regional health care delivery system, and Salick Health Care, Inc., a national provider of oncology management and consulting services.

Physicians practicing at the center are experienced, Board Certified oncologists who have an integrated multidisciplinary approach to the care and treatment of persons with cancer. The 100 plus member team includes medical, surgical, gynecologic, gastrointestinal, and radiation oncologists, pathologists, radiologists, radiologic technologists, pain management specialists and oncology nurses. Pharmacists, radiation therapists, radiation physicists, laboratory professionals, social workers, nutritionists, psychologists, financial counselors, support staff and trained volunteers augment the team of health care professionals.

"We try to provide a truly comprehensive program – a kind of one-stop shopping, if you will for cancer patients where everything is provided under one roof in a comfortable and patient friendly environment. Offering comprehensive resources means people don't have to leave the valley to receive high quality care," Michael Goldman, executive director, explains. "If a

patient is visiting the desert we will work directly with their hometown oncologist during their stay to provide continuity of care. Convenience, quality and compassion are all woven into a patient's experience."

Indeed, the emotional needs of patients and their families are addressed through psychosocial, individual and group counseling programs. The center has been designed for maximum convenience and comfort. Private treatment rooms have telephones, televisions, VCRs and comfortable seating. Waiting rooms also have televisions, VCRs, patient education materials and courtesy snacks and refreshments.

The center also includes The Desert Comprehensive Breast Center, a full-service breast care facility offering low-dose screening and diagnostic mammography, a high risk monitoring service, clinical breast examinations and instruction in breast self-examination.

The Center's multidisciplinary team includes specialists in breast imaging, medical genetics, pathology, breast surgery, medical oncology,

Comprehensive Cancer Center

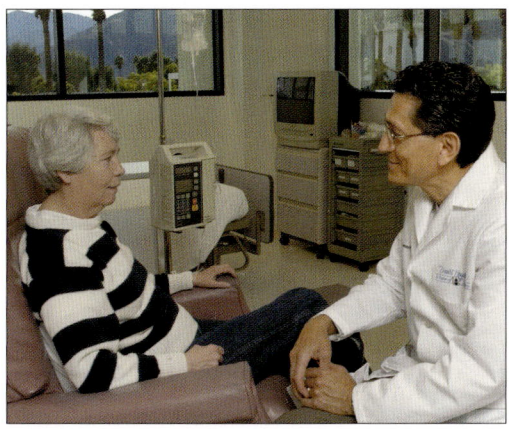 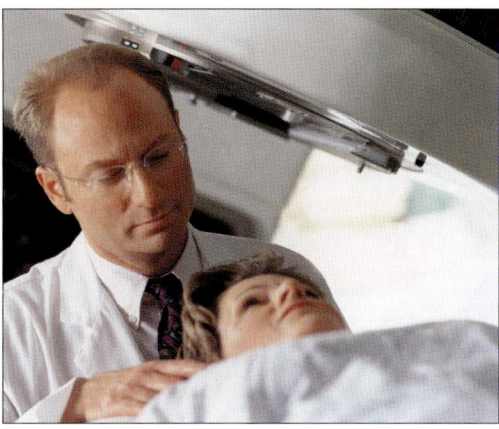

radiation oncology, surgical oncology, reconstructive surgery, pain management, radiology techs, nursing, counseling and community outreach.

Complementary medicine, which includes a broad range of alternative remedies such as herbal supplements and acupuncture, may be suggested to complement prescribed treatment.

And then there are therapies which are part of a clinical trial.

> "...everything is provided under one roof in a comfortable and patient friendly environment."

"Providing patients with access to clinical trials is an integral part of the comprehensive services offered at the Comprehensive Cancer Center. Currently we have more than 30 research (protocol) studies in place and a very sophisticated network of eight cancer centers throughout the country with 120 oncologists participating within this network. These physicians conduct investigator-initiated trials in addition to working with national cooperative groups and major pharmaceutical and biotechnology companies on phase I-IV clinical trials. We must always be pioneering in the area of cutting-edge research, to find a cure for cancer," Goldman says.

The center's new Thoracic Oncology Program is dedicated to the early detection of lung cancer, which is the leading cause of death for both men and women.

"The incidence rate of lung cancer is increasing in certain groups of people, especially women and African-American men," Walter Ehrman, M.D., cardiothoracic surgeon with the Thoracic Oncology Program, says. "Our Thoracic Oncology Program offers a spectrum of services so that we can follow each patient throughout the entire process from a minimally invasive biopsy to surgery, radiation, chemotherapy or other treatment, if needed."

The Program is also participating in the Early Lung Cancer Action Program (ELCAP), a lung screening research study with the purpose of detecting lung cancer early in high-risk patients. Local residents age 50 and older that smoke or have smoked a pack a day for at least 10 years, and have no personal history of cancer, may be eligible to enroll in the program.

Participants receive a low-dose computerized tomography (CT scan) screening exam. This type of scan maybe able to detect tiny spots on the lungs possibly years before they would show up on a regular chest X-ray. No injections or medications are needed.

The Comprehensive Cancer Center at Desert Regional Medical Center, through its multidisciplinary teams of healthcare professionals, is dedicated to providing patients and their families with the highest quality care and support.

For more information: www.desertccc.com or 760-416-4873.

(Above left)
Elber Camacho, M.D. serves as Medical Director of the Comprehensive Cancer Center.

(Above right)
Peter Greenberg, M.D., is Medical Director of Radiation Oncology Services.

Computer Payroll Company

(Above) Artist rendering of New Washington Street offices– 2003

Whether you have just one employee or 5,000 employees, Computer Payroll Company (CPC) can provide an efficient and accurate payroll service with good value to meet your business's unique needs.

Dena Brunskill, C.E.O. of CPC and her husband and business partner, Bill, began a payroll company in Orange County in 1969. They sold that company in 1985 to a Fortune 500 company and moved to the desert to be close to their elderly parents. Computer Payroll Company was started as a home-based business in 1992 and has since grown into a major commercial enterprise.

Currently CPC has over four dozen employees, including their son Richard. Construction of a new high-tech, 15,000-square-foot facility on Washington Street is underway. According to Dena, this business growth is due not only to good service and value, but also to "our high degree of involvement in the desert communities." Word of mouth and referral are the Brunskills most effective means of gaining new business. Much of this has resulted from their participation in local chambers of commerce events and important valley functions.

In their 10th year in the Coachella Valley, technology plays a crucial role in CPC's ability to provide up to 10,000 individual paychecks in one day. Volume that high requires a tight working relationship with vendors and suppliers, especially in the event of a crisis such as a power outage.

CPC is on top of the ever-increasing changes in tax law, assuring that clients and their employees are always in compliance. "In addition to staying on

> **"We never forget that sales bring revenue, but efficient, reliable, caring service adds the true profit to a company."**

top of current laws and taxes, one of our greatest accomplishments is staying abreast of technology," explains Brunskill. "Direct deposits, money transfers out of the country and deposits onto debit cards enable employees to have control over how they get paid, which is an attractive benefit offered by employers. With CPC's use of the current electronic technology that makes these options possible, even the smallest employer can now afford to offer these choices to their employees."

Computer Payroll Company is located in the desert but now has clients across the nation. One of the benefits of dealing on a national level is that CPC is in communication with other payroll experts who deal with situations similar to theirs daily.

As Dena Brunskill sums up, "We never forget that sales bring revenue, but efficient, reliable, caring service adds the true profit to a company." That explains why Computer Payroll Company is the desert's first choice for business payroll services. For more information: www.cpcpayroll.com or 760-779-1731.

Desert Hot Springs Chamber of Commerce

Executive Director Jo Lynn Slaughter spearheads the Desert Hot Springs, Calif. Chamber of Commerce. She sums up the chamber's duties succinctly: "We're a valuable resource for the community, with a very professional staff and volunteers who provide services to local businesses. We also operate the Visitor Center for the City of Desert Hot Springs, increasing business and job expansion and assisting in the orderly growth and development of our community."

This city of spas and resorts, nestled in the foothills of Joshua Tree National Park, is built over one of the world's finest natural hot mineral water aquifers. The city's drinking water has been rated time and again on appearance, odor, flavor and aftertaste in international competition. It has always placed among the top 10. In 1999 it was declared the "Best Drinking Water in the World." And its hot mineral waters are legendary, attracting visitors from all over the world in search of relief (from arthritis, stroke and injuries) as well as those just seeking relaxation.

Therefore, one of the Chamber's highest priorities is promoting the city's natural hot mineral water and award winning drinking water. It also takes responsibility for husbanding this precious resource. It established the Groundwater Guardian Team, a sub-committee organized to educate the community about how to protect the groundwater from contamination.

Serving the community more than fifty years, the chamber provides members with many benefits, such as networking, referrals, advertising and sponsoring special events. Their Festival of Waters celebrates the city's proudest natural resource with

> "We're a valuable resource for the community, with a very professional staff and volunteers who provide services to local businesses."

entertainment, vendors, activities for the children and special interest offerings. It's an event for residents and visitors alike. "We also sponsor the Holiday Parade," said Slaughter. In its 15th year, this parade is one of the longest running in the Coachella Valley.

Monthly mixers and Mayor's breakfasts are also offered as networking opportunities. The chamber enters a float into the Palm Springs Festival of Lights Parade every year, and participates in the Riverside County International Date Festival. It also sponsors blood drives to help surrounding communities and hospitals.

The chamber supports the All Valley Legislative Committee, organized by representatives of the seven Coachella Valley Chambers of Commerce, whose purpose is to maintain communication among its municipalities and keep businesses updated on topics like energy conservation, Workmen's Compensation, and other important legislative issues.

For more information: www.deserthotsprings.com or (760) 329-6403.

(Above)
Wendy E. Roberts, M.D., F.A.A.D.

Photos by Arthur Coleman

When five of your aunts are physicians, it might come as small surprise that you would follow a similar career path. Such was the case for Wendy E. Roberts, M.D., F.A.A.D., renowned dermatologist, dermatopathologist and founder of Desert Dermatology Medical Associates, Inc. in Rancho Mirage, Calif.

The path could have been different for Roberts. Her girlhood passion was ballet, which she studied as she was to study everything to come — with boundless enthusiasm. She danced with the Garden State Ballet in New Jersey and later performed with the world-famous Dance Theatre of Harlem.

In the end destiny prevailed, and Roberts went on to receive a Bachelor of Arts degree from Sarah Lawrence College in Bronxville, New York. Next she earned a medical degree from Stanford University School of Medicine, which was followed by a general surgery internship and residency at Highland General Hospital, one of the nation's top trauma centers located in Oakland, Calif. Roberts completed her dermatology residency at King/Drew Medical Center in Los Angeles. The highlight of her education was the completion of a Fellowship in Dermatopathology at New York University with Bernard Ackerman, M.D.

In 1994 she opened a multi-specialty dermatology office at Bob Hope Square. "I wanted to create a special place where outstanding results could be achieved in a caring, compassionate setting," Roberts explains.

Board Certified in both Dermatology and Dermatopatholgy, Roberts can perform surgery, dermatology and skin pathology in one convenient location. Desert Dermatology Medical Associates' primary services are cancer prevention and treatment, cosmetic dermatology, and skin, hair and nail disorders.

"I believe anyone can have beautiful healthy skin and maintain it throughout the course of life. It is important to have regular skin examinations. I take the time to listen to my patients. For me listening is as important as the examination. I take a detailed approach toward diagnosis and problem solving. And, I achieve outstanding results."

Among the many cosmetic services offered are body peeling for sun-damaged skin, laser facial resurfacing, leg vein laser/sclerotherapy, laser hair removal, collagen, Botox™, hand rejuvenation, skin rejuvenation CoolTouch™ laser, and the Total Skin Makeover.

In addition, Roberts has developed her own skin care product line called Dr. Wendy Dermatologic Solutions, which can be purchased at her office, on-line (www.e-drwendy.com) and by mail. The products are even available in Europe.

Desert Dermatology Medical Associates, Inc.

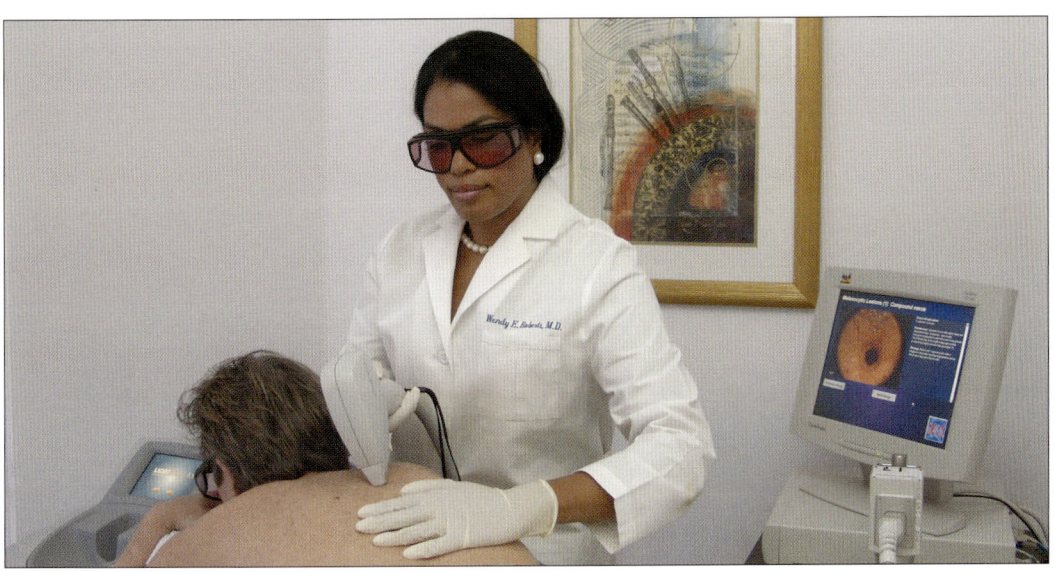

"I spent seven years developing these patented products. My patients have successfully used them and they are mostly available without a prescription. I am particularly proud of Clarity, my acne treatment, which contains no benzoyl peroxide. We also have cleansers, moisturizers and exfoliants, all of my products are more therapeutic than cosmetic and address specific skin problems such as excessive dryness, photo damage, uneven complexion and acne."

It is a continuing search for cutting-edge technology and science that drives Roberts.

"I am always looking for what's new in science and what is medically useful, and can take my patient's skin to the next level. New lasers, new computers, new chemicals are being perfected every year and I want to bring them into my practice as soon as they are proven safe and effective."

Roberts' recent technical acquisitions include digitized mole mapping, done with a computerized dermascope that creates a map of the moles on a person's skin by photographing, measuring and numbering each one. The computer detects the smallest of changes from one mapping to another.

For pre-cancerous spots, she has found photodynamic therapy with a blue light machine very effective. A special dye is painted on the targeted skin and the area is then exposed to special light, which destroys the pre-cancer cells.

Hair removal laser for light and dark complexions, new methods for infusing collagen, and state-of-the-art body peeling are also in her repertoire of up-to-the-minute treatments for her patients.

Being at the forefront is natural for Roberts, who is the founding director of the Section of Dermatopathology at Loma Linda University Medical Center. She also serves as assistant clinical professor of dermatology at the university.

She is on the board of directors of the prestigious California Dermatologic Society and serves on the Health Care Delivery Committee of the American Academy of Dermatology. Roberts is board president of the Desert Palms Area American Cancer Society and serves as director on the organization's California State Division Board. In addition, she was a featured speaker at the First International Women's Retreat at the World Congress of Dermatology in Paris. And, she has a talk show, With A Twist, on PAX-TV.

Roberts considers her mother, JoAnn, the ultimate role model. "She taught me to be self-sufficient and to think with an independent mind. She is the consummate professional woman, and with all of that, she is a very loving person. I would not be where I am today without my mother."

For more information: www.werobertsderm.com or 760-346-4262.

"...Roberts can perform surgery, dermatology and skin pathology in one convenient location."

(Above)
John F. Feller, M.D.
Co-Owner and
Medical Director of
Desert Medical Imaging

*D*esert Medical Imaging (DMI) is a family of locally owned and operated outpatient medical imaging centers in the Coachella Valley whose goal is to provide the highest quality outpatient imaging possible. Among the imaging services available at DMI are high resolution MRI, open MRI, multidetector computed tomography (CT), ultrasound, positron emission tomography (PET), and electron beam tomography (EBT). Heart disease, cancer, stroke, infection, causes of neck and back pain, and orthopedic injuries are just some of the illnesses detected and characterized with these powerful imaging tests.

Founded in 1998 with an initial office in Indian Wells, Calif., DMI now has additional imaging facilities in Palm Springs, Rancho Mirage and Indio. "We are basically the model for outpatient imaging centers here in the desert. No one else provides the spectrum of imaging services afforded by DMI," says Dr. John F. Feller, DMI's co-owner and Medical Director. "We really try to focus on 21st century digital solutions for providing patient care and service to our referring doctors."

DMI's main office in Indian Wells resembles a NASA command center. High speed secure internet access provides a backbone for transmitting images and reports between DMI's facilities. The office also hosts a secure, informative website where a patient's images and reports can be posted online and accessed only by the referring doctor or medical consultant located anywhere in the world.

DMI has many accommodations in its design aimed at meeting the needs of the unique clientele inhabiting the desert. Feller knew that much of the population here comprises either second-home owners or tourists. He wanted a user-friendly reporting system that recognized the transitory nature of the Coachella Valley's population as well as the growing year-round population. A CD-ROM writer was incorporated into the practice that "burns" the patient's medical images onto a CD-ROM. This CD-ROM is given to the patient and referring doctor, providing a portable archive that can be taken back to the patient's primary home. The patient's purse or briefcase becomes a portable, accessible x-ray file room, with his or her imaging studies viewable on any computer with a CD-ROM drive anywhere in the world.

Feller, an internationally recognized orthopedic radiologist and Assistant Clinical Professor of Radiology at Stanford University School of Medicine, said, "Most people don't know that a radiologist is a physician and that as such, can consult with patients regarding their imaging study results. This consultative service is yet another way DMI is able to be a partner in our patients' healthcare."

While DMI's equipment and digital solutions are certainly state of the art, "Our staff," Feller says, "is our #1 greatest asset." Selected for their friendliness, caring and technical expertise, many are also bilingual, another way DMI's centers are able to address the multicultural communities they serve.

Desert Medical Imaging

The newest addition to DMI's family of outpatient imaging services is a screening imaging center showcasing electron beam tomography (EBT), perhaps today's most significant screening diagnostic tool. The "gold standard" in noninvasive cardiac imaging techniques, EBT allows for the most rapid investigation of the body utilizing the least amount of radiation possible. The DMI Screening Center has the first GE-Imatron C300 EBT scanner in California. Recent hardware and software upgrades have doubled the speed of this system compared with previous EBT machines. Speed is important when imaging the heart, the fastest moving organ in the body. EBT has proved to be even faster than the fastest multidetector CT scanners.

"We are able to freeze-frame the heart and clearly detect calcium in the coronary arteries which correlates with atherosclerosis. Early detection of atherosclerosis is a critical factor in treatment and prevention of heart attacks," said Dr. Richard Seigle, Medical Director at DMI Screening Center. "If you wait until the symptoms start, it is often too late and you become one of the 150,000 people who die of heart disease each year with no warning. Coronary artery calcium scoring with EBT is a preventive service that costs less than $500 and is covered more and more by insurance," he adds.

For the first time in Riverside, San Bernardino and Imperial Counties, DMI will start doing electron beam coronary angiograms (EBA). Unlike a conventional coronary angiogram, which is invasive and carries some risk, this test requires only an intravenous dye injection in the arm. The entire heart with all the blood vessels is seen clearly and in three dimensions. The examination is so fast it is completed in only one breath hold. Being on the cutting edge of technology means DMI can offer this procedure to people who have had bypass surgery, angioplasty or stent placement that needs to be reassessed. Other uses include equivocal results following cardiac stress testing, as an alternative for people who fear an angiogram or have contraindications for an angiogram, and for evaluation of people with abnormal coronary artery calcium scores. Harbor-UCLA Hospital has been doing EBA for seven years, with no significant complications. In addition to doing the best heart scans available, DMI Screening Center can also do other screening imaging examinations including whole body scans and virtual colonoscopies.

"We continue to strive to combine caring and experienced staff with the newest technologies available to help us diagnose disease earlier, and more accurately, safely and comfortably than anyone else," Feller said. "We don't spare any expense to maintain those ideals as our highest priorities."

For more information:
www.desertmedicalimaging.com or 760-776-8989.

"We are basically the model for outpatient imaging centers...No one else provides the spectrum of imaging services afforded by DMI..."

> "Diagnosis, treatment, rehabilitation and continuing care are best accomplished by highly focused, experienced specialists."

Its history is as rich and fascinating as the community it serves. In 1948, the Desert Hospital District was formed and the Palm Springs Community Hospital opened. It was a single building with 33 beds, located on the grounds of the historic El Mirador Hotel, a favorite retreat for Hollywood celebrities that also served as an army hospital under General Patton during World War II.

Three years later the hospital closed and in 1951, the District opened Desert Hospital at the same location. For the next 50 years, the facility known today as Desert Regional Medical Center (DRMC), was to undergo a series of major expansions and improvements.

Milestones included the addition of the 220-seat Mark Anthony Sinatra Medical Education Center, a 10-suite surgical pavilion and the five-story Sinatra Patient Tower. In 1980, the hospital became the Coachella Valley's only designated Trauma Center, servicing over 800 miles to the Arizona border. In 1989 the desert's first and only Neonatal Intensive Care Unit was created to care for seriously ill newborns.

The 1990s saw the construction of the Richards Emergency Trauma Center and a floor dedicated to the Women and Infants Center. The Diagnostic Imaging Center, Special Care Unit, and a 150,000-square-foot facility, which includes the Comprehensive Cancer Center of the Desert, Outpatient Services and medical offices also came into being.

In 1997, the District voted unanimously to lease the hospital to Tenet Healthcare Corporation.

Today, the 393-bed acute care facility continues to meet the changing needs of our growing community. It is steadfast in its commitment to providing a full spectrum of quality healthcare for disease prevention, diagnosis and treatment.

The International Heart Institute of Palm Springs at Desert Regional Medical Center was created when the Valley was identified by Tenet Healthcare as being under-served in cardiac medicine. Today the Institute's services include the diagnosis and treatment of congenital and acquired heart disease in adults and children. Its medical director is Steven Gundry, M.D., an internationally renowned cardiac surgeon who believes in disease prevention and minimally invasive surgical techniques.

Desert Regional's cardiac surgeons soon hope to utilize robotic devices equipped with tiny surgical instruments to perform coronary artery bypass surgery through small "keyhole" incisions between the ribs – a procedure with which Gundry has extensive experience. The surgeon sits at a computer console and looks through lenses that are connected

(Above) Dedication of Sinatra Education Center
Photo by Mele R. Anguiano

Desert Regional Medical Center

to cameras inside the patient. He is able to direct the robot's movements with his hands and wrists, and the camera with his voice.

"The advantages of this minimally invasive surgery are less pain, less trauma, less bleeding and lower risk of infection for the patient," Gundry explains. Compared to conventional open-heart surgery, robotic patients have shorter stays in the hospital.

Neurosurgeons like Catalino Dureza, M.D., are also using new image-guided technology. They are able to perform difficult brain, spinal, sinus and orthopedic surgeries with greater precision. The new equipment is called the StealthStation Treon® and it gives surgeons a three-dimensional view inside the patient's skull or body, allowing them to pinpoint the location of their surgical instruments at all times. They can easily see where a tumor starts and stops, and where normal tissue is located. Previously, surgeons had to leave part of the tumor in the patient to avoid complications caused by removing healthy tissue.

In the fall of 2002, the Arthritis Institute was established providing a full range of orthopedic care at DRMC. Its medical director, Douglas Roger, M.D., is a former instructor of orthopedic surgery at Stanford University School of Medicine.

"A founding principle of the Institute is that diagnosis, treatment, rehabilitation and continuing care are best accomplished by highly focused, experienced specialists. At the Institute, these specialists work as a cohesive team," Roger says.

This includes all disciplines of orthopedic care –
internists, anesthesiologists, surgeons, physician assistants, a dedicated operation room team, skilled nurses and physical therapists.

The multidisciplinary team approach is also evident at the Comprehensive Cancer Center of the Desert, which focuses on programs and services for the detection, diagnosis, treatment, support and follow-up care of people with cancer. Services are on an outpatient basis. The facility also features the Desert Comprehensive Breast Center and participates in several research studies.

Through its Cancer Center, DRMC also has a Thoracic Oncology Program for treatment of patients with thoracic malignancy. The range of care includes screening, prevention, treatment and education.

Firsts are not unusual for DRMC, which has the Valley's only Acute Inpatient Rehabilitation unit providing services for stroke, spinal cord and brain injuries. It also houses the Valley's only hospital-based psychiatric, Home Heath and Hospice services.

DRMC is fully accredited by the Joint Commission on the Accreditation of Healthcare Organizations. Renowned nationwide, it has been featured on the Discovery Channel's "Champion of Industry."

For more information: www.desertmedctr.com or 760-323-6511.

(Left)
Before and after photos of 5-story Sinatra Patient Tower

Photo by Gayle's Studio and Anderson Photography

(Above) Stephanie Eichel and Dave Liniger, Founder and C.E.O. of Re/Max Int'l

Stephanie Eichel & Associates

Stephanie Eichel & Associates don't rely on a crystal ball to bring clients and property together, though many think they work magic. Eichel, La Quinta's leading Realtor at Re/Max Real Estate Consultants, attributes her success to the basic philosophy of communication, education and dedication.

A 12-year La Quinta resident, her familiarity with the community has enabled Stephanie to become a prominent Realtor in her home city. Her enthusiastic attitude reflects her passion for real estate, which is shared with clients each and every day.

Eichel graduated from California State University Long Beach with a degree in law and has an extensive background in marketing, setting forth a foundation exceeding the basic requirements to succeed in the real estate industry.

"I don't let any client ever feel like they are out of their element," she says. "I remember my first experience buying a home. I know it can be both exhilarating and terrifying. It is important to inform and guide each and every buyer through the experience making it a pleasurable one."

It's that kind of thinking that earned Eichel the prestigious Platinum Club Award five years running and her highest honor, that of being an inductee into the Hall of Fame. Because of her many accomplishments, many of her previous clients come back to her as they move up in real estate. This is both a blessing and a challenge for the popular Realtor in California's fastest growing city of La Quinta.

> "It is important to inform and guide each and every buyer through the experience..."

Eichel uses modern technology to gather information, but as she points out, "This technology can't open that door for you and walk you into the home that is matched to you because of a Realtor's leg work and research based on the buyer's desires and criteria."

The demand by tourists and future retirees craving a piece of paradise promotes a rich mix of choices for all clientele. In addition, "The Baby Boomer generation will continue to drive the growth in the Coachella Valley for many years," says Eichel, affirming the lure of the Valley's reputation for sun, fun, tennis and golf. The spirit of the game of golf brings celebrities, professionals, amateurs and the local community together, earning the desert a reputation as one of America's golf capitals.

Stephanie's husband Jason has become a significant asset to her team, contributing his cutting-edge knowledge of technology in helping the Eichel Team maintain its profile above the crowd, by offering a plethora of forward-thinking information about the Valley's future growth.

"Real estate is generally one's most significant purchase in life, Eichel says. "It continues to be my privilege to provide my expertise to gain my clients' confidence so they can achieve their piece of America's dream."

For more information: LQRealtor@aol.com or 760-275-8808.

(Above) Left to Right Pat Nesbitt, Julio Zavaleta and S. Trotz

Eldorado Polo Club

It is called the Game of Kings. And nowhere is this 2,000-year-old sport more revered and enjoyed than at the Eldorado Polo Club. Royalty, along with celebrities from the entertainment world, have played here. Prince Philip, Prince Charles and Major Ronald Ferguson as well as William Devane, Sylvester Stallone, Stephanie Powers and Tommy Lee Jones, have enjoyed this stunning venue, which is the largest in the country exclusively dedicated to polo.

Originally the club was located off Cook Street in Palm Desert, Calif., but in 1980 it moved to its present facility. At that time it consisted of four fields and acres of raw land, citrus and alfalfa. Today's facility encompasses 185 lush acres and includes a clubhouse, cantina and stabling for 1,400 highly bred polo ponies. There are 14 fields, including those leased from the Empire Polo Club.

Alex Jacoy, who has been general manager of the club for 25 years, says the facility has become a favorite setting for upscale social events. During the season the club is host to corporate events and charitable fund-raisers for nonprofits such as the Barbara Sinatra Children's Center, the American Cancer Society and Pegasus, a riding academy for the handicapped children.

Corporations utilize the venue to entertain clients as well as reward key personnel. Lucent Technologies, the American Bar Association and Toyota are among the many companies whose staff has been privy to an extraordinary evening of entertainment at Eldorado Polo Club.

"Royalty, along with celebrities from the entertainment world, have played here."

Many events are themed, such as Casino Night, Great Gatsby Night or A Royal Evening in the Winners Circle. The latter includes such entertaining touches as a we coming trumpeter, along with greeters who execute cross mallet salutes as guests make their grand entrance to the clubhouse. In yet another dramatic touch, clients are transported to tethered balloons in coal black coaches pulled by white horses.

One of the most popular events in recent years has been golf cart polo. After an exhibition polo match, professional polo players drive golf carts and serve as instructors while guests, outfitted with helmets and mallets, become the passengers/players. So popular has this variation on the traditional sport become that Jacoy is now considering introducing camel polo. Camels with handlers and 72-inch long mallets would be supplied for this unique game.

A member of the United States Polo Association since 1957, Eldorado Polo Club has become the winter capital for polo on the West Coast. Today it is a family affair, with something for everyone, including Pee Wee Polo for youngsters and social functions throughout the season. And at $6 general admission or $25 for clubhouse entry, it is a great way to spend a Sunday afternoon.

For more information: www.eldoradopolo.com or 760-342-2223.

Something to smile about – and a better smile with which to do so – is what Robert M. Maher, DDS is all about. His El Paseo Center for Cosmetic Dentistry, where he and his staff create dramatically improved smiles with virtually invisible dentistry, is his life's passion. Maher specializes in cosmetic and restorative dental services designed to extend the health of teeth, enhance wellness and physical appearance, and increase confidence.

Maher graduated from University of the Pacific School of Dentistry in 1970. In 1998, when he could have retired, he instead sold his Northern California practice and opened an office in Palm Desert. Today, he practices and trains experienced dental professionals in the art and techniques of leading-edge cosmetic and aesthetic dentistry.

(Above)
Robert M. Maher, DDS
El Paseo Center for Cosmetic Dentistry

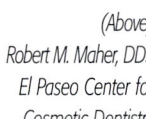

El Paseo Center for Cosmetic Dentistry

"I always had an interest in cosmetic dentistry, but only in the last 10 years have the necessary techniques, materials and training been developed,"

> "Dr. Maher specializes in cosmetic and restorative dental services designed to extend the health of teeth, enhance wellness and physical appearance, and increase confidence."

said Maher, a founding faculty member and instructor of aesthetic dentistry for the PAC-Live course at the University of the Pacific School of Dentistry in San Francisco. Dentists come from all over North America to learn state-of-the-art dental technology and procedures from him. This means that Maher continues to "amass a wealth of dental procedural knowledge gleaned from the phenomenal opportunity of working on more cases than most dentists see in a lifetime."

Maher and his staff love what they do. The front office is inviting – no windowed-partition-hidden desk in front of wall-to-wall, floor-to-ceiling patient files. Nor is there a waiting room crowd. Maher schedules one and only one patient at a time – Maher's unique Patient Privilege.

The walls of this dental care center are decorated with black-and-white photographs of people with beautiful smiles, along with color photographs of wildlife and natural

El Paseo Center for Cosmetic Dentistry

landscapes – signed by Robert M. Maher, photographer. This personal touch tells you a great deal about Maher's love of beauty in all of its manifestations. Who wouldn't want to be treated by a man with such a strong sense of the aesthetic?

The initial hour-and-a-half to two-hour exam is comprehensive – cancer screening, occlusion assessing, joint checking, decay and gum disease assessment, and digital X-Rays are routine.

What's not routine are the methods and materials used in this cutting-edge practice. For example, Maher has not used silver fillings in over 10 years. "Mercury expands and contracts and over a long period of time, it actually breaks the teeth. Most people with crowns probably had silver fillings there first. There are just far better materials available now." In this and dozens of other ways, Maher's attention to the latest developments in his field assures his patients get the best and only the best.

> "Dentists come from all over North America to learn state-of-the-art dental technology and procedures..."

Preventive Dentistry is emphasized at El Paseo Center for Cosmetic Dentistry, involving daily maintenance and nutrition, along with periodic exams and cleanings to diagnose problems as they arise. Maher and his staff are always on the lookout for gingivitis (or gum disease) and periodontal (or oral bone) disease. Their preventive regimen for both is extensive.

Their restorative dentistry encompasses replacing broken or leaking amalgams, crown and bridge design, bite realignment and implant integration. Orthodontic alternatives are also offered to answer a variety of needs. Depending on the severity of the situation, crowns, bridges, partials, bonding and veneers offer invisible solutions to orthodontic problems. Crooked or missing teeth as well as between-tooth gaps can also be corrected.

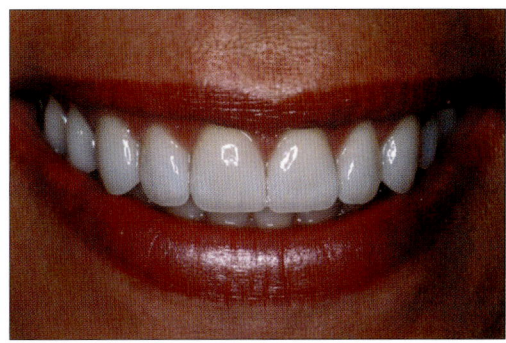

Implants offer a popular and permanent tooth replacement option that helps prevent gum shrinkage while providing a natural look and feel. The most natural-looking dentures are available at The Center, and using the safest and most reliable oral sedation for all procedures.

Maher is a member of the American Dental Association, California Dental Association, Academies of Cosmetic Dentistry, General Dentistry, Dental Organization for Conscious Sedation, and Laser Dentistry and Implantology.

Maher's El Paseo Center for Cosmetic Dentistry is comprehensive dentistry for the quality conscious. For those who don't have the good fortune to call the Coachella Valley home, Maher offers telephone consultations prior to scheduling an appointment. His staff will gladly assist in organizing the logistics of travel and accommodations.

For information: www.drbobmaher.com or (760) 836-0770.

"Live The Life You've Dreamed Of..."™

For every client of FLC Capital Advisors and Franklin Loan Center, "Live the Life You've Dreamed Of..."℠ is what David Neil and Max Briggs strive to achieve.

Neil is the president and Briggs is the chief executive officer of FLC Capital Advisors, the comprehensive wealth management firm they launched in 1994. Both are passionately dedicated to ensuring their clients enjoy a long-term, trusting financial relationship with FLC Capital Advisors.

"It's all about the FLC Experience," Neil explains. We are a boutique-style firm in the way we work with our clients and deliver our services. Compared to a major brokerage company, we are more of a family-type organization. You are never just a number here. We care about our clients' well-being."

FLC Capital Advisors recognizes that each client has unique goals, values, resources and circumstances. The firm's mission is to evaluate where a client is and where he or she wants to go. "A good financial plan is similar to a check-up that can help diagnose your financial health," Briggs says. "Financial planning initially may seem overwhelming when all facets of a good financial plan are considered. However, if a step-by-step approach is taken, the pieces come together to form a complete picture."

"This is why we call it a comprehensive financial plan. We tie up the loose ends. We take more of an all-encompassing approach to people's lives and financial well being. We tackle all the issues like one-stop shopping. A typical financial planner will do just one piece," Briggs explains.

"Our clients tend to come from a wide variety of

David Neil, President and Max Briggs, CEO

backgrounds, but have a few things in common. They are successful, they are very much entrepreneurial, and have accumulated a fair amount of wealth that they want to take care of," Neil explains.

Their clients generally fall into four groups. First are the affluent, high net worth individuals, who have worked hard to accumulate significant wealth and want to protect it. Second are successful professionals, including doctors, corporate executives, CPAs and attorneys. Third are small business owners who are helped both individually and also with their corporate needs, retirement plans and 401(k)s. Fourth are women investors.

FLC Capital Advisors focuses on four primary areas to assist clients: Retirement Planning, Wealth Accumulation, Tax Planning, and Estate Planning. "Truly one of the biggest concerns for people today

FLC Capital Advisors and Franklin Loan Center

is retirement planning," Neil says. "People are living longer, retiring earlier, staying healthier and remaining more active after they retire. They wish to retain a comfortable lifestyle but are worried about outliving their assets."

"That's where we come in," Briggs adds. "FLC Capital Advisors intends for its clients to sleep soundly, knowing that we are guiding them toward their financial goals."

"It's truly gratifying to know that we can make a difference. When clients become more confident as they understand why we are doing certain things, they enjoy greater comfort with their plans and goals. Having a long-term relationship with a long-term advisor can make all the difference in the goal to "Live the Life You've Dreamed Of...,"SM Neil explains.

Together, Neil and Briggs have more than 25 years financial industry experience in the Coachella Valley. In 1992 they purchased Franklin Loan Center. As CEO and President of this separate corporation, Neil and Briggs provided the leadership for growth that has made it the largest mortgage broker by loan volume in the Coachella Valley. The company specializes in residential home loans for the first-time buyer as well as the $10 million estate shopper.

"Buying a home is the biggest decision most of us ever have to make. It's the largest debt people take on," Neil explains. "We go way beyond helping someone obtain financing. The process becomes one of comprehensive financial planning."

According to Neil, the first thing one must ask is what is the best type of mortgage, if any, in a given situation? How big should the mortgage be? What will be the impact on cash flow, taxes, investments and retirement planning?

One must weigh all the options including the emotional aspect, which in some cases is the urge to pay cash. "If someone's goal is a long-term comfortable lifestyle, they should opt for a normal down payment and get a loan" Briggs states. "If their goal is for security, they should pay cash."

"There is an emotional side of the equation to consider. People need to be able to sleep at night, so we have to work out a happy medium so that the client has a healthy comfort level," Neil adds.

"It's all about educating the client and making sure they get the mortgage that's right for them. At Franklin Loan Center, clients can be assured that our Loan Officers will provide the highest level of personal attention and that they will get the best deal available," Briggs concludes.

For more information: www.flcapitaladvisors.com
For more information: www.franklinloancenter.com
or 760-779-8110.

> "We go way beyond helping someone obtain financing. The process becomes one of comprehensive financial planning."

(Above) Photo Credit Ethan Kaminsky

Kristi W. Hanson, Inc. Architect

From an early age, Kristi Hanson wanted a career in architecture. She would draw for hours and was fascinated with how buildings went together. Although her mother wanted her to be a graphic artist, Hanson stayed true to her passion. In 1987 she graduated from North Dakota State University with a bachelor's degree in architecture.

Hoping to ply her trade in warmer climes, Hanson sent her resume to architectural firms in selected southern cities. One month after graduation, Hanson was working in Palm Springs, California.

After a period of apprenticeship she struck out on her own in 1994. Operating out of the bedroom of her house and with no advertising, she found her phone ringing after a matter of a few days. "My business is word of mouth," she says, and apparently the word on the street was good enough that before long, Hanson's sister Jen had to be brought on staff. Jen suggested it was time to open an office, and so they did, launching Kristi W. Hanson, Inc., Architect from an office in Palm Desert. Hanson soon hired three additional employees.

"The fact that my business is woman-owned in a predominantly male field, and that I've been successful, makes my company unique. But why shouldn't women be successful architects? Women have a natural instinct for great design and for creating fun, innovative spaces that are functional, too."

Hanson explains that she doesn't have a signature "style." Because of this she's had opportunities

Custom residences at BIGHORN

to work on a wide range of projects. Although much of her work has been designing custom residences at upscale communities such as BIGHORN and Tradition, she has also designed projects such as Las Casuelas Quinta Restaurant, a seminary facility for the Catholic Diocese of San Bernardino, a social hall for the St. Louis Catholic Church, a real estate office, as well as classrooms and a library for the Marywood Country Day School.

"I really listen to what my clients are saying. People building in this area are often investing in a view. So I spend a lot of time on the lot visualizing where things will go. I design the site layout and the interiors up to the point of furniture. During construction, I visit the site and make myself available for the builder's questions. I further enhance my clients' outcome with a network of design professionals including landscape architects, metal and stone craftsmen and interior designers.

"My clients always begin with a dream, a vision. My job is to make their dreams come true!"

For more information: 760-776-4068.

> "My clients always begin with a dream, a vision. My job is to make their dreams come true!"

Hunt Weber Clark Associates, Inc.

The firm of Hunt Weber Clark Associates in the San Francisco world of communications is synonymous with high-level creativity and first-rate marketing solutions. One only needs to meet Nancy Hunt-Weber, agency president, to realize that the same commendable attributes are already starting to formulate in the Greater Palm Springs area's creative community.

Hunt-Weber's full-service design and marketing consultancy has been headquartered in the Bay Area for more than 16 years. Her fascination with desert living led her to open a second office a two years ago in Palm Springs.

"It's the best of two worlds. I have a seasoned staff in San Francisco, access to cutting-edge talent and established business networks and resources. In Palm Springs, I am partnering with some of the finest talent anywhere. Our mission is the same. It's all about collaborating, communicating and creating. In short, we translate a client's vision with the ultimate goal of increasing his revenue," Hunt-Weber explains.

Hunt Weber Clark Associates' primary specialties are branding, market positioning, strategy and creative implementation. Clients span from the West Coast to New York. The agency's expertise extends to the hospitality, restaurant and retail industries. Clients have included the Mark Hopkins Intercontinental Hotel, Wolfgang Puck's Postrio Restaurant and the Kimpton Hotel and Restaurant Group.

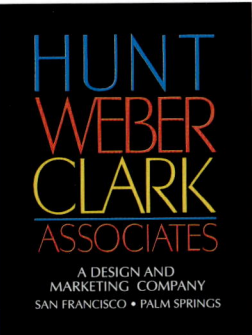

The agency has also designed award-winning concepts for the food, toy, and medical industries. Clients benefiting from highly individual design programs have included Joseph Schmidt Confections, Lewis Galoob Toys, Heritage Kitchens Specialty Foods, Natural Wonder Stores, and Blue Shield of America.

"It's the best of two worlds - A seasoned staff in San Francisco and partnering with some of the desert's finest talent."

National recognition and prestigious industry awards have been numerous. There have been 23 Awards for Excellence from American Corporate Identity, seven Creativity Awards from Art Direction magazine, 14 awards from Graphic Design: USA — and the list goes on and on.

For Hunt-Weber, marketing is a natural progression for her love of design. She has a bachelor's degree from California State College in Sacramento where she concentrated on fine art, and ongoing graduate courses at California College of Arts and Crafts in Oakland. She has also done graduate work in New York at the Parsons School of Design, Fashion Institute of Technology and the New School.

It was when growing up in Providence, R.I., that Hunt-Weber discovered her passion for drawing.

"I got in trouble drawing on the wallpaper."

After college, she rented a loft in New York and continued painting, which she supported by working in an art supply store.

Today agency business is conducted from her loft in San Francisco's trendy South of Market area and from her mid-century Palm Springs home, whimsically furnished in 1950-ish decor.

For more information: www.hwcinc.com or 760-318-6548.

Indio Chamber of Commerce

(Above) Ambassadors, boardmembers and staff help cut the ribbon at the opening of a new Indio Fashion Mall restaurant

The Indio, Calif., Chamber of Commerce is a growing, dynamic partner in the city's resurgence. "We're on a path of unprecedented expansion," says Indio Chamber CEO Sherry Johnson. "It's a prime time for Indio."

The Chamber welcomes the challenge of forging a premier position for Indio among the nine Coachella Valley cities. As the East Valley's largest business advocacy organization with 650 plus members, the Chamber has been proactive on many fronts. Chamber members benefit from referrals, networking events, advertising and publicity opportunities, workshops, seminars and the Chamber's award-winning East Valley Business Newspaper. The Chamber has also formed a political action committee to support and endorse candidates with a keen business understanding.

"Business is on the fast track," says Johnson. "Our focus is on economic development, community development, small business advocacy, government affairs/public policy and member services." The Chamber also functions as Indio's Visitor Center, getting the word out about the City of Festivals to tourists and those seeking to relocate.

> "Promoting a healthy business climate and a wholesome community..."

Indio's nationally recognized festivals play a major part in establishing its character and spurring growth. The long-running National Date Festival identifies the city as a legendary desert location built on agricultural success; the Tamale Festival shows Indio's pride in its Latin roots (USA Today named the Indio International Tamale Festival® one of the top ten food festivals in the nation); the critically acclaimed Southwest Arts Festival® now adds a touch of glamour and cachet. And other festivals such as the Native American Pow Wows, the Desert Circuit Horse Show and the Fourth of July Festival add their own unique flavors to the mix.

Southwest Arts Festival® patron displays a painting he just purchased at the 2002 festival

Since its inception 56 years ago, the Indio Chamber has spearheaded many successful programs, not least among them the Historic Mural Project. In the early 1990's when the city was in the doldrums, the Chamber financed the mural project to attract business into the Old Town District. Well-known muralists were hired to depict important moments in Indio's history. As the murals progressed, they both beautified the city and garnered attention from the media. It soon became apparent the colorful images had created more than an economic boost: Indio gained a revitalized sense of community pride.

As new chapters of Indio's past and present are portrayed in murals throughout the city, the Indio Chamber will be a proud partner and devoted community advocate. Promoting a healthy business climate and a wholesome community will continue to be the Chamber's main concerns. "It's gratifying to see Indio moving into this new phase of cultural and economic renaissance," says Johnson. "As the city moves ahead, the Chamber will move hand in hand with it."

For more information: www.indiochamber.org or 760-347-0676.

(Above) Frank Curry, M.D.

Indio Emergency Medical Group, Inc.

When Frank Curry, M.D. completed his training at Loma Linda University School of Medicine in Loma Linda, Calif., he asked his colleagues what they thought might be the most challenging emergency room in Southern California. The year was 1983. The answer was Indio.

It didn't take long for Curry to determine that not only was there no trauma center at John F. Kennedy Memorial Hospital, which serves the eastern end of the Coachella Valley, but that east Valley residents were using the emergency room to address problems that should have been handled at the primary care level.

Curry set out to right the situation. "I love to solve problems," says Curry, " and I never like to solve the same problem twice. However, all solutions must bring positive results and good for people."

Today Curry owns the Indio Emergency Medical Group, the Desert Urgent Care Medical Group, the Santa Rosa del Valle Medical Clinic and the West Shores Medical Clinic.

Indio Emergency Medical Group serves the emergency medical needs of the east Coachella Valley and eastern Riverside County at J.F.K. Memorial Hospital. Since its incorporation in 1994, three divisions have been introduced. West Shores Medical Clinic serves the primary health care needs of the rural, medically underserved community of Salton City in Imperial County, while the Santa Rosa del Valle Medical Group provides the same type of service for the underserved communities of Coachella, Thermal, Mecca and Oasis. Desert Urgent Care is a Workers' Compensation/Urgent Care site in Palm Desert.

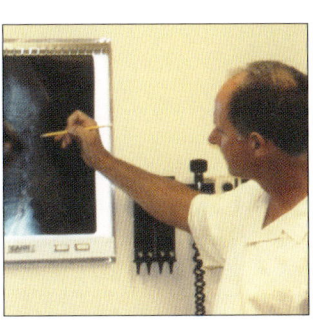

"We are unique in the continuum of care we provide, linking rural primary care to emergency medical services, and in our ability to manage workers' compensation injuries from the emergency stage to their resolution," Curry explains.

> **"We are unique in the continuum of care we provide, linking rural primary care to emergency medical services."**

In addition, the non-profit Santa Rosa del Valle Foundation was created to assist in funding health care needs. Currently, the foundation has purchased two mobile health care units that go directly to migrant farm labor communities to administer primary health care. Notes Curry, "These are people who rideshare to the fields and generally don't have their own transportation."

Board certified in Emergency Medicine and a Fellow of the American College of Emergency Medicine, Curry is Chairman of the Board of the J.F.K. Memorial Hospital. Curry is also chief of the Department of Emergency Medicine and chief of J.F.K. Urgent Care, which he jointly opened with the hospital on its campus. Curry also serves as chairman of the Medical Quality Review at J.F.K. Memorial Hospital, and is a member of the Child Abuse and Neglect Task Force, Riverside County.

Dedicated, caring and with a broad range of interests, Curry defines success as "doing good things for other people while you're having fun yourself."

For more information: www.iemginc.com or 760-775-4181

When KMIR-6 was purchased by Journal Broadcast Group in August 1999, a commitment to excellence was born. Just a few short years after the acquisition, the NBC affiliate became a state-of-the-art, Emmy Award-winning television station.

"We didn't worry about ratings," says General Manager Larry Blackerby. "We just started creating a better product." Blackerby tells his staff: "First be best, then be first."

For the 65 employees of the station who became part of the oldest employee-owned company in America, the year 2000 marked not only a new millennium but a defining year for their station. New equipment was purchased. A new newsroom was built. A new set was launched. More local newscasts were added to the schedule. "We delivered on what we said we were going to do," says Blackerby." Viewers noticed and ratings have been climbing ever since.

The KMIR-6 staff is grounded in such bedrock values as integrity, customer focus, accountability and respect for individuals. The station's mission is to be the best local broadcast company in the Coachella Valley. That goal is met by creating relevant, locally targeted news programming, which becomes a magnet for effective advertiser marketing. It's a strategy for success that has tapped the motivation and innovative spirit of KMIR-6's employees, providing the kind of environment that inspires one's best work.

As a broadcasting entity, KMIR-6 has two clients: viewers and advertisers. Both customers receive the highest quality product. For advertisers, the sales team offers superior customer service. Blackerby explains, "We don't just sell spots, we sell audiences. If you're looking for a certain demographic, our sales team will work with you to find the best way to reach that demographic on our air." For viewers, KMIR-6 presents local news, sports and weather gathered by experienced journalists and delivered by established anchors Karen Devine, Cal Ahlers and Bryan Scofield.

The news team plays an integral role at the station. Highly motivated producers, reporters and photographers concentrate on local news and respond to residents' concerns. Good storytelling techniques are utilized and news is delivered in a style that's clear, compelling, accurate and informative.

This professionalism has been recognized with prestigious awards. The station won two Best Newscast Emmy Awards in 2002. KMIR-6 is the first station in the Coachella Valley to receive regional Emmy Awards. Other awards include a Golden Mike, Media Woman of the Year for Anchor Karen Devine, and Addy Awards for creative commercial production.

KMIR 6

Bryan Scofield
Karen Devine
Cal Ahlers

A lot has changed in the industry since Blackerby first got hooked on media as a St. Louis teenager, listening to Jack Buck on KMOX radio. "All the equipment I learned to operate is probably in a museum someplace," Blackerby jokes. Working his way up through production and programming ranks, Blackerby says he's held just about every job at a TV station. When he walks through the KMIR-6 building and visits with his staff, he has a genuine curiosity about their jobs and how the day's going for them. He believes a hands-on approach, knowing his employees, and "removing obstacles" are crucial to his job.

> "...KMIR presents local news, sports and weather gathered by experienced journalists and delivered by established anchors..."

"The most fun I've had in this business has been at KMIR-6," says Blackerby. "I absolutely love my job. I have an absolute passion for it." It's not just the achievements and growing ratings, he adds, but the people and culture created within the studio. It's an environment that delights Blackerby. It's also a source of pride. "To see every person in an entire building come together and do it the right way; to work with people who know what they're doing and – more importantly – enjoy what they're doing – that really makes me feel good."

In addition to providing news and entertainment, KMIR-6 is actively involved in the community. Blackerby is on numerous boards for non-profit organizations. Others in the company also volunteer or participate in outreach programs and fundraisers. This commitment to the community is one of the principles handed down by Journal Broadcast Group. "We're not just here in Palm Desert doing news and selling advertising," says Blackerby. "We live here and try to help the community where we can."

With the economic climate of the Coachella Valley strong and the population growing, KMIR-6 is positioned to be a vital link in the valley's future. The staff is prepared to meet tomorrow's challenges with continued dedication, determination and success. "I like to compete and I like to win," says Blackerby. "But I want to be Number One because we're doing a good job and providing the valley with what they want from their local television station."

KMIR-6 broadcasts four hours of local news programming, plus hourly updates, on weekdays. The station airs two hours of local news on weekends. For more information: www.kmir6.com or 760-568-3636.

*I*n the mid-1960s, John F. Kennedy Memorial Hospital began providing medical care and services to the residents in the Central/Eastern Coachella Valley at it present site on Monroe Street. Then it was known as Indio Community Hospital. In 1975 the hospital merged with Valley Memorial Hospital.

In 1984, the hospital was renamed John F. Kennedy Memorial Hospital. Eunice Kennedy Shriver spoke at the dedication ceremony. Today the hospital is owned by Tenet Healthcare Corp., and is fully accredited by the Joint Commission on Accreditation of Healthcare Organizations.

With the phenomenal boom in residential building in the East Valley over the last decade, health care services have struggled to keep pace with needs of an ever-expanding population. JFK Memorial's proactive, dynamic development policies have kept it ahead of the curve.

In Spring 2002, the hospital unveiled a $13.4 million, two-story intensive care and medical/surgical tower. The new addition provides a 16-bed intensive care unit (ICU) and critical care unit (CCU) on the main level and a 24-bed dedicated surgical unit on the second floor, specializing in surgical and orthopedic patients. This has brought the hospital's total number of licensed beds to 162, allowing it to expand existing programs and add news ones.

Not only does the tower offer an extra 20,000 square feet of space, it also marks the first time the hospital has had an elevator. There is also a healing garden for both patients and staff. The garden was inspired by staff members, many of whom were grieving over deceased colleagues while the facility was being built.

The ICC/CUU unit features private rooms with state-of-the-art bedside monitors equipped with EEG, arrhythmia, pulse oximetry, respiration and continuous cardiac output and arterial-line monitoring. There is also a centralized monitoring station with flat screen monitors where doctors and nurses can review graphic representations of patient data.

Other features of the ICC/CUU and dedicated surgical unit are a computerized medication delivery system to promote patient safety, blanket warmers for patient comfort and isolation rooms to prevent transmission of diseases.

Also in 2002, John F. Kennedy Memorial Hospital opened the Arthritis Institute, in response to a growing patient population of aging baby boomers. The Institute provides a wide range of services using a team approach, including education, diagnosis, treatment and rehabilitation.

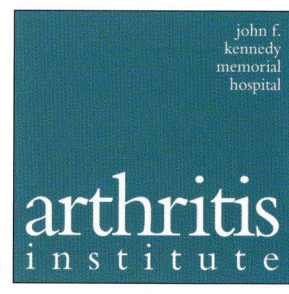

From surgeons to nurses to administrators, everyone is specially trained in arthritis and other forms of joint disease.

Advanced equipment including CAT scan, MRI, bone scan and ultra sound/Doppler machines, helps Arthritis Institute doctors diagnose the many varieties of joint disease. A wide range of medical treatment options is available.

Dedicated to education and prevention, the Institute sponsors arthritis seminars, and its

John F. Kennedy Memorial Hospital

physicians regularly speak at community functions. The medical team also conducts research on arthritis and joint disease to better understand and manage these conditions.

> **"Our integrated team approach to treating arthritis works for everyone..."**

Jonathan Braslow, M.D., medical director of the Institute, believes the Arthritis Institute is a tremendous asset to the community. "Our integrated team approach to treating arthritis works for everyone – the patient, the medical staff, and even the health insurance companies, who are pleased that we are streamlining care without compromising quality," Braslow said.

The Institute participates in Operation Walk, a non-profit program where one day of the year is devoted to performing free surgeries on patients in need of hip or knee replacement who can't afford to pay for surgery.

John F. Kennedy Memorial Hospital is also known for it busy pediatric unit and a family-oriented obstetric department. Approximately 2,500 babies a year are delivered at the hospital. Prenatal care, breastfeeding, counseling and parenting classes are offered through its Healthy Beginnings Program.

The hospital's cardiac services are equally renowned. A Cardiovascular Catheterization Laboratory is available for diagnosis and treatment of cardiac and vascular diseases. Its comprehensive services also include therapeutic procedures for pacemakers, emergency stenting and emergency angioplasty.

Emergency Services are provided 24 hours a day, 7 days a week. JFK Urgent Care, located on the hospital campus, is staffed with qualified medical professionals available to treat non-life-threatening conditions.

Rehabilitation services, diabetes management and patient education opportunities are also offered, along with a wide variety of additional inpatient and outpatient services.

The hospital's continued commitment to its community is evident in its interactive Web site, which offers a wealth of information on all of its services. There is also a popular "E-mail a Patient" feature that allows individuals to e-mail their friends and loved ones who are being treated at JFK. True to its more than 30 years of providing health care with a personal touch, messages are then hand-delivered to the patients.

For more information: www.jfkmemorialhosp.com or 800-343-4JFK (4535).

(Above)
Jonathan Braslow, M.D., Director of JFK Hospital's Arthritis Institute.

Photo by Scott Windus Photography

John F. Kennedy Memorial Foundation

Not long ago the visionary board of directors of the John F. Kennedy Memorial Foundation commissioned a needs assessment survey. They were interested in finding out whether the needs of newborns and young children were being met in the Coachella Valley. Survey results indicated a lack of services in the central valley, where there were no pediatricians who accepted Medi-Cal, no WIC (Women, Infants & Children) nutritional programs and no educational pre-natal care programs.

Through a combination of hard work and major gifts, the Well Care Clinic was born. In January 2002 the $1.25 million clinic opened its doors in Palm Desert, Calif. and during its first six months, 2,800 pediatric visits were provided.

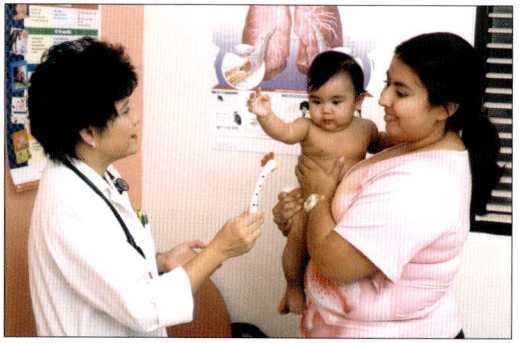

Dr. Nieves Go consults with a mom and her baby.

The John F. Kennedy Memorial Foundation is "dedicated to enhancing the physical, emotional and intellectual health and wellness of Coachella Valley children and families."

The emphasis is placed on helping young children, from birth to three, have a healthy, happy and safe start in life. With that as its goal, the Foundation provides parenting education and health care services to the under-served. It also administers the Ophelia Project, that mentors adolescent girls to achieve their dreams through education.

The Well Care Clinic is the brainchild of Foundation Executive Director John Shields.

"The emphasis is placed on helping young children, from birth to three, have a healthy, happy and safe start in life."

"We offer health care for moms and kids through prenatal care, pediatric care, WIC and parent education programs. We are non-profit and our policy is not to turn away anyone," Shields says. "What we have done with the Well Care Clinic is to assemble multiple maternal and child health care services under one roof. We have implemented a new approach where we integrate child development assessments and parent education into the pediatric practice. When parents bring their baby for a well baby check up, they will see the pediatrician and child development specialist. This is a critical time in that a baby's brain is still developing in response to outside stimuli. It is also a time when parents are most responsive to outside help."

Shields, with 30 years experience managing successful family-serving nonprofit organizations, is the founding director of the Barbara Sinatra Children's Center and has earned national recognition in the field of child abuse.

"For me, the Well Care Clinic is one of the most exciting efforts I have taken on," Shields says. "It is such a positive thing to be involved with young families at the time of the birth of a baby. We can prevent problems and make a tremendous difference at such a strategic time. I have never had so much fun in my life."

For more information: www.jfkfoundation.org or 760-776-1600.

(Above) Photo by Kaminsky Productions

Anne Kerpon Interior Design

Interior Designer Anne Kerpon is ready for any design challenge.

Experienced in designing commercial as well as residential spaces, Anne Kerpon prides herself on her ability to work in a range of styles, tailoring what she does to every client's specific needs. "It's important to be versatile," she says. "Today's clients are sophisticated, and many prefer a particular style but want to personalize it. So you have to know the basics of all of the different styles, while being able to add eclectic elements that bring out each style's intrinsic excitement. It's a real challenge.

"I thrive on it, frankly," she laughs. "It keeps me fresh. I always want to stay on the cutting edge and to offer my clients the very latest looks."

Kerpon begins by spending time with her clients, reviewing design references and resources to get a sense of their tastes. Once she feels she understands a client's preferences from the inside out, she will stop at nothing to find what they want. She spends hours trolling the markets in nearby Los Angeles; she scours the Internet searching for the latest patterns and designs. And, if it doesn't exist, she will design it personally on paper and have it made.

Communication between client and designer is key, Kerpon says. "I have to be a listener and a translator," she explains. Her first questions for a client are about their real lives and their fantasy lives. Next is what they want from her. Her services range from simply choosing paint colors for their walls to designing their entire homes. Personal attention from beginning to end is her motto. She shepherds a project every step of the way.

Anne Kerpon

"I always want to stay on the cutting edge and to offer my clients the very latest looks."

A member of the American Society of Interior Designers, Kerpon received her training in Newport Beach at the Interior Design Institute. She gained practical experience working with some of the Coachella Valley's most prominent designers. "This valley is a crucible for contemporary design work," she says. "It so happens that this region attracts some of the nation's most skilled architects, and the spaces they build call for discerning, savvy interior design. Add to those elements a population of knowledgeable clients, and what you end up with is a working community of extremely rare and fine visual talent. My colleagues here are among the best in the country. I'm proud to be a part of this scene."

For more information: 760-771-4267.

Professional sports for women changed forever in 1972 when a national corporate sponsor hooked up with magnetic popular entertainer Dinah Shore to launch a golf tournament today known throughout the world as the Kraft Nabisco Championship.

The location was the new Mission Hills Country Club, Rancho Mirage, with its challenging 18-hole Desmond Muirhead golf course. Trees, which today tower in clusters to charm and bedevil golfers, were as sparse then as nearby condo landscaping. Rancho Mirage itself was a relatively unknown residential neighbor of established Palm Springs and more than a year away from cityhood.

Today, Rancho Mirage is known for exclusive country club living, health care, shopping and dining and, of course, its postcard tournament beamed across the U.S. and many parts of the world when the ground is still frozen and golf clubs are stashed for the winter.

The Kraft Nabisco Championship is one of only four LPGA Major Championships in the world.

Kraft is finding new ways to take their Major Championship to even higher levels. The hospitality culture required for such a successful destination event is a natural for a top international food company. Kraft further supported the event in 2003 when it raised the purse by $100,000 to $1.6 Million and the winner's share to $240,000.

Corporate sponsorship prize money, televised exposure with Dinah Shore hosting and global

> **"Some of the greatest names in entertainment, sports and politics exert their seniority boasting rights at every event."**

media attention distinguished this event from the start. The original purse set by Colgate Palmolive was $110,000 with a first prize of $20,000, then a stunning amount for women's sports and a giant step toward parity with the men's tour. Paydays were so meager Kathy Whitworth commented in 1972, "It's expensive to play on tour – I'd say you have to win at least $8,000 to break even."

The first major on The Tour, the Kraft Nabisco Championship is steeped in tradition from awesome records compiled on a legendary course to the winner's victorious jump in the lake, a Sunday afternoon rite started by three-time winner Amy Alcott and her caddie in 1988.

Another tradition is the Walk of Champions across the bridge at Mission Hill Country Club's 18th green. Long the most famous walk in women's golf, it was the

Kraft Nabisco Championship

(Above) Two-time champions and perennial favorites, Annika Sorenstam and Juli Inkster

culmination of every event until Amy Alcott decided to add "the splash heard 'round the world." Now the walk is a prelude with a chanting crowd urging the winner to take the big leap.

Mickey Wright, Kathy Whitworth, Sally Little, Jane Blalock and other great women golfers dominated early play. A decade later sunbelt players Nancy Lopez, Betsy King, Juli Inkster and Amy Alcott joined popular Pat Bradley and JoAnne Carner in attracting huge galleries. Sweden's back-to-back winner Annika Sorenstam and a galaxy of sensational international players such as Australia's Karrie Webb or Korea's Se Ri Pak brought the newest wave of fairway stars, bridging generations and faraway oceans.

The world of sports zeros in on the Kraft Nabisco Championship every spring but the tournament impacts its desert host city and the region year around through its charity ties and volunteer preparation.

The tournament has donated more than $5 Million to desert charities since its inception. Charity selection in the early 1970s was designed to serve the broadest base and meet future needs as well. The founders did a thorough job. Even though the area's population has mushroomed, the major charities have remained constant. They are Desert Healthcare Foundation, United Way of the Desert, the Boys and Girls Club of Palm Springs and the Palm Springs Kiwanis Club.

Volunteer chair often serve for 20 years or more and there is a waiting list for the tournament's 700 volunteer positions. Resignations are rare and most volunteers treasure their collections of official caps, jackets and other memorabilia.

Celebrities also have strong ties. Some of the greatest names in entertainment, sports and politics exert their seniority boasting rights at every event. Many have made such close friends, dating back decades, the event has become an annual homecoming.

The Kraft Nabisco Championship is a desert wonder for more than the lucky folks who attend in person. Thanks to the media, images of majestic mountains, perfect fairways and superb competition are shared with grateful golf fans everywhere.

For more information:
www.kraftnabiscochampionship.com
or 760-324-4546.

La Mariposa Aristokatz, Mosaic

In another time she might have been an explorer charting paths for those to come. Today, Diane Matzner owns not one, but three highly successful boutiques in Palm Springs.

La Mariposa, offering unique women's apparel and accessories, has been delighting customers for 20 years. Aristokatz, a cat lover's paradise, is celebrating its 12th year. Mosaic, a gift emporium, is the newest in her collection and has been open for four years. Both La Mariposa and Mosaic are located in the Mercado Plaza, which boasts an old-world marketplace ambiance. Aristokatz is nearby in the historic Oasis Plaza.

Born and raised in Long Beach, Calif., Matzner has always been a high-energy person with a strong sense of her future. In fact, she kept a diary in junior high and wrote it in that she would someday own her own business.

"I have been very fortunate to make a living doing what I love," says Matzner. "At a young age I discovered that retail was the perfect outlet for my entrepreneurial spirit. A passion for buying, merchandising and relating to people came very naturally to me."

Her success has been recognized. In 1998, she received the prestigious Athena Award when the Palm Springs Chamber of Commerce named her Entrepreneurial Businesswoman of the Year.

"I take great pride in being a small, independent, woman-owned and -operated business. I like to believe the people I employ and the customers that have supported us for 20 years respond to that attitude."

Matzner also has a strong sense of community. She is a board member of the Palm Springs Chamber of Commerce and the Palm Springs Economic Development Corporation, and a committee member of the Palm Springs Police Community Task Force. She also serves on the advisory board for the City of Palm Springs Tourism.

She has played a vital role in bringing Art in Public Places to Palm Springs. She convinced the city, architectural review board and her landlord to allow her to commission the famous "Cat Bench" that sits in front of Aristokatz. Her own cats, Dusty and Pepper, were models for artists Gwen Hughes and Rick Barber as they crafted the whimsical bench. Today another piece of functional art, "Mosaic Bench," an extraordinary tile-encrusted cement love seat by Harvey J. Silverman, sits permanently in front of Mosaic.

"My goal is to provide a shopping experience. To me retail is an emotional thing – a romantic connection with the way things look, feel and smell. Inspiration from my travels and a colorful imagination help me keep things fresh and new. The bottom line is, what I do makes me very happy."

For more information call: 760-322-0833.

"To me retail is an emotional thing – a romantic connection with the way things look, feel and smell."

La Quinta Chamber of Commerce

The La Quinta, Calif., Chamber is your primary c-o-n-n-e-c-t-i-o-n to prospective clients and customers. The Chamber offers valuable resources and a professional staff to assist you in planning, coordinating and implementing a cost-effective marketing plan. The Chamber sponsors events and programs that support the needs of the local business community and foster business-to-business and business-to-customer relationships.

Nestled in the heart of the Coachella Valley, the La Quinta Chamber prides itself on a diverse and dynamic membership that has doubled in recent few years. The Chamber's mission is to promote and enhance business growth, civic well-being and a sound quality of life. The La Quinta Chamber is prepared to help you grow your business.

Valerie J. Smith, CEO of the La Quinta Chamber of Commerce, describes the momentum driving one of the fastest growing Chambers in the valley. "The phenomenal growth and development in La Quinta have set a challenging pace for our Chamber. We pride ourselves in providing the resources and business connections needed to support and sustain the growth of the city's business community."

2002 marks a year of celebration! The La Quinta Chamber celebrates its 52nd anniversary of serving the business community. Incorporated in 1982, the city of La Quinta is celebrating its 20th anniversary. This hallmark event celebrates the city's rich history and planned approach to growth and prosperity. The city and Chamber partner in promoting economic development and publishing a monthly newsletter distributed to all La Quinta residences and businesses.

Under Smith's leadership, the Chamber encourages and supports the active involvement of the Board of Directors and members of the Events and Programs, Legislative and Community Affairs, and Member-ship Services committees. One powerful idea that was generated and proved most successful is the Power Lunch, a members only, one-of-a-kind Chamber leads group.

The Chamber's annual membership directory promotes Chamber members and business owners. A powerful marketing tool for both the city and the Chamber is the 2003 edition, *Celebrate La Quinta*, highlighting economic expansion, quality of life and a comprehensive business directory and resource guide.

Unique to the Coachella Valley is a coalition of Chamber executives who meet monthly to advocate legislative measures and provide a leadership forum. Programs include Leadership Coachella Valley, the All Valley Chambers Legislative Committee and an annual All Chamber Legislative Luncheon.

The La Quinta Chamber of Commerce's board of directors and professional staff are dedicated to achieving their business mission and serving their members. Smith believes that "the Chamber provides a strong foundation for businesses to build upon. The La Quinta Chamber is truly your primary c-o-n-n-e-c-t-i-o-n to prospective clients and customers."

> "The La Quinta Chamber celebrates its 52nd anniversary of serving the business community."

For more information:
www.laquintachamberofcommerce.com
or 760-564-3199.

Kim Lombardelli
RE/MAX Real Estate Consultants

Kim Lombardelli, Real Estate Consultant

In a business based on referrals, it helps to have a warm personality, great sense of humor and a passion for problem-solving. Kim Lombardelli is a real estate agent with generous amounts of all three.

Lombardelli also has a wealth of experience. For 15 years she has sold real estate in the Coachella Valley. For the last seven years, Lombardelli and her husband, Lorenzo, have been owners and operators of five RE/MAX offices here and three in San Diego. Lombardelli's focus is on what she enjoys most, listing and selling.

Today they have 158 agents working out of offices in Rancho Mirage, La Quinta, and Palm Springs. Two offices, including their headquarters at One El Paseo, are in Palm Desert, Calif.

"I love finding people the perfect home. I also enjoy the marketing, negotiating and problem-solving aspects of the business. Overall, I try to keep everything smooth and simple. From the very beginning of any transaction, it is all about trust, integrity and listening," Lombardelli says.

"The greatest compliment that a customer has ever given me about my work is that I listened. It's

> **"I love finding people the perfect home. I also enjoy the marketing, negotiating and problem-solving aspects of the business."**

when they come back to work with you again that you realize you've done a good job."

She has surrounded herself with professionals so that she can have the time to focus her personal attention fully on the client. Her team includes three buyers' agents and three coordinators who specialize in transaction, escrow and marketing.

Lombardelli definitely has real estate in her blood. Her father and mother as well as her grandmother had their own real estate offices.

Today, Lombardelli enjoys spending time with her grandmother Dotte who lives in the desert.

"She's my mentor, my supporter and best friend. She is such a good businesswoman, and throughout my career she has given me great advice. I just love being with her."

Lombardelli, who is on the board of directors of the Board of Realtors, is a top producer and a RE/MAX Hall-of-Famer who has been honored for earning more than $1 million in commissions. She has also been recognized with a certificate of appreciation from the Riverside County Department of Mental Health Services for her work with the Foundation for the Retarded of the Desert.

RE/MAX's newest offices have been designed to be 100% accessible to people with special needs, and two people from the Foundation have been employed at their offices.

Lombardelli has also been involved with fundraising for Habitat for Humanity. In addition, over the years she has financially assisted deserving families to obtain their dream homes.

"It's all about giving back."

For more information: www.deserthomesellers.com or 760-862-2977.

(Above)
MSA's Senior Management Team
Front: Bob Mainiero, Sandy Fox, Bob Smith, Margo Thibeault, Michael Oehlbaum
Back: Chuck Harris, Paul Sepulveda, Marv Roos, Julian De La Torre, Steve Van, Ulrich Sauerbrey, Bruce Kassler, Cherie Murphy

Photo By
Tom Brewster

Mainiero, Smith and Associates, Inc.

Incorporated in 1976, the firm of Mainiero, Smith and Associates, Inc. (MSA) has not only been part of the Coachella Valley's phenomenal growth, it has played a major role in making it happen.

The company specializes in land planning, civil engineering and surveying services for both private developers and public agencies. The MSA team plans, designs and surveys commercial, residential, resort and institutional projects with more than 85 percent of its projects concentrated in the desert.

Over the past quarter century the MSA team has completed some 1,500 projects, representing a full spectrum of clientele ranging from small commercial developers to the nation's largest homebuilders to the federal government.

"MSA combines many of the advantages of a large national consulting firm with those of a small local company familiar with the uniqueness of the Coachella Valley," comments founding principal Bob Smith. "We have a large staff with the talent and horsepower to tackle complex projects and demanding time schedules, yet we have a strong working knowledge of the local agencies and design standards. Moreover, all the decisions are made here, quickly, as we are not beholden to corporate headquarters in Irvine or San Diego."

MAINIERO, SMITH AND ASSOCIATES, INC.
PLANNING / CIVIL ENGINEERING / LAND SURVEYING

And it has been since the very beginning, a team effort.

"We were long on enthusiasm and short on experience," explains Smith, who was 25 years old when he and Bob Mainiero, who was 30, launched the company. After a 20-year partnership, Smith purchased Mainiero's interest in 1997, but Mainiero stayed on as a consultant, managing his own clients' projects and providing mentoring and support to the younger staff.

> "The company specializes in land planning, civil engineering and surveying services for both private developers and public agencies."

Hiring and retaining talented senior management as well as cultivating leadership positions among the younger professionals has been part of MSA's culture since its doors first opened.

"We like to hire people looking for careers as opposed to just jobs. The longevity of our staff is unique for this area in that our key staff members average over 12 years with the firm. I also think we work hard at identifying the strengths of the individuals on our team and playing to those strengths while working around weaknesses with help from others. People are happiest doing what they do best," Smith says.

A "do what it takes" approach is also very much a part of the MSA philosophy. Smith likens it to a circle of success where a happy client translates to repeat work and referrals, which in turn bring in more work and interesting projects. And with that comes professional and financial growth for everyone involved, not to mention a motivated staff.

Mainiero, Smith and Associates, Inc. – it's all about teamwork.

For more information: www.mainierosmith.com or 760-320-9811.

There is a quiet spirituality about Marcel Bassirian, proprietor of the splendid Marcel de Claremont, an award-winning rug gallery in Palm Springs, Calif.

One senses this from his dramatic advertising, that is seen throughout the world. For the few who might have missed it, the ads feature Marcel, all in white, sitting cross-legged on a floor with a picture book about rugs in his hands. But Marcel is not alone. He is sharing the spotlight with Lika, a regal Dalmatian friend. Both Marcel and Lika appear to be very involved in some type of discussion – one assumes they're talking about the ancient art of rug-making.

"I provide the most essential element in the home," claims Bassirian, "which is rugs – hand-woven, imported rugs. I design most of these rugs based on the elements and colors that we are surrounded with in the desert. I travel to far countries two times a year to order and buy these rugs," Marcel says.

And indeed, the fruits of his travels can be seen in his exquisite Marcel de Claremont showroom – winner of three Desert Beautification Awards – located at 250 East Palm Canyon Drive in Palm Springs. Here one can view hand-made antique and new rugs, custom-made rugs, contemporary and traditional designs, Aubussons, needlepoints, kilims as well as tribal and nomadic rugs from many countries.

When people marvel at what Bassirian and his weavers have been able to create, he responds that There is no such thing as impossible in my business. Whatever is in your mind can and will be translated in the form of rugs. I take some of the ancient designs of rugs and translate them using today's

> **"Marcel is not only revered by his customers and industry associates, but by his community."**

colors such as terra cotta, olive, and tobacco. If you are a contemporary person, you have no idea what we can create for you."

Marcel's incredible passion for his trade took root during his high school years when he worked summers for a rug company. His ear for languages served him well – he is fluent in Persian, English, Hindi, Urdu and Kashmir – as he dealt with buyers from around the world.

He was awarded a bachelor's degree in commerce from the Western Australia Institute of Technology and a master's degree in business from Kashmir University in Kashmir, a historic region partitioned between India and Pakistan.

A thirst for knowledge lies at the center of Marcel's life. He likes to relate the story of a man perched high on a brick wall. The man is parched. Beneath him is a crystal clear river beyond reach. The man scratches at the bricks until they begin to loosen and fall into the river, splashing him with water.

Marcel de Claremont Rug Gallery

Before he knows it, his feet have reached the water.

For Marcel, the message of this simple parable is that water is knowledge. This is a philosophy shared with the Persian poet Rumi, one of the great spiritual masters. Mowlana Jalaluddin Rumi was born in 1207 and today has a large following. It is said the poet's name stands for love and ecstatic flight into the infinite.

Bassirian feels he is living in a place that nurtures spirituality. "Palm Springs, or the valley in general, is a powerful place," he claims. "It is magical, it is spiritual, and there is an incredible source of energy oozing out from these mountains. It gives us comfort and a feeling of security at home."

It is not for no reason that Bassarian showcases his one-of-a-kind rugs in the desert. "There is mysticism inherent in the business of creating heirlooms," he claims.

"Think of the thoughts that the weaver puts into his work," he continues. "He or she has an eye on every knot. Each knot is eyesight. A rug is not only a work of art, it is the soul of the weaver."

After a rug is purchased, Marcel makes sure the buyer knows that he can come back to him should anything happen to the rug. It is this strong element of trust that has made him a sought-after resource by the insurance industry. He is one of a handful of recognized, reliable rug experts. He has trained many insurance claim agents in what to look for regarding flood damage and other calamities that can befall rugs.

Marcel is not only revered by his customers and industry associates, but also by his community. Just hours after the horror of 9/11 he was on the phone with the local Red Cross, offering the use of his parking lot for the mobile blood bank. But he felt he needed to do more, so he began to design a 12 x 18 foot rug that portrayed the American flag with the Twin Towers. He mobilized his weavers who worked night and day and created in nine months a gift that normally would have taken two years to complete.

The rug was presented to the City of Palm Springs on July 4, 2002. As part of the ceremony, La Quinta High School student Credence Anderson dedicated a song entitled "God Will Always Bless America." Palm Springs will, in turn, present this heirloom to the President of the United States. After that, the rug will make its way to the Memorial Building in New York, where it will remain.

Even if you don't know what you want, buy something, to be part of the exchanging flow. Start a huge foolish project, like Noah.

It makes absolutely no difference what people think of you.

-- Rumi, These Spiritual Window-shoppers

For more information: www.marceldeclaremont.com or 760-322-7847

(Above) Albert T. Milauskas, M.D., founder of Milauskas Eye Institute, and Dorothy Milauskas.

Compassionate eye care and cutting-edge technology are the hallmarks of the Milauskas Eye Institute. By staying at the forefront of change in Ophthalmology, the Institute has been able to offer residents of the valley the best and most advanced care possible. This has given Institute patients quicker access to the latest in eye care.

Albert T. Milauskas, M.D. FACS, founder of the Milauskas Eye Institute, offers his insight into the accomplishments of the practice. "The most important means of maintaining a competitive edge is by providing caring, compassionate patient care that advocates excellence on all levels." The Institute maintains its high standards by providing patients with the best doctors and latest technology. For instance, the Institute remains the only Ophthalmology practice in the desert with a permanently installed excimer laser for laser vision correction. It was also the first practice in the desert to employ the GDx instrument for advanced glaucoma detection.

Dr. Milauskas founded his practice in 1980, working from a single office in Palm Springs. Since then, the practice has expanded into facilities in Rancho Mirage, La Quinta and downtown Palm Springs. "The practice has grown because we've been able to anticipate growth in the valley and what the demands for services would be. By expanding into Rancho Mirage and La Quinta, we kept ahead of the growth patterns in

> **"The Institute has the only permanently installed excimer laser surgery center located in the valley."**

the valley," Dr. Milauskas explains.

Dr. Milauskas continues, "We are the largest Ophthalmology practice in the Coachella Valley. We have five Ophthalmologists and five Optometrists on our staff. They work together very closely to provide our patients with the best care possible." With a staff of over 70 employees, and four locations across the valley, Milauskas Eye Institute can provide eye care to

Milauskas Eye Institute offers full service optical dispensaries at all of its locations

Milauskas Eye Institute

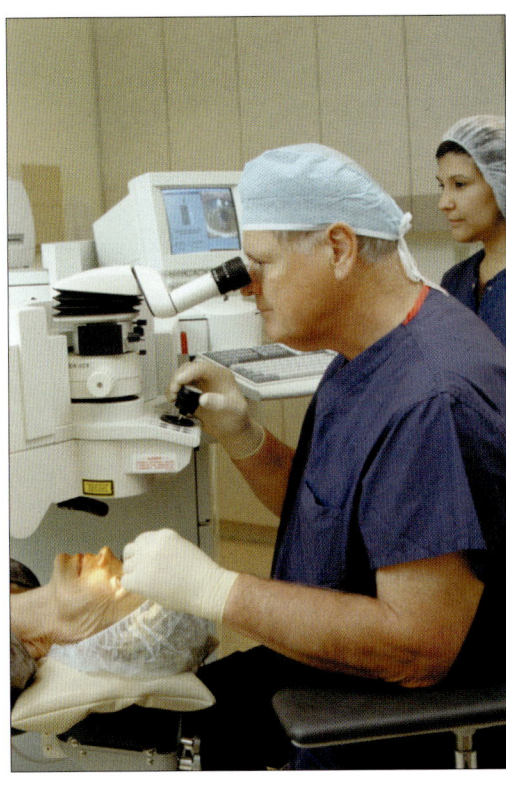

Milauskas Eye Institute is a comprehensive Ophthalmology practice. The physicians and surgeons at the Institute handle everything from routine eye exams to treating complex diseases of the eye. On the surgical end, the Institute provides the finest care in cataract surgery, glaucoma surgery, and laser vision correction. Each office also has a full service optical dispensary and contact lens service.

Innovation and technology are crucial to keeping the practice on the cutting edge. "When we built the La Quinta office three years ago, we determined that we would create a world class refractive surgery center there. To do so we became the first, and remain the only practice with a permanently installed excimer laser. The laser we use, the VISX Star S3, with eye tracking, is the most advanced FDA approved laser available. We are also the first practice in the desert to have the VISX Waveprint, which allows us to take laser vision correction down to the individual level by allowing for custom ablations based upon the uniqueness of each person's eyes."

Education is also critical at Milauskas Eye Institute. "We strive for excellence through teaching and clinical research," says Dr. Milauskas. Education is one of the primary means of fostering preventive medicine. Dr. Milauskas is a Clinical Professor of Ophthalmology at the Jules Stein Eye Institute at UCLA. He also lectures on behalf of several Ophthalmic pharmaceutical companies.

In addition to its clinical practice, the Milauskas Eye Institute incorporates an accredited ambulatory surgical center at its Rancho Mirage location. The Eye Surgery Center of the Desert provides patients with state-of-the-art outpatient surgical care catering exclusively to the eye surgery patient.

Milauskas Eye Institute is dedicated to offering its patients the best. From the best physicians and staff to the latest in technology, Milauskas Eye Institute continues to be the leader in eye care in the Coachella Valley.

For more information: www.milauskas-eye.com or 760-340-Eyes.

(Top left)
Dr. Milauskas performs laser vision correction at the La Quinta office

(Top right)
Janet Hartzler, M.D. is one of the many talented doctors at Milauskas Eye Institute

Orr Builders

After 20 years in commercial, industrial and residential construction, Brian Orr is just as enthusiastic and dedicated as he was when he started. As president of Orr Builders, his firm is one of the Coachella Valley's largest general contractors, having constructed well over three million square feet of living and working space.

Orr Builders' list of clients is as long as it is prestigious – Canyon National Bank, Desert Golf Business Park, Bircher Valley Metroplex, North Palm Springs Business Center, Washington Business Park, Village Court Plaza, Mirada Interiors, Merrill Lynch, A.G. Edwards, PaineWebber, Big League Sports Park, Pacific Western Bank and One El Paseo Plaza – to name a few.

The company provides a full range of professional construction and construction management services, from build-to-suits with consultation at the design phase, to the build-out of tenant improvements. It has a stellar reputation for maintaining aggressive project schedules while delivering job site safety, high quality and cost-competitive products.

Orr relies on his long-term relationships with the Valley's most reputable subcontractors for his highly coordinated, efficient project teams. This enables the company to work smart, staffing up or down to save his client money.

Indeed, it is the client who always comes first.

> "We recognize that today we are building our clients' tomorrows. Our craftsmanship must stand the test of time."

"We recognize that today we are building our clients' tomorrows. Our craftsmanship must stand the test of time. We must be timely without fail in meeting the demands of building schedules and budgets. And timeless in meeting the design, and construction expectations of our clients for years to come," Orr says.

Ever since he was a teenager, Orr has gotten great satisfaction from working with his hands. He's always been intrigued by watching construction projects come to life. His father's involvement in construction and real estate was very intriguing. Enough, that Orr found himself spending weekends and summers working as a general laborer for various companies in Orange County, Calif. Orr relished the hands-on experience and being part of a team.

"The concept of joint leadership is appealing," he says. "You're taught to delegate, to be dedicated and to be committed. You feel that no matter at what level, everybody is equal at a certain point."

So appealing was it all that Orr got his contractor's license when he was just 20. He established his own business in Orange County in 1982 and relocated to Palm Desert, Calif. in 1986.

Since that time, Orr Builders has played a large role in not only building the community but in making it better. The company has donated its services to such worthy causes as the Palm Desert Holocaust Memorial and the John F. Kennedy Memorial Foundation's Well Care Clinic and more.

For more information : 760-360-6632.

Pacific Western Bank

(Above)
William Powers, President & Chief Executive Officer

Bill Powers, president and CEO of Pacific Western Bank, has a true understanding of the word "community." This very funny, very friendly and very successful man has intimate ties to both the local business community and local non-profit groups. "We are an excellent business bank," asserts Powers. "We really work hard at being friendly by hiring people who know how to smile and who have a sense of humor. When you call us, you hear: 'Thank you for calling Pacific Western Bank.' You can't say 'Thank you' and be mad. We want you to hear the smile in our voice when you call," Powers said.

Pacific Western Bank specializes in commercial and real estate loans with six branches located in LaQuinta, Indian Wells, Twentynine Palms, Palm Springs, Cathedral City, and Yucca Valley. It is a wholly owned subsidiary of First Community Bancorp and boasts an ever-growing number of Southern California locations.

Prior to moving to the Coachella Valley in 1986, Powers enjoyed a 21-year career with Bank of America, during which time he supervised as many as 30 branch offices, including many in the Los Angeles region.

As a youngster, Powers attended five different high schools. Therefore he determined that when he moved to the desert, his kids would stay put. Taking an immediate liking to the area, "I felt that now I could make an impact in the community, help my bank and have some fun all at the same time."

And what an impact Powers has made! He has served as president and tournament chairman (and still remains on the board) of the Bob Hope Chrysler Classic. He is a board member of the Desert Community Foundation, the Board of Trustees for the McCallum Theatre, and the founding director/officer of the Desert Town Hall Speakers Forum. Powers is a

> "We are an excellent business bank. We really work hard at being friendly..."

(Left - Right) John Shields, Executive Director, Nieves Gutierrez, Clinic Pediatrician, William Powers, Chairman, JFK Memorial Foundation, Jose Marquez, Program Officer

past president of the United Way of the Desert, American Cancer Society, Palm Desert Chamber of Commerce, College of the Desert Foundation and Indian Wells Desert Symphony, remaining active on many of the boards. He is also founder/past president/director of the Yucca Valley Economic Partnership, a past president/director of the Coachella Valley Economic Partnership, and a director of the City of Indian Wells Promotions Committee.

As president of the John F. Kennedy Memorial Foundation he spearheaded the $1.25 million Well Care Clinic which assists the underprivileged with pre-natal and early childhood medical care. He is also past chairman of the Board of Governors for the hospital and a member of the Board of Directors.

Powers and his wife Anita live in Indian Wells. Their two grown children, David and Christie, both live in Palm Desert and work at Powers Awards, the family business.
For more information: www.pwnb.com or 760-836-0870.

(Above) Scene from annual World Famous Palm Desert Golf Cart Parade

Palm Desert Chamber of Commerce

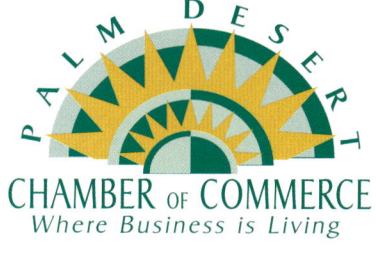

When skyrocketing electricity prices threatened Palm Desert merchants, they didn't call the power company, they called the Palm Desert Chamber of Commerce. Staff responded by dispatching trained energy auditors to help reduce their load, taking advantage of rebates, saving money and keeping their businesses open.

Not your typical image of a local Chamber, usually viewed as the place where tourists go to get maps and information. But the Palm Desert Chamber of Commerce – like the city itself – isn't typical.

"We are a business support and economic development membership organization," explains Chamber President/CEO Susan Harvey. "We know that a strong business community begets a strong community overall. Our mission is to be a good community partner."

The Western Association of Chamber Executives recognized PDCC's unique response to the energy crisis and cited it as an outstanding new program. Harvey credits PDCC's publicly acknowledged success to an innovative board of directors and staff, committed to enhancing business prosperity, civic vitality and quality of life.

Established in 1954, the valley's largest chamber represents more than 1,400 diverse and ethnically broad-based businesses. Among its services are networking, special events, publicity, promotion, seminar and personal growth opportunities and government advocacy on local and national levels.

The Chamber remains relevant and pro-active, honed to react to new challenges as they occur. Their motto, says Harvey, is "under-promise and over-deliver."

Members are kept apprised through newsletters and by the staff, which fields about 12,000 calls a year. Its award-winning Web site helps thousands of visitors each month. Referrals number more than 15,000 a year.

"Positive synergy is what makes Palm Desert special," Harvey says. "While our special events aim to benefit our members, we seek to involve the entire community."

Among those events are the World Famous Palm Desert Golf Cart Parade, a fantastical show attracting more than 25,000 to the city's main shopping street, El Paseo. Another popular event is Putt Putt on El Paseo, when locals play a miniature golf game that winds its way through 18 businesses. The Peace Officer & Public Safety Appreciation Day is the Chamber's salute to dozens of officers, firefighters, 911 dispatchers and citizens for outstanding service in the Coachella Valley.

As the city's demographics shift toward more families and year-round residents, the Chamber will continue to adapt to changing business and cultural demands.

"We focus on tangible business benefits that don't involve a great deal of investment by the business people, so they can focus on what they do best and still have time for their families," Harvey says.

For more information: www.pdcc.org or 760-346-6111.

> "The Chamber remains relevant and pro-active, honed to react to new challenges..."

Palm Springs Chamber of Commerce

(Above) Photo by Al Iorli

The Palm Springs Chamber of Commerce is a sturdy thread weaving economic growth throughout the fabric of the Coachella Valley.

"The sole purpose, energy and mission of the Palm Springs Chamber of Commerce is to promote our Chamber members, their location, their products and their services," explains Palm Springs Chamber of Commerce CEO David K. Aaker, A.C.E.

Implementing these goals has become the primary focus of the Palm Springs Chamber. The Chamber also operates as a Business Development Center, offering resources to encourage economic growth. One of its successes, the Chamber's bi-annual business expo, is a valuable promotional tool that features 135 member businesses. Exposure to thousands of residents and community visitors occurs throughout the day-long event. Other strategies serving the business community include business mixers, Chamber breakfasts, the monthly publication "Business Matters," legislative advocacy and the Sister Chamber program.

PALM SPRINGS Chamber of Commerce
partners for success

Membership has consistently grown in both quantity and quality. This is in part due to the efforts of the Chamber's annual membership drive. Aaker reflects that "When people join, they understand that through participation, their business is amplified, therefore increasing their marketability." Member businesses are marketed on a daily basis when the Chamber answers inquiries for referrals, hotel reservations, attractions and locations. Tom Mulhall, 2002-2003 president of the Palm Springs Chamber of Commerce, notes, "One of the things the Chamber has done in recent years is to become involved in advocating the interests of its members." If a significant legislative issue arises, the Chamber's government liaison voices the position of commerce. "It is important to point out that we serve the entire business community with a promotional focus on our members. Our goal is to promote business in Palm Springs," Mulhall emphasizes.

> "The mission of the Palm Springs Chamber of Commerce is to promote our Chamber members."

Not only does the Palm Springs Chamber promote local businesses, it also boasts global membership. "If a company does business in or around the Coachella Valley, we can bring them additional business through their membership," Aaker asserts, noting that Palm Springs is one of nine chambers in the Coachella Valley.

The Chamber is built upon a solid foundation, with an active membership constantly on the lookout for economic opportunity. It currently has a waiting list of members wishing to serve on the board.

Aaker sets his sights on future success and envisions a bright future for Palm Springs businesses. "The Chamber will grow for decades to come," he asserts.

For more information: www.pschamber.org or 760-325-1577.

(Above)
Michael E. Platt, M.D.

Dr. Michael E. Platt, located in Palm Desert, Calif., has earned a reputation as the physician of choice for those interested in wellness and preventive medicine.

Platt is a board certified internist who is nationally recognized in the field of natural hormone replacement.

Platt's medical approach differs from other doctors' in that he focuses on the causes of illness, rather than primarily treating symptoms. For example, adult-onset diabetes, the most common type of diabetes, Platt believes is very often curable. However, the usual focus by most physician is to treat it, not eliminating it.

The major unifying element in Platt's treatment program is the utilization of natural hormones. "Hormones control every system of the body," Platt explains. "A deficiency of one hormone often leads to alterations in other hormones. Balancing the body's hormones helps people feel better, often eliminating chronic illnesses."

According to Platt, doctors receive relatively little information on hormones in their educational training. "This is because medical schools teach doctors patient care that is based on research done by drug companies," Platt says. The typical medical approach is to treat patients with drugs, rather than preventing or eliminating illness.

An area that has always interested Platt is obesity. Metabolic weight control, examines all elements that cause the body to retain fat.

Platt firmly believes in putting his patients back in

"...nationally recognized in the field of natural hormone replacement."

control of their bodies. Patients are taught the causes of weight gain and are given the knowledge, correct hormones and medication adjustments to eliminate fat. Two registered staff nutritionists teach patients to adjust their eating patterns to allow their bodies to burn fat and keep it from returning.

"Obesity is the second leading preventable cause of death, and is prominently associated with other serious conditions," Platt explains. "In spite of this, doctors traditionally fail to treat obesity as a disease and continuously provide patients with faulty information and useless weight-loss approaches. This has created the obesity epidemic now present in this country."

Platt advocates natural progesterone for both women and men, stating that progesterone is the only hormone that must replace. Platt rarely

Michael E. Platt, M.D. Internal Medicine

advocates the use of estrogen in women and has been taking women off estrogen for many years. Women never stop making estrogen – it is made by fat cells, skin cells and the adrenal glands. Platt maintains that estrogen has exceptionally few benefits when given as hormone replacement therapy.

On the other hand, progesterone (please note: not medroxyprogesterone) has numerous benefits as a replacement hormone. It prevents and treats osteoporosis, prevents heart disease, is a natural anti-depressant, prevents Alzheimer's and prevents the six cancers caused by estrogen. When treating men, Platt uses progesterone to prevent prostate cancer (another estrogen-induced cancer).Because progesterone lowers insulin levels, it is useful in controlling weight for men.

Platt also states that progesterone removes PMS, cramps, breast tenderness and migraine headaches in pre-menopausal women. It eliminates asthma in men and women.

Testosterone cream is prescribed for men and women if the patient exhibits certain symptoms . In men, the hormone prevents coronary artery disease, improves muscle strength and stamina, eliminates depression, improves libido, lowers insulin levels and prevents Alzheimer's. When testosterone cream is utilized correctly, women experience a nearly 100 percent success rate in eliminating urinary incontinence within one week of use.

The natural hormones Platt utilizes are obtained by prescription from Town Center Drugs in Palm Desert. The compound pharmacy is staffed by pharmacists specially trained and licensed to compound natural hormones, as well as other medications that may be compounded into various formulations – creams, pills, suppositories, etc.

Platt says: "Getting hormones into balance is the key to wellness. As people get older, their hormones decline, which is why aging occurs. The correct and logical replacement of hormones helps alter the aging process. It is aging that causes a decrease in hormones; it is a decrease in hormones that causes aging."

For more information: www.drplatt.com or 760-836-3232.

Town Center Drugs and Compounding Pharmacy

Mort Farina, RPH, and his staff of compounding pharmacists at Town Center Drugs custom-prepare medications to satisfy individual patient needs. They blend powders, creams and liquids into specific formulas tailored for each individual patient, based on his/her particular chemistry and deficits. Town Center Drugs is a significant part of the triad among patient, doctor and pharmacist.

Compounding pharmacists are not your normal everyday pharmacist! They are independent, trained to think for themselves, well versed in the art of taking people to the next level of vitality through the use of pharmaceuticals. Compounding pharmacists offer an integrated approach to medicine that examines the diet, history, hormones and other pertinent factors related to each individual patient. After consulting with the patient and his/her doctor, the formula is then combined, which requires thought, precision and time. Farina says, "We work with the patients and their doctor to remedy their ailments by creating a formula specific to their particular need."

"Our goal is for Bio Identical hormones to work together in unison, which in turn helps the patient feel better." Farina and his staff rely heavily on topical applications that target specific areas of the body, such as creams, ointments and gels. These dissolve directly into the skin, thus bypassing the intestinal system and creating fewer side effects as a result. This approach ensures more safety for the patient. Farina prides himself on his ability to target specific ailments, thus providing an uncommon type of health care for his patients.

Town Center Drugs and Compounding Pharmacy is open seven days a week and is located in the Westfield Palm Desert Mall. The pharmacy offers both standard medications as well as the personally designed prescriptions.

For more information: 760-341-3984.

(Above) Left to Right
Mark Nickerson, Carl Sam Maggio, and Chuck Hodges

Prime Time International

They are nutritious, delicious and very popular. "They" are red, yellow and green sweet peppers grown by Prime Time International, a fully integrated produce company headquartered in Coachella, Calif.

What is unique about the agricultural company's feature commodity is that it is offered on a year-round basis. PRIME TIME® premium peppers are shipped from four locations in California and three in Mexico. The company's other core products are seedless watermelons, cantaloupes and various mixed vegetables.

"The 12-month availability of our sweet peppers really separates us from our competitors," Carl Sam Maggio explains. Maggio, along with Chuck Hodges and Mark Nickerson, are the operating partners of Prime Time International.

In business since 1987, the Coachella-based Sun & Sands Enterprises and its marketing and sales division, C.H. Sales, merged operations in 1998 under Prime Time International, a name derived from its renowned PRIME TIME® label.

Today the company has 50 employees, which can mushroom to 300 as field workers are brought in for harvesting. Many employees have been with the company since its beginning.

"We've created an environment where they're proud to be with us," Maggio explains.

It is not only the work environment that gets attention, it is the field environment, too. Prime Time International uses an advanced drip irrigation system that minimizes the use of chemicals, fertilizers and water, on average using 25 percent less than typical industry rates.

An integrated pest management system is also in place. In addition to maintaining constant detailed growing field supervision to spot pest infestations early when they are localized and easier to control, Prime Time International uses natural methods, particularly natural predators that are both crop – and environment-friendly. The company also partners with PrimusLabs.com, specializing in pesticide

> "What is unique about the agricultural company's feature commodity is that it is offered on a year-round basis."

residue analysis and a certification program. Customers can visit the Primus' Internet site to assure that they are buying certified-safe products.

Prime Time International's mission statement declares that it is "committed to providing premium produce to the public and to being recognized as an exemplary corporate citizen."

For six years straight, the company has participated in the Palm Springs Festival of Lights Parade with a John Deere tractor festooned with 10 miles of lights. The entry has won the parade's top prize, the Chairman's Award, three times.

The company also supports Hidden Harvest, which is operated by a non-profit organization called Desert Cities Hunger Action. The program's objective is to retrieve produce left behind in fields and orchards and to distribute it over 30 agencies that feed the hungry.

"We are committed to being a good business partner in the Coachella Valley," Maggio says.

For more information: www.primetimeproduce.com or 760-399-4278.

(Above) Barbara and Jim Gammon

Pro Realty & Investments, Inc.

It was a defining moment when Barbara and Jim Gammon moved to The Lakes Country Club in Palm Desert, Calif. in 1990. They relocated to the desert from La Jolla, where Jim was president of Gammon Company, a firm specializing in the acquisition and pre-development of land for resale to merchant builders and/or commercial developers in Southern California.

In 1992 the couple launched Pro Realty & Investments at 41-905 Boardwalk in Palm Desert and in 1999 acquired the on-site sales office at the Lakes Country Club. The Lakes is a 380-acre private community and club located across from Marriott's Desert Springs Resort & Spa. It has 902 condominium homes surrounded by spectacular amenities.

Pro Realty & Investments is involved in 95 percent of all transactions in the club. In addition, the firm handles active listings and home sales (both new and existing) in country clubs, communities and home projects throughout the Coachella Valley. Seasonal and long-term leasing and home care services for absentee owners are also provided.

Jim, who has an extensive background in the development of office, commercial, high-density multi-family residential and mixed-use projects, is also active in land, commercial and investment property brokerage and consulting. Pro Realty & Investments also offers development advisory services for land owners, developers, builders and investors.

"We pride ourselves on market and product knowledge, professionalism and integrity..."

"We pride ourselves on market and product knowledge, professionalism and integrity based on my 35 years experience in real estate development, sales and financial management serving sophisticated clientele," Jim says.

And it's a team effort, for Barbara is consistently in the top one percentile of all valley agents.

In fact, the company just may be, on a per agent basis, the most productive in the area, with eight out of 10 of its agents receiving The Desert Sun's Top Producer Status for the first half of 2002.

Barbara and Jim have never recruited agents. It is a source of pride for the owners to watch how former staff assistants have developed into successful agents and how an enthusiastic team-based working environment has resulted in incomparable service to clients and customers. The company will soon be adding eight newly licensed agents to their team.

"I love to come to work every day," Jim says. "I have the best people to work with – clients, staff, vendors and consultants."

Married 43 years, he considers Barbara a great influence and inspiration. "She is very wise and has terrific business sense."

"We both love the desert and what we do."

For more information: www.proinv.com or 760-773-4464.

*I*f a documentary were to be made featuring Rozene and Ric Supple, it might be entitled, "Palm Springs — We Love You." For decades, this visionary husband and wife team has embraced the desert community through pioneering forays into radio production and heartfelt philanthropy.

Rozene came to Palm Springs in the 1930s as a teenager. Her family lived at Smoke Tree Ranch and Rozene attended Palm Springs High School. Ric, a San Francisco native, considered becoming an attorney like his father, but instead pursued a 40-year career in the insurance business. Both Rozene and Ric attended Stanford University, but they didn't become a couple as undergraduates. They became reacquainted at their 25th year class reunion, and their partnership began there.

After surmounting numerous hurdles, Rozene purchased KPAL-Radio in Palm Springs in 1968. Today, 35 years later, the Supples count four popular radio stations in their R. & R. Corporation: KDES 104.7 - The Oldies Station; KPSI - Newstalk 920; MIX 100.5 - Adult Contemporary Hit Music, and KGAM 1450 -Talk Radio. Their hands-on involvement has brought quality local and national programming to the desert, provided career opportunities for locals and given promotional support to many community events.

Always interested in broadening the desert's cultural menu, the Supples got involved with the Nortel Networks Palm Springs International Film Festival as soon as it began. They have continued supporting it through the years, both as financial contributors and board members. Each of them has served terms as board chairman.

When the Film Festival lacked major sponsors (but still had to pay for theatre rental) the Supples came to the rescue. In 1998 they purchased the 36 year-old Camelot Theatres, giving the Film Festival a permanent home and relieving it of about $50,000 a year in theatre rental fees.

Renovation began on the old theatre, located on the south side of

> "...This visionary husband and wife team has embraced the desert community through pioneering forays into radio production and heartfelt philanthropy."

R & R Radio Corporation and Camelot Theatres

the Palm Springs Mall, and the name was changed to the Festival of Arts Theatres. The $3.5 entertainment complex premiered with state-of-the-art sound and projection equipment. Comfortably seating 870, the large house boasts three screens plus a stage for live performances. Next door is Ric's Café, where filmgoers can enjoy fresh salads, sandwiches, gourmet coffees, beer and wine. There is even a cocktail Cine-Lounge, perfect for receptions. And parking is easy.

When the Palm Springs Festival of Short Films was born, the Supples donated the use of their theatres to a second annual festival. "It is our gift to the community," Rozene says.

Aware of a growing market for first-run foreign, independent and art films, the Supples built a solid relationship with Laemmle Theatres of Los Angeles, a top presenter of art films. In 2002, the Festival of Arts Theatre was re-christened Camelot Theatres, to recapture some of the panache it had achieved in its glory days.

Its short history has been phenomenal, screening such acclaimed films as "Oh Brother Where Art Thou," "Monster's Ball," "My Big Fat Greek Wedding," and of course, "Sordid Lives."

"We got lucky with Sordid Lives," says Ric.

"Nowhere in the United States has it taken off like it has in Palm Springs. Today we have filmgoers literally arriving by the busload. And we've had cast members on hand to chat with our audiences. In some cases, filmgoers will dress up as their favorite character."

The Supples continue to touch lives in their community. Rozene's major gift helped establish the trauma center emergency department at Desert Regional Medical Center. She made the gift in memory of her father, the late G. A. Richards, a Detroit media and sports entrepreneur. Ric has served as treasurer, vice chairman and chairman of the Desert Hospital District Board for more than 16 years, and both have been key supporters, officers and board members of the Desert Medical Regional Health Foundation since the mid-1970s. In addition, the Supples are members of the Founding Fifty of the McCallum Theatre.

They have been recipients of the Spirit of the Valley Award, the Anti Defamation League Award and have been named Distinguished Citizens by the Palm Springs Area Boy Scouts of America.

For more information: www.camelottheatres.com or 760-325-2582.

Ramada Inn Resort and Conference Center

Nestled in the wind protected "Smoke Tree" area of Palm Springs, California. The Ramada Inn Resort and Conference Center, since 1969 continues to be one of the Coachella Valley's favorite vacation and business havens.

With two new Jacuzzi therapy pools, a putting green and an outdoor pool bar beside the Olympic-size swimming pool, the Resort has the facilities to pamper in the true Palm Springs style. Situated on 3 acres with views of the San Jacinto Mountains, the guests are surrounded by lush gardens and cooled by refreshing mist, with strategically placed air misters offering them extra comfort for their fun in the sun. Two hundred forty one guestrooms and 14 suites are tastefully decorated, featuring a patio or balcony, in-room coffee, refrigerator, hair dryer and iron and ironing board.

Ramada Inn Resort and Conference Center boasts 2 popular restaurants: Leon's Bar and Grill, which serves dinner nightly and features a piano bar; and Tony's Café, open for breakfast and lunch and known for delicious home-style cooking. Everything from cheeseburgers to fine Italian cuisine can be found right on the premises, and both restaurants offer outside catering services as well.

RAMADA® INN

RESORT & CONFERENCE CENTER

There's something for everyone here, whether you're a business traveler or someone looking to immerse yourself in the luxurious art of relaxation. Amenities include a new fitness facility, a quaint gift shop, saunas, massage therapy, a spa and 8,000 square feet newly remodeled meeting space. "This huge playground is a center of activity in Palm Springs," notes Barbara Lyons, Director of Sales and Marketing.

The Resort is very locals-friendly, hosting Chamber of Commerce breakfasts and mixers – a great way to introduce the Ramada to those who are new to the area or unfamiliar with the property's extensive recent remodel. A bonus of this community focus is that the restaurants are gaining in popularity. As the Coachella Valley continues to thrive, "We embrace the new ideas and opportunities that come with growth," said Lyons. "It is exciting news to announce new ownership and a management team who are working to provide outstanding service."

> "...A great way to introduce the Ramada to those new to the area or unfamiliar with the property's extensive recent remodel."

The Ramada Inn Resort and Conference Center's longevity is largely due to its strong customer service ethic. "Honesty over the phone with the client is where it begins," comments Lyons. "As a result, people leave here thanking us for an outstanding time."

The Ramada Inn Resort and Conference Center will continue to succeed because of its visionary owner, Phil Barney, and its management team, who see enhancing the customer's experience as their mission. With its superb new renovations, guest satisfaction is assured for many years to come.

For more information: www.psramada.com or 760-323-1711.

Rancho Mirage Chamber of Commerce

"I like to tell people that we are in the ring business," says Stuart Ackley, Executive Director of the Rancho Mirage, California Chamber of Commerce. "We make telephones and cash registers ring."

Incorporated in 1955, the Rancho Mirage Chamber acted as an ad hoc planning commission until the city's incorporation in 1973. Today it is in the business of providing service, networking and information to businesses in Rancho Mirage. Through public relations, event planning and the creation and distribution of a variety of publications, the Chamber attracts, then supports a wide range of business interests.

Known for its uniquely personal approach, the Chamber offices don't use voice mail but always have a live person answering the phone – often Ackley himself. Phone inquiries are treated with respect. Even when the question coming in doesn't concern businesses within the Rancho Mirage city limits, this Chamber endeavors to locate a resource to help the caller. The word "No" is not in their vocabulary. Not surprisingly, the Rancho Mirage Chamber of Commerce holds the unique distinction of being the first chamber in the Coachella Valley to stay open on Saturdays – all year long.

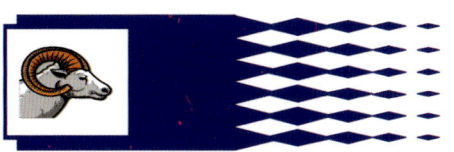

The number of businesses in Rancho Mirage has increased by 70 percent since 1997. Ackley cites cooperative efforts between the chamber and city as the reason for this remarkable growth spurt.

> "...Rancho Mirage has become an upscale dining destination that pulls in visitors from faraway places."

Boasting 42 restaurants, Rancho Mirage has become an upscale dining destination that pulls in visitors from faraway places. The chamber operates the Rancho Mirage Restaurant Association to market the city's diverse and thriving "Restaurant Row."

Community events add to the list of reasons to live and do business in Rancho Mirage. The chamber and city co-host Rancho Mirage Art Affaire, an upscale art and music festival begun in 2001 that is now held every November.

The River at Rancho Mirage, the Valley's newest shopping, entertainment and dining colonnade, will host the chamber's 2003 "Bits and Bites," an annual event which began in 2000. At "Bits and Bites" residents and tourists alike come to sample the fare of over 20 restaurants at the unique complex, whose meandering water features have made it a must-see desert attraction. The event recently raised $30,000 for local charities. The River has become the new hub for shopping, dining and movie going in the Coachella Valley, enriching the Rancho Mirage business scene and exerting a positive influence on the Chamber.

The Rancho Mirage Chamber of Commerce's mission stands firm, according to Ackley: "We're here to make lives and businesses prosper. We're here to serve."

For information: www.ranchomirage.org or 760-568-9351.

(Above)
Laine Rinker,
President

Rinker Financial

When Laine Rinker launched Rinker Financial in 2000, his goal for the Indian Wells Calif.-based mortgage company was straightforward.

"We take our motto, 'Home Loans Done Right,' seriously," Rinker says. "When you are concerned about financing your home, you want to go to people you can count on. We take care of every financing need with courtesy and quality. That is because we truly care about the borrowers for whom we work. Simply put, we are all about making it easier and quicker for someone to achieve the dream of owning a home."

Rinker, a tell-it-like-it-is guy, brings to his company 19 years of experience in mortgage banking.

"A big thing with me is trust. I tell people the truth. I let them know what we're doing and what we're trying to do. I don't really try to sell. Instead I try to find out what people's needs are, explain the products available and narrow it down to what suits their needs. You have to take an interest in people, take care of them and treat them right."

This philosophy was nurtured at an early age. Growing up on a family-owned flower farm in Stuart, Fla., Rinker began working in the chrysanthemum fields at the age of eight. At the age of nine he started playing golf. By the age of 19, he had acquired a real estate license in Florida.

Bothered with allergies, Rinker headed West and got his California real estate license while working on a bachelor's degree in finance at California State University, Fullerton.

He toyed with the idea of becoming a golf pro, but left that up to two of his brothers and his sister who are all professional golfers – two are still on the golf Tour.

Rinker met his wife Kellii at Junior World, a golf tournament for rising stars. After he graduated from college, they married. Kellii turned pro in 1981 and together they set off on the L.P.G.A. Tour.

Settling in the Coachella Valley in the mid-80s, Rinker began his on-the-job financial education working as a loan officer for Great Western Bank and as a mortgage banker for Palm Springs Savings Bank and Oak Tree Mortgage. He then joined Mission Hills Mortgage, where he was a top producer for nine years.

Hard work and a sincere concern for other people are the foundation for Rinker Financial.

"My mom and dad taught me a strong work ethic. On a flower farm if the flowers aren't ready on Valentine's Day, you've missed it. It's just like a loan. People need to close on time because they've got to move."

For more information: www.RinkerFinancial.com or 760-779-9300.

> "...Making it easier and quicker for someone to achieve the dream of owning a home."

Rothermund Rudman
Because There is a Difference

They have been known to complete each other's sentences. They have been partners and friends for 18 years. They are the best-selling team of Rothermund & Rudman.

Joan Rothermund and Brenda Rudman have been phenomena in local real estate since the early 80s. In 1980, Rothermund joined one of the desert's leading residential real estate companies and was named "Sales Agent of the Year" five times. In 1986 she was selected Palm Desert-Rancho Mirage-Indian Wells Realtor of the Year. Rudman joined the same company in 1982 and by 1984 she and Rothermund had formed an in-house partnership.

In 1987, along with Rudman's husband, Mel, they created Rothermund Rudman, Inc., Realtors and became renowned for glamour listings, record sales and skilled marketing.

Then in 1993, along with Jerry Smith, they launched the Palm Desert office of Prudential California Realty, an independently owned and operated member of Prudential Real Estate Affiliates, Inc. Since its inception they have built a Corporate Center headquarters in Palm Desert, Calif., which is home to their 65-member family of agents, and have a second office in La Quinta.

"We've been around longer than Regis and Kathie Lee," Rudman jokes. "And we haven't changed our philosophy of providing integrity, value and service. Our motto continues to be Because there is a difference. Actually it's more than a motto, it is our corporate and personal attitude toward our profession and our clients."

Rothermund and Rudman share a passion for what they do and agree that experience, honesty and hard work are the keys to their success. And a sense of humor helps, too.

> "...Experience, honesty and hard work are the keys to their success. And a sense of humor helps, too..."

"We get as much joy selling a first-time buyer a $75,000 condo as we do selling a multi-million dollar estate," Rothermund says. "Our average-priced home is $500,000 but we enjoy working with all price ranges."

Indeed the dynamic duo regards their clients as family. They have established trusting relationships that don't end with a sale and consider repeat business and personal referrals a mainstay.

However, it's not all work and no play. In addition to their desert homes, the Rudmans have a vacation home in San Diego and Rothermund keeps a pied-á-terre in Los Angeles.

"We have a rule that if one of us is on vacation, they are not to call the other unless they sell a house over $1 million," Rudman laughs. "Seriously, there's great comfort in knowing one of us is always available."

Their uncanny chemistry has been recognized through numerous honors including the prestigious Chairman's Circle Award presented annually to the top 3 percent of agents in the Prudential Real Estate Network. They have won it four times.

For more information : www.homespalmsprings.com or 760-773-1011.

Salon 119
A Day Spa

(Above)
Michele Lassak
and Wende Rae

Photo by
Tom Brewster

Combine close to four decades of experience, a fantastic location and a passion for their work and their clients, and the result is one of the hottest hair, nail and days spas in town – Salon 119.

Michele Lassak and Wende Rae are partners in the salon, with Lassak owning the salon and Rae the day spa end of the business. The salon's name comes from its location at 119 North Indian Canyon Drive.

"We adore Palm Springs and think it is absolutely charming. Prior to opening our salon we had developed a Palm Springs clientele while working at other places, so it was just a natural for us to open here," Rae explains.

"It took us two years to find the right spot and we couldn't have chosen better now that construction is underway for the $90 million Spa Resort Casino," adds Lassak.

Salon 119 is a partnership that was meant to be. Lassak and Rae share a similar vision and each brings her unique expertise to the enterprise.

Lassak had owned two Palm Springs salons before teaming up with Rae. In the business for 27 years, she travels at least three times a year to places like Las Vegas, New York and Los Angeles, as well as Europe, for hands-on workshops where she can continuously be educated on the latest products, styles and techniques.

"Hair coloring is my passion," Lassak says. "And, I love to have my own hair done. Everywhere I travel, I have my hair done."

> "Lassak and Rae share a similar vision and each brings her unique expertise to the enterprise."

Rae is equally passionate about her work. "I always wanted to do skin care. My mother was a big influence on me because she always took such good care of her skin with facials and sun protection."

Rae specializes in Epicuren facials and trains other aestheticians in the use of the product. Epicuren is a highly regarded enzyme product noted for its ability to nourish, replenish and energize skin cells. Many of Rae's facials include hand and foot massage.

"We never leave the client once we begin a facial," says Rae. "We want them to feel totally pampered and special. It's so much more than getting debris out of the skin. I have a really wonderful touch and I want my clients to enjoy their treatments. When they leave they should feel as though they've gotten away for awhile."

"We try to bring a little happiness to everyone," Lassak adds.

Little wonder that after only two years in business, Salon 119 is expanding by adding 1,300 square feet of upstairs space for additional treatment rooms, a lounge area, oxygen bar and a magnificent view of the San Jacinto Mountains.

For more information: www.salon119.com or 760-327-4800.

Sensafine, Inc.

*Cindy Davis-Anderholt
Proprietor, Sensafine Inc.*

Her style is defined as eclectic. One might use the same word to describe designer Cindy Davis-Anderholt herself. She is the proprietor of Sensafine Inc. in Palm Desert. The firm is also known as C. L. Davis & Associates.

Sensafine is an Italian word meaning "timeless" or "classical."

"Good design looks good 50, 75, 100 years from now," Davis-Anderholt says. "In taking a timeless design approach, any project will look good for many years to come."

The focus of her firm, which was established in 1984 and now includes an art gallery, is creating complete custom furnishings and architectural details for home, offices, clubhouses and restaurants not only in the desert but throughout the world.

Says Cindy, "Many of the homes we have gone on the market completely furnished and have sold in a matter of days at a substantial profit."

Often her custom pieces have been inspired by her extensive travels throughout Europe, Asia, Africa, and Mexico. In 1978 she had been in southern Iran for two weeks working on interiors for several restaurants and hotels when martial law was declared. She stayed for an additional five months to complete her work.

This is a long way from Iowa where the designer grew up. During her junior year at West Marshall High School, Davis-Anderholt's basketball team went to the state finals. She netted all-state honors three years in a row.

Today she enjoys horseback riding and night scuba diving. She observes nature's stunning color combinations and incorporates them into her design.

"Often the first time you meet with a client, the person will subconsciously be wearing the color they want to use. You need to tap into a sixth sense and listen. After all, it's their home."

Davis-Anderholt studied business and interior design at Iowa State University in Ames. Then she studied clothing design at the Fashion Institute of Design & Merchandising in Los Angeles. In 1977 she went to work for celebrity fashion designer Bob Mackie.

"I was a runway model. I'd love to get back into clothing and create realistically-sized mix-and-match casual wear for today's women."

That may have to wait, because currently she is creating an indoor/outdoor furniture line utilizing such things as sunbrella fabric to create an area without environmental delineations.

Active in philanthropic events, she and her husband, attorney John Anderholt, have won a Desert Spirit award for their fund-raising efforts on behalf of the American Cancer Society.

When she was four years old, her dad jokingly asked, "Do you think you'll ever amount to anything, kid?" She answered, "Yep." And she was right.

For more information: www.sensafine.biz or 760-346-8219.

> "Sensafine is an Italian word meaning timeless or classical."

The combined elements of creative vision and business strategy comprise the company that is Thane International, headquartered in La Quinta, Calif. William F. Hay, chairman and CEO, and Denise DuBarry-Hay, chief creative officer, are co-founders of one of the world's foremost direct marketing and wholesale distributing companies.

Thane's successful business enterprise is directly related to the promotion of unique, first-rate products and the company's commitment to its customers. "One of Thane's primary goals is to offer innovative, high-quality products and to make our customers very satisfied with our service and products," DuBarry-Hay states.

Thane became a publicly traded company in May 2002 with the acquisition of Reliant Interactive Media Corp. In March 2002, Thane International acquired Krane Products Inc., which markets continuity-based home maintenance products in addition to operating seven out-bound telephone call centers. Thane International hopes to continue acquiring companies and further developing its stance as a global competitor. "We are scouting companies that would be good acquisition targets, complementing both our company philosophy and goals," DuBarry-Hay explains.

Thane International is now one of the largest direct response and retail marketing companies in the world. Estimates suggest that the 600-employee company has revenues approaching $400 million.

Thane's distribution channels in the United States, and through its 186 international distributors and strategic partners in 80 countries around the world, include direct response TV, home shopping channels, catalogs, retail, print advertising, credit card inserts and the Internet. In addition, Thane develops and acquires products, arranges low-cost manufacturing and plans the marketing strategy.

A significant portion of Thane's success may be attributed to the business climate of the Coachella

> **"The combined elements of creative vision and business strategy comprise the company that is Thane International..."**

Valley. A dedicated business community that is supportive of local development, the valley helped foster much of Thane's growth.

In return, Thane expresses its appreciation of and commitment to the Coachella community by contributing to Martha's Village and Kitchen, Women in Film and Television and the Palm Springs Film Festival. "It is important to give back, especially when we are so blessed," DuBarry-Hay says.

In fact, when Hay and DuBarry-Hay won the Ernst & Young 1998 Entrepreneur of the Year award for the Inland Empire region, Hay gave much credit to the desert. "There has never been a day when we have regretted moving here and doing business here," says Hay. "The desert has allowed us to build a great team of good people."

Having worked in front of the camera as an actress in the 1970s and 80s, DuBarry-Hay followed

Thane International, Inc.

her entrepreneurial spirit and began developing feature films. DuBarry-Hay's business savvy led her to perfect her skills in securing funds and organizing specialized partnerships. This experience provided the knowledge to develop and market her first infomercial in 1987 – Play the Piano Overnight – a video that became the model for the popular music-instruction series. "I decided to create and produce an infomercial and take the marketing into my own hands. It was a huge hit," DuBarry-Hay recalls.

The success and popularity of this premier infomercial prompted DuBarry to partner with Hay in 1990 to form Thane International. Hay's experience in building companies and organizing a strong management team balanced DuBarry-Hay's talent for selecting products and creating successful marketing

messages. As Chief Creative Officer, DuBarry-Hay determines which products to take to market, how to position them, what type of offer to create and who to cast in the infomercial. With a background in the entertainment industry, Bill Hay adds to the formula broad-business acumen.

As a director and executive committee member of the Electronic Retailing Association, Hay is a respected industry leader. He is the visionary and driving force for Thane's continued placement as a leader in the direct response industry.

Thane International brands include Thane Housewares, Thane Fitness, California Beauty and Ageless Wonders.

To maintain a competitive edge while serving the global market, Thane has offices worldwide: Thane Direct, an international division in Toronto; European markets in Frankfurt and London; DRTV Sales in La Quinta, Calif.; Thane Direct Response Group in Tampa; Thane Distribution Group in Philadelphia; Concept and Product Solutions (CAPS), a product-development team in Santa Monica; and Thane Internet Group in La Quinta.

In 1996, Thane launched a retail Internet site that has reaped prestigious awards. The Electronic Retailing Association lists Thane International as one of the "Best Web sites." It is also ranked No. 1 for e-commerce for as-seen-on-TV products. The marketing and selling of products on Thane's Web site has garnered a high customer response, with more than 10 million visitors each month.

With such a diverse business portfolio, the future success of Thane International is guaranteed. For more information: www.thane.com or 760-777-0217.

(Top left)
Denise DuBarry-Hay,
Chief Creative Officer

(Top right)
William F. Hay,
Chairman and CEO

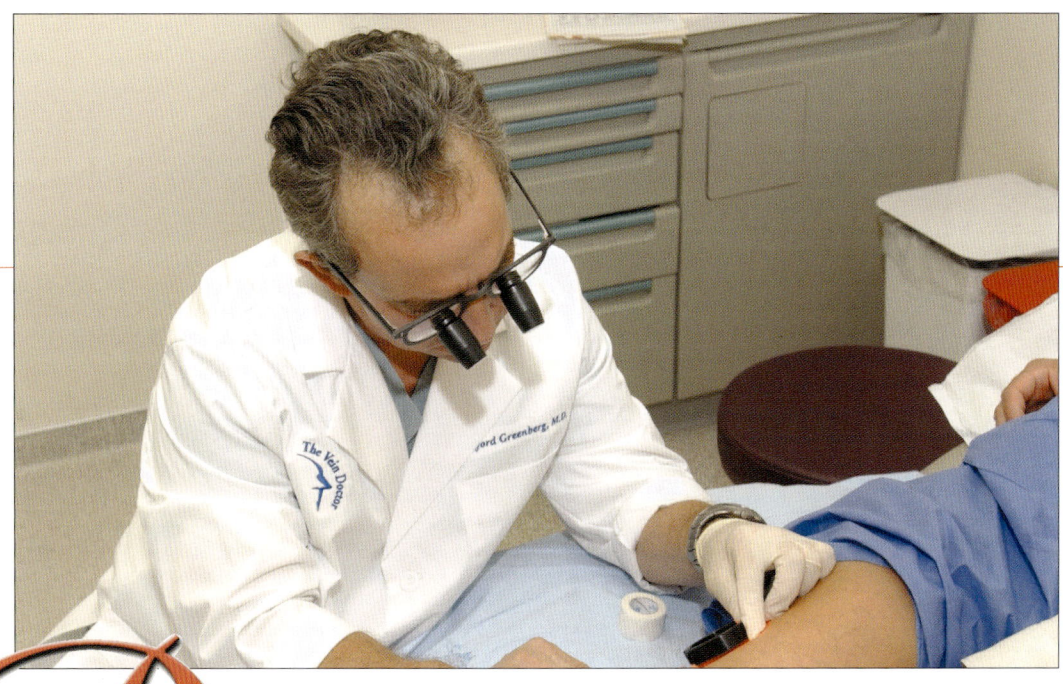

(Above) Sanford J. Greenberg, M.D

Photo by Ed Lee

Painful, embarrassing and unattractive varicose and spider veins need no longer prohibit one's activities nor dictate one's wardrobe. While treatments for these conditions have been around for over 80 years, never before have they been so effective and noninvasive, boasting incredibly quick recovery time.

Sandy Greenberg, M.D., Medical Director of The Vein Doctor and founder of the Vein Cure™ method, offers quick solutions to common diseases such as varicosis (varicose veins that are dilated) venous reflux (damaged veins that allow blood to pool and flow in reverse, resulting in enlargement and bulging of the vein), rosacea (veins and capillaries in the face that cause facial flushing and blushing), and treatment for sun-damaged skin.

These afflictions can be caused by pregnancy, hormone replacement therapy, birth control pills, heredity, faulty valves in the legs, even age and minimal exercise. Prolonged periods of both standing and sitting can contribute to varicosis.

Vein reflux is also a cosmetic concern. Painful symptoms include legs that ache, swell, burn, and feel heavy and tired. Untreated, leg varicosis can cause changes in the skin resulting in eczema, pigmentation, and ulceration and bleeding. Millions of people are afflicted by vein reflux, but today more men and women are doing something about it.

The Vein Doctor's Vein Cure™ method, perfected by Greenberg over the last 12 years, is the premiere treatment for vein disorders, using methods that

"The Vein Doctor's Vein Cure™ method...is the premiere treatment for vein disorders..."

re-route blood flow to healthy veins after delivering radio frequency or laser energy to the diseased vein, causing it to close. Symptoms improve immediately.

Compare this to the traditional practice of "vein stripping," in which the veins are removed completely. This involves anesthesia, hospital stays and side effects such as bruising, hematoma, numbness and the possibility of infection. Greenberg's VNUS Closure, EVLT (Endovenous Laser Treatment), intense pulsed light, and sclerotherapy create predictable results in less time, with far less risk – explaining over 1,000 happy patients he treats annually.

Greenberg's success in the non-surgical elimination of varicose and spider veins on the legs, hands, and face can be credited to his ability to accurately diagnose causes during the consultation phase. Using duplex ultrasound testing, he assesses the source of the problem, thereby preventing the recurrence of damage. His method of sclerotherapy injects the most diluted solution of medicine needed (his

The Vein Doctor

VeinCure™ solution), greatly reducing risk and still effecting the disappearance of varicose and spider veins.

Greenberg uses other vein eradicating technologies, including EndoVenous Laser Treatment (EVLT) for greater saphenous vein incompetence, using diode laser energy within the vein via a minute laser fiber, as well as VNUS Closure™, which uses radiofrequency energy to seal the vein shut. These are minimally invasive non-surgical treatment alternatives to traditional vein stripping, resulting in less pain and rapid recovery time, with a decrease in potentially adverse side effects and no scarring.

Greenberg also specializes in a facial treatment that results in dramatically smoother, softer skin with fewer wrinkles, reduced redness and smaller pores. PhotoFacial™ significantly reverses redness associated with rosacea (veins and capillaries on the face that cause redness and sometimes painful flushing), sun damage and age spots through a series of computerized pulsed light treatments. Sun-damaged skin is restored to a healthier, brighter, more youthful condition. The computerized pulses eliminate congested blood vessels and unwanted skin discoloration. Results vary, but are usually reported as successful between treatments three and six, with positive clearing of unwanted blood vessels and pigment. Small acne scars, large pores, circles under the eyes and fine lines are reduced through PhotoFacial™ treatments.

Staying ahead of ever-changing technological advances is a high priority to Dr. Greenberg. Greenberg's techniques are being disseminated throughout the country as he trains practitioners in his methodology. Some doctors may treat vein conditions as part of their practice, but Dr. Greenberg is the preeminent example of successfully specializing in the field. His goal is to continue expanding into other cities so that everyone may take advantage of the services he provides. The sheer volume of satisfied patients referring others is increasing demand for these treatments exponentially.

The office is inviting and comfortable in every respect, located at 44-300 Monterey, Suite B in Palm Desert, Calif. The staff is exceptionally friendly and warm, proof of the success achieved by those who are passionate about their work!

For more information: www.theveindoctor.com or 760-340-2200.

(Top left)
Sanford J. Greenberg, M.D.
Medical Director

(Top right)
Staff Members

Photos by
Ed Lee

For Jeff Walker, senior pastor at the inter-denominational Victory Christian Center, "It's been a wonderful journey."

Walker, who was living in Mattoon, Ill., back in the early 80s, visited a former classmate in Burbank, Calif. The two young men, who together had attended the Rhema Bible Training Center in Broken Arrow, Okla., were driving past a Palm Springs exit sign when the friend said that Walker should consider starting a church there.

Although Walker was reared in a religious home and had had a personal commitment to the Lord since the age of six, he felt he really wanted to be a banker. His dad, whose best friend was a bank president, had helped him get a job at the local bank when he was just out of high school.

For Walker, it was a time to pray. He asked, "Lord, what do you want me to do?"

He also spoke of his dilemma to an acquaintance who owned a home in Palm Springs and asked if he might be so kind as to rent him a room. The gentlemen offered him his home on Araby Drive, rent free.

So with $100 and a Toyota, Walker heeded the call and arrived in Palm Springs in December 1981. An introduction to a wonderful Christian lady, Connie Diaz, was a turning point. Mrs. Diaz offered to have services held in her living room, and the Victory Christian Center was born. Five people, including Pastor Walker, attended the first service in February 1982 and continued to worship there through October, when they rented a building in Cathedral City. The congregation now numbered 15. Its weekly budget was $50 for rent and $26.50 for an ad in the local newspaper.

"We focus on practical Bible teaching with a worship experience that is very dynamic and spirit-filled..."

The congregation continued to grow and outgrow its quarters. When membership had grown to 300, Pastor Walker believed it was time to move forward and build a church. In 1985, land was purchased on Bob Hope Drive. In 1991, the first multi-use building was completed to accommodate children and youth activities, classrooms, fellowship functions and a sanctuary to seat approximately 400.

Victory Christian Academy classes were held in trailer facilities on the campus until 2001, when a 6,500-square-foot wing was added, housing classrooms, kitchen, bookstore, choir, prayer room and a pastor's and guest speaker's retreat. Sixty additional seats were also added to the sanctuary, for now the

Victory Christian Center

(Top right) Jeff and Melissa Walker

congregation numbered 1,200, which necessitated three Sunday morning services.

Not only has the congregation grown, so have the ministries. Since 1990, the Church has operated the Bread of Life Food Bank, which provides food and clothing to approximately 300 people each week. Most of the food is purchased with donations, although some comes from F.I.N.D. (Food in Need of Distribution).

Victory Christian Center's preschool and academy for youngsters kindergarten through 5th grade were launched in 1994 and 1995, respectively. Today there are 54 children enrolled in the preschool, which is served by four teachers. Seventy students are enrolled in the academy, which is administered by five teachers.

In 1999, the 180 Youth Program, an outreach program for young people aged 12 to 18, was initiated. The name suggests a 180-degree turnaround, achieved through positive activities supervised by youth pastors. About 75 kids meet Sunday and Thursday evenings in a facility in Cathedral City.

The Victory Christian Center is renowned for its uplifting services.

"We focus on practical Bible teaching with a worship experience that is very dynamic and spirit-filled," Pastor Walker explains. "We have great musicians who are here each Sunday and we are very expressive."

Each Sunday, it is not unusual to welcome 20 new visitors to the Church. To become a member of the congregation, it is necessary to participate in a six-hour study program. Today most new congregants are invited by friends, although a variety of advertising media direct newcomers to the Church.

Even with the phenomenal increase in congregants and ministries – along with the additional work – Pastor Walker feels as committed as when services were held in Mrs. Diaz's living room.

"I have a total commitment to the vision. I do feel a calling and God has given me the grace to do what I'm doing. I'm having fun. I love every day of my life."

When Pastor Walker is not teaching, he is learning. In 2002 he earned a doctor of ministry degree from Oral Roberts University in Tulsa, Okla., and he is currently studying for his doctorate in clinical psychology at Trinity College for Graduate Studies in Anaheim, Calif.

In between, he serves as chaplain for the Riverside County Sheriff's Department, where he has been a reserve deputy since 1991. He considers it a "nice diversion" from his day-to-day duties. Pastor Walker, and wife Melissa with their three children reside in Rancho Mirage, Calif.

For more information: www.victorychristian.org or 760-328-3313.

(Above)
Kate Spates, Director of Operations and Stacy Thetford, Director of Sales and Marketing

WebSites 2000

WebSites 2000 is everything its name suggests and more. This upbeat, full-service web site development company is dedicated to educating its clients on the most effective use of the Internet in today's high-tech world.

Its focus is on how the power of the World Wide Web can be used as a marketing, advertising and communications tool for small to medium-sized businesses and professions looking to increase profits by making their products/services known and available to millions of consumers locally, nationally and indeed, worldwide.

The company was created in 1996 when Tom, Brent and David Spates acquired WebOriginals, an Ohio-based firm that was founded by a family friend. The Spates, who were busy running Spates Fabricators, a truss-manufacturing yard in Thermal, Calif., changed the name from WebOriginals to WebSites 2000 and named Brent's wife, Kate, director of operations.

Kate Spates had nearly a decade of hospitality operations experience at the Marriott's Desert Springs Resort. She grew the company at a steady rate and in 1999 welcomed Stacy Thetford as director of sales and marketing.

Thetford also brought a wealth of local hospitality experience to WebSites 2000 having worked 11 years for the Ritz-Carlton in Rancho Mirage. Together the dynamic duo's forte became customer service coupled with a strong commitment to quality and the ability to translate the technical aspects of website development into user-friendly terminology.

"We are professionals that understand the importance of first impressions. We make getting online and understanding the benefits of the Internet easy for our clients. We guide them through the process and allow them to focus on what's important to their business.

"Our strengths lie in very clean web site presentation with fast-loading graphics and consistent navigation throughout. We create our sites to be search engine friendly and continuously monitor and track their progress," Spates explains.

WebSites 2000 provides a complete range of Internet services with a strong emphasis on Complete Secure E-Commerce Solutions. Services include consulting, web site creation or redesign of an existing site, hosting services, domain registration, e-mail services and site marketing.

Most of its new business comes by referral. Notes Spates: "What better way to grow your business, but with satisfied customers who want to share their great experience. Our other successes have come from our community involvement."

The company has been honored with an Addy Award from the Advertising Federation of the Desert for the Bob Hope Chrysler Classic web site design (www.bhcc.com). The Western Association of Chamber Executives also recognized WebSites 2000 when it awarded its 1st Place Quality Award to the Palm Desert Chamber of Commerce's web site (www.pdcc.org).

For more information: www.ws2k.com or 760-779-0066.

The Westin Mission Hills Resort

It is the dramatic entry that captivates at first. Guests come upon a stately palm-dotted lawn sprinkled with colorful bursts of flowers. As they approach the porte-cochere they are greeted by sunlight dancing off polished domes, majestic arches and the intoxicating scent of citrus.

"We are truly an exotic desert sanctuary," says Bill Feather, general manager of the 512-room, AAA Four-Diamond resort. "Not only are we unique in our splendid Spanish-Moorish architecture, we provide incomparable amenities to enhance the guest experience."

The resort boasts two world-class golf courses designed by legends Pete Dye and Gary Player. Both have been awarded four and a half stars out of a possible five in Golf Digest's guidebook, "Places to Play 2002-2003." Golf Digest also lists the resort among its top 75 golf resorts in America.

The Westin Mission Hills Resort has been a Golf magazine Silver Medalist as well as a recipient of Meeting & Conventions magazine's Gold Tee award. The tennis facility has been honored by Tennis magazine, which ranked it among the top 25 adult tennis camps in the country.

> **"Not only are we unique in our splendid Spanish-Moorish architecture, we provide incomparable amenities to enhance the guest experience."**

All of the guestrooms have contemporary Spanish Mission decor and all have been twice blessed with Heavenly Beds and Heavenly Baths. Each is equipped with high-speed Internet access and a private patio. Sparkling swimming pools are close by.

In 2001 the resort introduced a new 34,000-square-foot conference center, bringing its total indoor function space to 65,000 square feet. Most recently, the beautiful Westin Mission Hills Resort Villas with their own Seasons restaurant were introduced, providing guests the opportunity for vacation ownership.

The full-service Spa at Mission Hills features exotic wellness rituals, a fully equipped fitness center and a hair and nail salon.

Bella Vista restaurant offers Continental cuisine and the option of inside or patio casual dining. For a quick bite, the Lobby Lounge offers the perfect respite, with its circular fire pit and magnificent views. The resort's James Beard House-honored chefs have been known to dazzle guests with splendid catering menus for events such as the Bob Hope Chrysler Classic Gala.

"We encourage our 500 associates to become involved in their desert communities," says Feather. "We were delighted to assist the United Way of the Desert's fund-raising drive by donating the use of The Pete Dye Resort Course for a tournament. We want the Westin to be not only a showcase for corporate programs and social events, but a place where desert residents feel welcome to stop by, play golf, dine and just enjoy our exotic desert sanctuary."

For more information: www.westin.com or 760-328-5955.

They are affectionately known as "The Bobs." They are Bob Bennion and Bob Deville, owners of Windermere Real Estate Coachella Valley.

Currently they have offices in Palm Springs and Desert Hot Springs, with another planned for Rancho Mirage in 2003. They handle all types of real estate including residential, commercial, investment property, relocation, and property management.

Windermere Real Estate was founded in Seattle in 1972. The founders and their families are still an integral part of the organization, which today boasts more than 6,500 experienced sales associates in some 285 offices throughout the western United States and British Columbia. Indeed, it is one of the largest real estate networks in the country, with this region's most extensive selection of homes available for sale.

Integrity, professionalism and community service are a way of life for the Windermere organization and for Bob Bennion and Bob Deville.

"For us, uncompromising integrity and the highest standards of professionalism are tops. We're not a company for every real estate agent. We take pride in finding the right people to be part of our team," Deville says.

Partners since 1993, Bennion and Deville have each accumulated more than 20 years of real estate experience. Today they are among the top producers in the Seattle and Northwest areas. Deville emphasizes that they do not specialize in any specific sector but rather represent properties in all price ranges. They own their Windermere Coachella Valley offices, and do not actively list and sell because they strongly believe that owners/brokers should not compete with their agents.

In addition, they pride themselves on their excellent rapport with agents from other offices.

"Presentation is everything, and we pride ourselves on our marketing materials. Our Web site is a tremendous tool for us, property buyers and agents. We want what's best for the seller and/or buyer regardless of who sells the property. It's all about servicing the client and giving ALL of our properties full exposure," Deville explains.

As for their staff, they insist that all personnel obtain and maintain active real estate licenses within six months of their hire date. Both Bennion and Deville know that a solid understanding of the real estate industry can only raise the level of professionalism within their offices, regardless of whether or not one chooses to sell real estate.

"We are so happy with what we've been able to create in such a short period of time," says Deville. "Our agents are so hungry for knowledge, new marketing techniques and advanced technology.

Windermere Real Estate Coachella Valley

Windermere has all of this to offer, and by putting these tools to use we've really seen a difference. In fact, 95 percent of our agents have doubled their commissions since joining our team. We're only as good as the agents we have working for us. This team is the best I've seen anywhere, and I've been in a lot of real estate offices. It's just so rewarding."

Few companies can match Windermere's commitment to the neighborhoods and communities they serve. Every Windermere agent is required to give a portion of each commission dollar to the Windermere Foundation. This is matched dollar for dollar by the agency owners. The Windermere Foundation has contributed millions of dollars to nonprofit organizations dedicated to providing housing and related services to homeless and low-income families. Less than one percent of contributions go to administrative costs. (Contributions are also made by salaried employees and managers, as well as by the general public.)

Locally, monies have been used to support The AIDS Assistance Program (AAP) in feeding families with children who have the burden of living with AIDS. Two Windermere Scholarship Programs help fund continuing education or high school completion for Palm Springs residents. The focus has been on parents with young children who have expressed a sincere desire to return to school. Windermere has also bought classroom equipment for the Boys and Girls Club of Desert Hot Springs, and helped them though direct donations.

In addition, Windermere has an annual Community Service Day where all Windermere agents work on neighborhood improvement projects. Typical duties might include home repair, roof installation, painting and landscaping.

"This is not a one-transaction company," says Deville. "We look forward to the opportunity to build your trust today and handle all of your real estate needs in the future. We're here for the long haul."

And that is good news for many.

For more information:
www.WindermereCoachellaValley.com or
760-327-3990.

> "This team is the best I've seen anywhere, and I've been in a lot of real estate offices."

PROFILES OF EXCELLENCE *Index*

A&M Construction **104**
P.O. Box 366
78070 Calle Cadiz
La Quinta, CA 92253
760-564-4832

Aaker & Associates **105**
P.O. Box 509
Palm Springs, CA 92263
760-323-4600
www.davidkaaker.com

Aaronson Plastic **106**
Surgery Center
1221 North Indian Canyon Drive
Palm Springs, CA 92262
760-325-5255
www.saaronson.com

Advance Hearing Systems **108**
42-382 Bob Hope Drive
Rancho Mirage, CA 92270
760-341-9619

All About Massage **109**
74-121 Highway 111
Palm Desert, CA 92260
760-346-7949
888-772-2442 (Toll Free)
www.allaboutmassage.com

Agua Caliente Band **110**
of Cahuilla Indians
650 E. Tahquitz Canyon Way
Palm Springs, CA 92262
760-325-3400
www.aguacaliente.org

Agua Caliente Casino **110**
32250 Bob Hope
Rancho Mirage, CA 92270
760-321-2000
www.hotwatercasino.com

Michael G. Allen **112**
"Special Agent"
610 South Belardo Road, Suite 300
Palm Springs, CA 92264
760-325-2526
E-mail: santabigmike@aol.com

The Ames Group **113**
81-711 Highway 111, Top Floor
Indio, CA 92201-5489
760-345-2555

AristoKatz **148**
121 South Palm Canyon Drive
Palm Springs, CA 92262
760-322-8666
888-322-6369 (Toll Free)
www.aristokatz.com

Becker & Becker Realty **114**
44-311 Monterey
Palm Desert, CA 92260
760-346-5593
800-347-2732
www.palmspringsdeserthomes.com

Tom Brewster Photography **115**
399 W. Cabrillo Road
Palm Springs, CA 92262
760-320-3684
www.tombrewsterphotography.com

Camelot Theatres **164**
2300 Baristo Road
Palm Springs, CA 92262
760-325-6565
www.camelottheatres.com

Canyon National Bank **116**
1711 East Palm Canyon Drive
Palm Springs, CA 92264
760-325-4442
www.canyonnational.com

Cathedral City Chamber **117**
of Commerce
68-845 Perez Road
Suite 6
Cathedral City, CA 92234
760-328-1213
www.cathedralcitycc.com

Carole, Serge & Toni **118**
Fred Sands Desert Realty
70380 Highway 111
Rancho Mirage, CA 92270
760-779-4393
800-801-6403
www.sergeandtoni.com

The Classic Touch Fine Jewelry **119**
Marriott Desert Springs Resort
74-855 Country Club Drive
Palm Desert, CA 92260
760-341-9331

Comprehensive Cancer Center **120**
1180 N. Indian Canyon Drive
Suite E218
Palm Springs, CA 92262
760-416-4873
www.desertccc.com

Computer Payroll Company **122**
74-200 Highway 111
Palm Desert, CA 92260
760-779-1731
877-446-4272 (Toll Free)
www.cpcpayroll.com

Desert Hot Springs Chamber **123**
of Commerce
11-711 West Drive
Desert Hot Springs, CA 92240
760-329-6403
800-346-3347
www.deserthotsprings.com

Desert Dermatology **124**
Medical Associates, Inc.
39700 Bob Hope Drive, Suite 115
Rancho Mirage, CA 92270
760-346-4262
www.werobertsderm.com

Desert Medical Imaging **126**
74-785 Highway 111, Suite 101
Indian Wells, CA 92210
760-776-8989
www.desertmedicalimaging.com

Desert Regional Medical Center **128**
1150 N. Indian Canyon Drive
Palm Springs, CA 92263
760-323-6511
www.desertmedctr.com

Stephanie Eichel & Associates **130**
RE/MAX Real Estate Consultants
78-411 Highway 111
La Quinta, CA 92253
760-564-8188
760-275-8808
E-mail: lqrealtor@aol.com

Eldorado Polo Club **131**
50-950 Madison Street
Indio, CA 92201
760-342-2223
www.eldoradopolo.com

El Paseo Center **132**
for Cosmetic Dentistry
73-640 El Paseo
Palm Desert, CA 92260
760-836-0700
877-836-0700 (Toll Free)
www.drbobmaher.com

FLC Capital Advisors **134**
44-800 Village Court
Palm Desert, CA 92260
760-779-8110
888-763-6867 (Toll Free)
www.flccapitaladvisors.com

Franklin Loan Center **135**
44-800 Village Court
Palm Desert, CA 92260
760-779-8100
www.franklinloancenter.com

Kristi W. Hanson, Inc., Architect **136**
44850 Las Palmas
Suite A
Palm Desert, CA 92260
760-776-4068
kristiwhansonarchitect@verizon.net

Hunt Weber Clark **137**
Associates, Inc.
2410 Alhambra Drive
Palm Springs, CA 92264
760-318-6548
415-546-2091
www.hwcinc.com

Indio Chamber of Commerce **138**
82503 Highway 111
Indio, CA 92201
760-347-0676
800-444-6346
www.indiochamber.org

Indio Emergency **139**
Medical Group, Inc.
81-893 Dr. Carreon Blvd.
Suite 4
Indio, CA 92201
760-775-4181
www.iemginc.com

KMIR 6 **140**
72920 Park View Drive
Palm Desert, CA 92260
760-568-3636
www.kmir6.com

John F. Kennedy **142**
Memorial Hospital
47-111 Monroe Street
Indio, CA 92201
760-347-6191
800-343-4535
www.jfkmemorialhosp.com

John F. Kennedy **144**
Memorial Foundation
73-555 San Gorgonio Way
Palm Desert, CA 92260
760-776-1600
www.jfkfoundation.org

Anne Kerpon Interior Design **145**
78-365 Highway 111
Suite 362
La Quinta, CA 92253
760-771-4267
E-mail: kerpon@aol.com

Kraft Nabisco Championship **146**
Two Racquet Club Drive
Rancho Mirage, CA 92270
760-324-4546
www.kraftnabiscochampionship.com

La Mariposa **148**
155 South Palm Canyon Drive, A-2
Palm Springs, CA 92262
760-322-0833

La Quinta Chamber **149**
of Commerce
78-371 Highway 111
La Quinta, CA 92253
760-564-3199
www.laquintachamberofcommerce.com

Kim Lombardelli **150**
RE/MAX Real Estate Consultants
74-199 El Paseo
Suite 101
Palm Desert, CA 92260
760-862-2977
760-641-6671
www.deserthomesellers.com

Mainiero, Smith and **151**
Associates, Inc.
777 East Tahquitz Canyon Way
Suite 301
Palm Springs, CA 92262-6784
760-320-9811
www.mainierosmith.com

Marcel de Claremont **152**
Rug Gallery
250 E. Palm Canyon Drive
Palm Springs, CA 92264
760-322-7847
www.marceldeclaremont.com

Milauskas Eye Institute **154**
555 E. Tachevah Drive, Suite 101
Palm Springs, CA 92262
760-327-1561
www.milauskas-eye.com

Mosaic **148**
155 South Palm Canyon Drive
Suite A1
Palm Springs, CA 92262
760-322-3485
E-mail: ematz@earthlink.net

Orr Builders **156**
77-570 Springfield Land
Suite D
Palm Desert, CA 92211
760-360-6632
E-mail: orrbuilder@aol.com

Pacific Western Bank **157**
74-750 Highway 111
Indian Wells, CA 92210
760-836-0870
www.pacificwesternbank.com

Palm Desert Chamber **158**
of Commerce
73-710 Fred Waring Drive
Suite 114
Palm Desert, CA 92260
760-346-6111
www.pdcc.org

Palm Springs Chamber **159**
of Commerce
190 West Amado Road
Palm Springs, CA 92262
760-325-1577
www.pschamber.org

Michael E. Platt, M.D. **160**
Internal Medicine
73-345 Highway 111
Suite 203
Palm Desert, CA 92260
760-836-3232
www.drplatt.com

Prime Time International **162**
86-705 Avenue 54, Suite A
Coachella, CA 92236
760-399-4166
www.primetimeproduce.com

Pro Realty & Investments, Inc. **163**
41-905 Boardwalk, Suite X
Palm Desert, CA 92211
760-773-4464
www.proinv.com

R & R Radio Corporation **164**
2100 Tahquitz Canyon Way
Palm Springs, CA 92262
760-325-2582
www.camelottheatres.com

Ramada Inn Resort and **166**
Conference Center
1800 E. Palm Canyon Drive
Palm Springs, CA 92264
760-323-1711
800-245-6904
www.psramada.com

Rancho Mirage Chamber **167**
of Commerce
42-464 Rancho Mirage Lane
Rancho Mirage, CA 92270
760-568-9351
www.ranchomirage.org

Rinker Financial **168**
74-760 Highway 111, Suite 204
Indian Wells, CA 92210
760-779-9300
800-340-7227
www.rinkerfinancial.com

Rothermund Rudman **169**
Prudential California Realty
72-895 Fred Waring Drive
Palm Desert, CA 92260
760-568-9275
760-773-1011
800-998-8977
www.homespalmsprings.com

Salon 119 A Day Spa **170**
119 N. Indian Canyon Drive
Palm Springs, CA 92262
760-327-4800
E-mail: salon119@msn.com

Sensafine, Inc. **171**
41-625 Eclectic Way, Suite P
Palm Desert, CA 92260
760-346-8219
www.sensafine.biz

Spa Resort Casino **111**
140 N. Indian Canyon Drive
Palm Springs, CA 92262
760-325-3400
www.sparesortcasino.com

Thane International, Inc. **172**
78-140 Calle Tampico
La Quinta, CA 92253
760-777-0217
www.thane.com

Town Center Drugs and **161**
Compounding Pharmacy
72-840 Highway 111
Palm Desert, CA 92260
760-341-3984

The Vein Doctor **174**
44-300 Monterey, Suite B
Palm Desert, CA 92260
760-340-2200
866-437-8346 (Toll Free)
www.theveindoctor.com

Victory Christian Center **176**
34500 Bob Hope Drive
Rancho Mirage, CA 92270
760-328-3313
www.victorychristian.org

WebSites 2000 **178**
41-865 Boardwalk, Suite 207
Palm Desert, CA 92211
760-779-0066
www.ws2k.com

The Westin Mission Hills Resort **179**
71333 Dinah Shore Drive
Rancho Mirage, CA 92270-1508
760-328-5955
www.westin.com

Windermere Real Estate **180**
Coachella Valley
850 N. Palm Canyon Drive
Palm Springs, CA 92262
760-327-3990
www.windermerecoachellavalley.com